FR NCH

FR

FRENCH LITERATURE
FROM 1600 TO THE PRESENT

W. D. Howarth, Henri M. Peyre
and
John Cruickshank

Revised and reprinted
from
France: A Companion to French Studies
EDITED BY D. G. CHARLTON

METHUEN

FRANCE: A COMPANION TO FRENCH STUDIES
first published in 1972
by Methuen & Co Ltd
11 New Fetter Lane London EC4
Printed in Great Britain
by Richard Clay (The Chaucer Press), Ltd
Bungay, Suffolk
These chapters revised and first published as a
University Paperback in 1974
This edition © 1974 Methuen & Co Ltd

ISBN 0 416 81640 1

Distributed in the USA by
HARPER & ROW PUBLISHERS INC
BARNES & NOBLE IMPORT DIVISION

CONTENTS

EDITOR'S PREFACE

The chapters in this volume first appeared in *France: A Companion to French Studies* in 1972 (London, Methuen, x + 613 pp.). That work – ranging over French history and society, thought, literature, painting, sculpture and architecture, music, and politics and institutions from the Renaissance to the present – is inevitably lengthy and proportionately costly. It has thus been suggested that particular chapters which together provide a very useful treatment of their subject should be made available in cheaper format. That is the aim of the series to which this book belongs, covering respectively:

1 *French History and Society: The Wars of Religion to the Fifth Republic*
   (Dr Roger Mettam and Professor Douglas Johnson)
2 *French Thought since 1600*
   (Dr D. C. Potts and Professor D. G. Charlton)
3 *French Literature from 1600 to the Present*
   (ProfessorW. D. Howarth, Professor Henri M. Peyre and Professor John Cruickshank)
4 *French Art and Music since 1500*
   (Professor Sir Anthony Blunt and the late Mr Edward Lockspeiser)
   (with illustrations not included in the original volume)
5 *Contemporary France: Politics, Society and Institutions*
   (Professor Jean Blondel, in an expanded treatment of his subject)

Each study has been revised, with additional material where necessary, and the original brief bibliographies have been expanded into the form of bibliographical essays. Given 'the chastening insight [in Professor Sir Ernst Gombrich's words] that no culture can be mapped out in its entirety, but no element of this culture can be understood in isolation', one may regret that these chapters should be torn from their original context, and it is greatly to be hoped that those interested in individual elements of French culture will refer to the total volume to complete their understanding. Yet it is the Editor's belief, even so, that this present book provides, at a price which most would-be purchasers can afford, a widely informative, up-to-date guide and evaluation.

D. G. CHARLTON

Department of French Studies
University of Warwick
February 1974

FRENCH LITERATURE
FROM 1600 TO 1750
W. D. Howarth

Introduction

This period may be said to be the beginning of the modern era. It saw
none of the great technological innovations which, from the early
nineteenth century onwards, have accelerated the pace of human
progress; and, sandwiched between the last of the great dynastic civil
wars of Europe and the first of the great revolutions based on political
ideologies, it brought about no violent social upheaval in France. Yet
it was during this period, nevertheless, that the most decisive political
and social changes came about in the development from feudalism to
bureaucracy, from the medieval to the modern way of life. For between
1600 and 1680, as a result of the deliberate policies of Richelieu and
other statesmen, the great feudal families were deprived of their
effective political power. This was a relatively painless process, in spite
of such outbreaks of resistance as the Frondes; and although France
was still far from an egalitarian society based on constitutional monarchy
and parliamentary democracy, the unity of the State was consolidated
in the person of the monarch, the foundations were laid for an efficient
internal administration, and the seventeenth and eighteenth centuries
were a period of relative social stability for France.

One way in which this stability was reflected was in the encouragement it gave to a more active cultural life. Whereas the unsettled
climate of the Wars of Religion had been unfavourable to learning,
culture and refinement, particularly in Paris and at court, the first half
of the seventeenth century saw the beginnings of the *salons* as focal
points of the social and intellectual life of the capital, the foundation of
the Académie Française, and the establishing of the first permanent
theatres in Paris. Similarly, at court, the rough military type gradually
disappeared, to be replaced by something more nearly resembling

Castiglione's ideal courtier, versed in the social graces and able to take an intelligent interest in literature and the arts.

In these favourable conditions, French classical literature took shape and grew to maturity in a brief half-century or so of creative activity which still today, in the eyes of the most iconoclastic modernist, represents the finest flowering of the native French literary genius. The qualification 'native' is important, because this was a remarkably self-contained phenomenon, produced at a time when French cultural and intellectual life was probably more insular than at any other period in its history. The literature of this age forms in this respect a complete contrast with a truly European movement such as Romanticism: it was hardly fed at all by other contemporary cultures, and while it did depend heavily on links with the literature of antiquity, this influence was so blended with other local and contemporary stimuli as to make of French 'classicism' something unique in modern literature.[1] That this creative achievement should so soon be followed in certain genres by a falling-off into imitative mediocrity was no doubt due as much to the continued stability of social conditions, and to reluctance on the part of over-cautious writers to question the basic structure of society,[2] as it was to a complacent refusal to vary the formulae which had produced the masterpieces of the 1660s and 1670s. At any rate it is easy to see that the authors who counted in the decades leading up to 1750 were those who were willing to look abroad for new ideas and styles, and who were in the vanguard of the new cosmopolitanism which characterizes the literature of the mid-eighteenth century.

The Baroque Age 1600–1640

At the beginning of the seventeenth century, the full flowering of the classical manner was still far off; but before the century is very old, it is possible to see various indications of the new tendency towards order, stability and refinement. First, as regards the preparation of the reading

---

[1] As Professor Peyre has remarked, it would be easy to write a history of other modern literatures, Italian, Spanish, German or English, without ever using the word 'classical'; '. . . mais on ne peut concevoir une histoire de la littérature française où ce mot commode ne désigne les grands écrivains du XVIIe siècle' ('Le Mot *classicisme*', in J. Brody (ed.), *French Classicism: A Critical Miscellany* (Englewood Cliffs, N.J., 1966), pp. 104–13).
[2] As La Bruyère points out (*Caractères*, XIV, 65), it was not a question of there being no 'grands sujets', but of these being 'défendus'.

public: the widespread desire for self-improvement, for refinement and culture, is reflected in the numerous manuals of 'politesse' which appeared throughout the first half of the century, the most celebrated of which was *L'Honnête Homme, ou l'Art de plaire à la Cour* (1630) by Nicolas Faret (*c.* 1600–46). More important, from the point of view of strictly literary culture, the celebrated 'chambre bleue' of Madame de Rambouillet (?1588–1665) went a long way towards bridging the gap between men of letters, mostly of bourgeois origin, and the nobility and leaders of fashionable society. Here, writers and noblemen seem to have mixed in an easy relationship, without pedantry or affectation, enjoying the pleasures of the mind in the widest, freest sense. Other *salons* may have been more exclusively literary, more highbrow in tone; none had the reputation of the Hôtel de Rambouillet. These regular gatherings of like minds did much to refine the literary language, and to focus the attention of writers on the study of real human relationships; more generally, they helped to prepare a cultured public for the serious analysis of moral and psychological problems.

The earliest imaginative literature which catered for – and at the same time stimulated – this new taste was that written in imitation of the pastoral literature of Italy and Spain. The masterpiece of this genre, and a favourite with readers throughout the century, was *L'Astrée* by Honoré d'Urfé (1567–1625), of which three parts appeared in 1607, 1610 and 1619, parts IV and V being published in 1627 by his secretary. Manners are stylized and settings conventional; the plot is full of complicated contrivances; and the ideal of courtly love assumes the character of a quasi-religious ritual. But when the author analyses the sufferings of the shepherd Céladon, separated by misfortunes and misunderstandings from his beloved Astrée, there is genuine psychological realism.

While this is the primary interest of *L'Astrée*, it also shares the tendency, notable in almost all genres, towards a more polished and harmonious form of expression. Other prose-writers who catered for this new public of cultured readers, though in very different ways, were François de Sales (1567–1622), whose style, harmonious and full of agreeable imagery, not of pedantic abstractions, matched his purpose: to persuade his reader to adopt a 'dévotion' purged of its more extreme austerity and asceticism; and Guez de Balzac (1597–1654), who acquired tremendous fame as a letter-writer and moralist. Balzac made of the epistolary art not the spontaneous expression of the writer's personality, but a self-conscious exercise in literary style: his skilful combination of prose rhythms, oratorical periods and contrived rhetorical effects likewise aimed at clarity, harmony and *agrément*; and his collections of letters, published from 1624 onwards, became veritable best-sellers.

Refinement of the language of poetry was the self-imposed task of François de Malherbe (1555–1628). He was as resolutely opposed to the exalted conception held by the Pléiade of the poet as an inspired favourite of the Muses, as he was critical of the actual poetic works of Ronsard and his followers. His place in literary history is due not so much to his own creative writing, which was rarely distinguished, as to his critical doctrine; principally embodied in his *Commentaire sur Desportes*, and in his friend Racan's *Mémoires pour la vie de M. de Malherbe*, this was imposed on his fellow poets by word of mouth and by force of personal example. Malherbe called for a simple, harmonious metre, in which the grammatical unit of the phrase or sentence should coincide with the metrical unit of the line of verse, and a sober, almost prosaic vocabulary, pruned of the extravagances and idiosyncrasies of imaginative flights of poetic fancy. His own practice was less extreme than his precept; cf. for instance his use of metaphor, not only in his early 'Larmes de Saint-Pierre', but also in his later occasional poems: love poetry (written on his own behalf, or on behalf of Henri IV), 'consolations' or other *vers de commande* written for various patrons and protectors. However, even in practice, he was seldom more than a conscientious craftsman. His influence was to help to make of French lyric verse, for nearly two centuries, something elegant and harmonious, but lacking the imaginative inspiration of true poetry; though on the credit side it is only fair to recognize that the alexandrine as he envisaged it – clear, measured, energetic – was a metre marvellously suited to be a vehicle for Corneille's dramatic dialogue.

While certain prominent poets of the time such as Honorat de Bueil, Seigneur de Racan (1589–1670) or François Maynard (1582–1646), who can be counted as disciples of Malherbe, wrote occasional odes and conventional love poetry illustrative of that doctrine which, at any rate in its broad lines, was to find most favour with following generations, the opening decades of the century witnessed a great variety of poetic activity on the part of other, more independent writers, some of whom have only recently begun to emerge from a long period of unjustified neglect. Jean de La Ceppède (1548–1623) wrote a long sonnet-sequence on Christ's Passion (*Théorèmes sur le sacré mystère de notre Rédemption*,

1613 and 1622), whose religious symbolism, biblical erudition and intellectual conceits make him the French poet most nearly comparable to the metaphysical tradition represented by Donne and his contemporaries in England. Mathurin Régnier (1573–1613), a nephew of Desportes and a determined champion of the old order against Malherbe's restrictive innovations, confined himself almost entirely to the writing of satire. Colourful, vigorous and realist, his verse gives a caustic picture of the society of his times, in the manner of a modern Juvenal; his portrait of Macette, the hypocritical bawd, in Satire XII, has always been an anthology piece. But the most distinguished of these 'independent' poets was Théophile de Viau (1590–1626), who not only represents opposition to Malherbe in matters of style and technique, but also exemplifies, as regards subject-matter and intellectual content, that *libertin* current of thought which continued the materialism of the Italian Renaissance. His verse, which has an engaging flavour of spontaneity and sincerity, is marked by a materialist's delight in physical sensation and the world of natural phenomena. The expression of his ideas may not seem unduly provocative to the modern reader; and indeed when he was brought to trial by the Jesuits for impiety, it was largely on the basis of anonymous poems of which it is doubtful whether he was the author. But Théophile's whole way of life was a provocation to the *bien-pensants* of his time: he was at the centre of a freethinking bohemia of young noblemen and men of letters, completely emancipated from the hypocrisy and intolerance of orthodox religion, and practising a new social ethic based on an Epicurean philosophy of nature. The poet's persecution, imprisonment and early death put an end to all this: *libertinage* went underground, and repressive orthodoxy was solidly entrenched for another century or more. Several surviving members of the *libertin* group judged it prudent to make public profession of orthodoxy; the conformist supporters of the establishment centred round Richelieu had their hand strengthened; while Théophile's former patron, the Duc de Montmorency, was to be one of the most notable victims of the Cardinal's desire to curb the power and privilege of the great noblemen.

From a purely literary point of view, the poetry of Théophile and others who resisted Malherbe's influence provides one of the principal manifestations of that manner to which modern criticism has given the name 'baroque'. Definitions of this term, as applied to the literature of the period in France, vary considerably in the emphasis given to different characteristics: style, structure, subject-matter, moral purpose; perhaps one of the most helpful (particularly if one is considering lyric poetry) is the following:

> poetry in which, although the problems of the age are reflected, the perfect poise between intelligence and sensibility is either destroyed or not achieved or not attempted, with the result that the poet has a distorted vision of life, distorted through imagination and sensibility, without any apparent care for proportions or balance.[1]

Thus, while in the case of a Malherbe, sensibility is strictly controlled by reason, and imagery submitted to the test of common sense, Théophile and other baroque poets, such as Antoine de Saint-Amant (1594–1661), embellish their nature descriptions by vivid, spontaneous imagery, or indulge in subjective flights of fancy which may even in some cases assume an absurd or surrealist flavour. The picture they offer of the world may be either serious and visionary, or imaginative and playful; but it is an intensely personal one, far removed from Malherbe's cliché-like generalizations.

Drama in the latter half of the sixteenth century had remained a bookish affair. Such plays as were acted were performed in the colleges or in private houses; it is probable that many were not performed at all; and the divorce between the humanist playwrights and the professional theatre was almost complete.

Alexandre Hardy (c. 1572–1632) was nothing if not a man of the theatre. He was the first professional dramatist, *poète à gages* to the Comédiens du Roi; he wrote several hundred plays, of which thirty-four were published (1623–8). As well as writing tragedies on traditional themes (e.g. *Didon se sacrifiant, Mariamne, Coriolan*), Hardy was instrumental in developing the tragi-comedy and the pastoral which were to become the most popular genres throughout the first three decades of the century. Generally speaking, his tragedies, as well as the plays belonging to other genres, fully exploit the possibilities of contemporary stage practice (the *décor simultané*, symbolic rather than representative, which involved the use of separate compartments, like medieval 'mansions'): structure is episodic, there is little unity of time or place, and the interest is focused on striking – often sensational – events (cf. *Scédase*, a 'free' tragedy showing rape and murder on stage; or *La Force du sang*, a tragi-comedy whose heroine is miraculously able to

---

[1] O. de Mourgues, *Metaphysical, Baroque and Précieux Poetry* (Oxford, 1953), p. 74.

identify, and marry, her repentant ravisher and father of her seven-year-old child).

But though Hardy's plays have something of the vigour and colour of English Elizabethan and Jacobean drama, his style is extremely uncouth and unattractive; and in the theatre as elsewhere, the pastoral was to be one of the chief refining influences, developing dramatic language as a vehicle for the subtle analysis of feeling, without bombast or crudity. This was the achievement of Racan in his *Bergeries* (1625) and of Jean Mairet (1604–86) in his *Silvie* (1628), two very successful adaptations to stage requirements of the style and subject-matter of *L'Astrée*. What stands out in both plays, in spite of the conventional artifices of plot, is the delicate portrayal of natural feelings, aided by an appeal to the notion of a sympathetic nature. However, the most attractive play of the 1620s is not a pastoral but a tragedy, although Théophile's *Pyrame et Thisbé* (1623) does share certain features with the plays of Racan and Mairet, particularly their fresh, lyrical charm. If it is hardly a tragedy in the Aristotelian sense, lacking both inevitability of outcome and tragic guilt (it presents the pathetic fate of two innocent lovers, victims of a family feud, and the 'catastrophe' is brought about by the untimely arrival of a lion), it has a poetic intensity and imaginative force lacking in the pastoral. Indeed, this imaginative quality led to the unjust depreciation of the play for centuries, following an egregious example of 'common sense' criticism on the part of Boileau.

While the highly personal imagery of Théophile's tragedy represents one baroque feature of the theatre of this period, it is generally agreed that it is tragi-comedy that is the baroque form *par excellence*. Here, the favourite themes of disguise, mistaken identity and false appearances, the ubiquitous figure of the magician, the disjointed, episodic structure and such devices as the 'play within the play' all reflect the essential characteristics of baroque art: instability, impermanence, superficial brilliance and ostentation, lack of aesthetic unity.[1] Whereas tragi-comedies still outnumbered other types of play in the 1630s, this was the decade in which the real struggle was taking place between the adherents of the freer, irregular type of drama which can conveniently be called 'baroque', and those who were already turning to a more refined, more disciplined and simpler alternative. The choice crystallized, in theoretical discussion, round the 'rules' – the three unities of

[1] The subtitle given by J. Rousset to his *Littérature de l'âge baroque en France* (Paris, 1954) is 'Circé et le paon': the sorceress represents themes of magic and metamorphosis, the peacock ostentation and display.

time, place and action which modern theorists mistakenly claimed to derive from Aristotle – but the *bienséances* (conventions regarding subject-matter and style) were as important as the 'rules' themselves in settling the form and the linguistic idiom that the mature classical theatre was to adopt. The view once held of playwrights unwillingly forced into obedience to pedantic theorists and critics has now been thoroughly exploded: to begin with, at any rate, the unities were eagerly accepted by a group of young avant-garde writers as a means of appealing to the *cognoscenti*. The first play written consciously and deliberately in observance of the rules was Mairet's *Sylvanire*, composed to please his patron in 1631. This was a tragi-comedy; but in general, when writing tragi-comedies dramatists preferred not to be hampered by such restrictions, and it was in tragedy and comedy that the unities and other conventions became established.

Comedy suffered something of an eclipse at the beginning of this period; but the genre was given a new lease of life around 1630, and here again, the influence of the pastoral was of the greatest importance: indeed, it could be said that these new comedies are no more than the transposition of *Les Bergeries* into an urban setting. The definition of comedy by Pierre Corneille (1606–84) as 'une peinture de la conversation des honnêtes gens' is illustrated by his first play *Mélite* (1629), a genteel imitation of the speech and manners of ordinary men and women, with a complicated plot concerning the traditional obstacle to the happiness of a pair of lovers. This was a style sharply distinguished from that of popular farce with its extravagant characterization; and indeed, after *Mélite*, Corneille wrote a series of comedies in which there is no 'comic' writing at all. Other dramatists followed suit, and *la comédie littéraire* was rapidly consolidated along these lines. But at the same time, these ambitious young playwrights, competing for public favour and the patronage of the two Paris theatre companies at the Hôtel de Bourgogne and the Marais, did not neglect other genres. Regular tragedy was inaugurated, Mairet's *Sophonisbe* (1634) being outstandingly successful and influential, along with *Hercule mourant* (1634) by Jean de Rotrou (1609–50), *La Mariane* (1636) by Tristan l'Hermite (1602–55), and Corneille's *Médée* (1635). The first three of these plays could be called backward-looking, in that there is little dramatic conflict, and the tragic, or pathetic, event is predetermined – though *Sophonisbe* is a particularly poetic evocation of the fate of two lovers, crushed by the power of Rome; but Corneille's first tragedy, adapted, like Rotrou's, from Seneca, not only appeals to the lingering taste for the spectacular, but also foreshadows in the character of the legendary sorceress the poet's later preoccupation with strong-willed individualists.

However, it was some time before Corneille, any more than his competitors, was to profess an exclusive allegiance to regular tragedy, and the eclecticism of his early years is further illustrated by *Clitandre* (1632), a vintage tragi-comedy of episodic construction, crowded with action, and *L'Illusion comique* (1635), which the author himself described as 'un étrange monstre'. Although labelled 'comédie', it has much in common with the tragi-comedies of the time, and perhaps more than any other play epitomizes the spirit of the baroque theatre: it is one of the most successful examples of the 'play within a play', and illustrates on several levels, from the hollow boasting of Matamore, the braggart soldier, to the portrayal of theatrical illusion which gives the play its title, that preoccupation with the interplay between truth and fiction, reality and illusion, which characterizes much of baroque art.

The point at which these two trends come together in Corneille's theatre is *Le Cid* (1637). Often described as the first classical tragedy in France, it is in fact less regular in form, and less 'classical' in spirit, than for instance *Sophonisbe*. It was labelled a tragi-comedy when first published, and although the way in which the dramatist has chosen to develop the principal dramatic conflict in the minds of Rodrigue and Chimène, whose love is threatened by the claims of family loyalties, suggests the concentration and psychological exploration in depth proper to tragedy, nevertheless the profusion of external events, the superfluous role of the Infanta, and the happy ending, all indicate the affinities of *Le Cid* with the freer, less disciplined genre. But if *Le Cid* is a tragi-comedy, it represents a very considerable development since *Clitandre*. The emotional range that Corneille achieves with his verse, from the poignant expression of Rodrigue's dilemma in the *stances* of Act I to the jubilant self-congratulation of the conquering hero, and from Chimène's energetic cry of vengeance for her father's death to the tenderness and spontaneity of the lovers' duet in Act III – this is something unmatched in any previous play, whether tragedy or tragi-comedy. No wonder that 'beau comme *Le Cid*' became a proverbial expression: contemporary audiences at once recognized the play as a masterpiece, and Corneille's fellow authors did him the honour of a critical attack such as no other play had ever faced.

Much of what passed for comment in the 'Querelle du *Cid*' was spiteful and petty; but the controversy caused such a stir in the world of letters that it led to the intervention of Richelieu. The Cardinal had a genuine interest in the theatre (he built the first theatre in Paris specifically designed as such, for premises used as theatres were usually converted tennis courts) and serious ambitions as a dramatist: he engaged a team of writers, the 'Compagnie des cinq auteurs', to which Corneille, Mairet and Rotrou all belonged, and legend has it that Corneille's restiveness in this role earned him Richelieu's disapproval. It seems more likely, however, that Richelieu intervened as a mediator rather than as a partisan, and it was possibly with largely disinterested motives that the play was submitted on his orders to the newly created Académie Française as an opportunity to exercise its judgement.

Classicism: the Formative Years 1640–1660

The formation of the Academy, the earliest of the moves to place cultural activities under State patronage, occurred in 1635 when the private gatherings of a small group of individuals with literary interests gave way to the more formal meetings of an officially constituted body of forty members. The examination of *Le Cid* on the Cardinal's orders was in one sense an exception to the normal functions of the Academy, which was from the beginning primarily concerned with the standardizing of the French language. The major fruit of this work was to be the Academy's own *Dictionnaire* of 1694, though the search for clarity and regularity had by this date also produced rival dictionaries: in 1680 by César-Pierre Richelet (1631–98), and in 1690 by Antoine Furetière (1619–88) – the latter being expelled from the Academy for his show of independence. A similar desire for codification and standardizing of linguistic usage animated Claude Favre de Vaugelas (1585–1650), also an academician, whose *Remarques sur la langue française* (1647) provide an analytical record of 'la façon de parler de la plus saine partie de la Cour, conformément à la façon d'écrire de la plus saine partie des auteurs du temps'. And in the field of poetic and dramatic theory the same kind of methodical application of reason and *bon sens* produced the *Poétique* (1639) of Hippolyte-Jules de La Mesnardière and *La Pratique du théâtre* by François Hédelin, Abbé d'Aubignac (c. 1604–c. 1673), both of these treatises, which played an influential part in the establishment of 'classical' doctrine, being due to the personal patronage of Richelieu (the *Pratique*, though not published until 1657, was begun in 1640). Meanwhile, another protégé of Richelieu, Jean Chapelain (1595–1674), was already beginning in the 1630s to exert an influence not unlike that of Malherbe a generation earlier. Chapelain resembles Malherbe in that his reputation did not depend on any important doctrinal work: instead, he made his mark in the salons, in his correspondence and in sundry occasional writings. Destined to be a prominent butt of Boileau's satire on account of his epic poem *La Pucelle*, and to be discredited by later generations because of the pedantic critical attitudes he was thought to have represented, Chapelain nevertheless counts as one of the most important architects of French classicism. And as recent scholarship has acknowledged,[1] his attitude to poetry was much more liberal than that of Malherbe: he made full allowance for that intangible element that no rules can produce, and that he knew his own verse did not possess.

It was to Chapelain that the Academy entrusted the task of adjudicating between Corneille's play and Scudéry's hostile *Observations sur le Cid*: an invidious task, given the enormous popular acclaim for the play on the one hand, and the interest shown by the Cardinal on the other. The *Sentiments de l'Académie* represent a prudent compromise; but it is possible to discern beneath the pedantry and triviality of some of the comment a genuine feeling for that harmony between simplicity of subject, regularity of form and purity of diction which classical tragedy was about to achieve.

The result of the *Querelle* on Corneille's development as a dramatist is unmistakable. While he remained to the end of his career remarkably flexible and adaptable in his attempt to please the public, there were to be no further examples of the irregular, episodic construction of tragi-comedy, and all his experimentation was henceforward to be carried out within the stricter classical formula. After a gap of three years, *Horace* (1640), *Cinna* (1640) and *Polyeucte* (1641) followed in quick succession. These three plays, together with *Le Cid*, have always been considered the high peak of Corneille's achievement, but *Pompée* (1642), *Rodogune* (1644) and *Nicomède* (1650) do not fall far short. This remarkable spell of creative activity constitutes a triumphant justification of the formula which Mairet and others had helped to develop, but which Corneille himself, responding to the stimulus of the 'Querelle du Cid', perfected. The essence of classical tragedy is a single action, seized at crisis-point: this is what distinguishes the new genre from the concentrated, but static, tragedy of the previous century on the one hand, and from the complex interrelations of plot and sub-plot which characterize tragi-comedy on the other. Despite the prominence always

[1] See in particular E. B. O. Borgerhoff, *The Freedom of French Classicism* (Princeton, 1950), pp. 31–46.

given by literary historians to the unities of time and place, it is the unity of action that gives the essential character to classical tragedy: the others merely help to make unity of action more effective. Unity of action – or, as Corneille calls it, 'unité de péril'–means that the plot must contain nothing to distract the spectator from the central tragic issue, which yet remains in suspense until the end because of the balance of opposing forces. *Horace*, indeed, was later criticized by Corneille himself, because the hero escapes from one *péril* – death at the hands of the enemy, when the Horatii fight the Curiatii – only to fall into another, when he is arraigned for the killing of his sister, who has insulted the name of Rome. *Cinna* and *Polyeucte*, however, leave nothing to criticize in this respect, and by the middle of the 1640s Corneille's own brand of classical tragedy, in which sublime effects are created by the confrontation of attitudes subtly analysed or heroically proclaimed, was firmly established.

This move towards a highly intellectualized form of drama was not followed by all playwrights, of course. While regular tragedies on subjects from mythology or ancient history become more and more numerous, tragi-comedy continues to provide a popular alternative; though of the most talented writers, only Rotrou still shows in the 1640s the eclecticism which Corneille and others had shown in the previous decade. Rotrou's *Le Véritable Saint-Genest* (1647) makes an interesting contrast with Corneille's *Polyeucte*: both are religious tragedies, but whereas Corneille takes the baptism of his hero as his starting-point, and shows the effect of divine grace by a clash of intellectual attitudes presented with a high degree of abstraction, Rotrou on the other hand, as a baroque artist, prefers to portray a visual enactment of a conversion as the climax of his play, when the actor Genest, taking the part of a Christian martyr, is himself visited by divine grace: pretence becomes reality, and he is led away to his own martyrdom. The play on the theme of reality and illusion, the richness of the imagery and the structural feature of the 'play within a play' combine to make *Saint-Genest* the last, and perhaps the most noteworthy, example of the French baroque drama – a kind of dramatic writing which has more real affinity with our own Elizabethan drama, or with the drama of the Golden Age in Spain, than with the classical forms that were to supplant it.

Rotrou, however, is something of an *attardé*, or at least an independent; he was much less susceptible than many of his contemporaries to those standardizing influences in the social and intellectual life of the country which brought about the change from a baroque to a classical literature. For a variety of reasons, from about 1640 onwards, writers seem to have become more and more responsive to these influences, and the results of this can be seen in several ways. Descartes's *Discours de la méthode* (1637), with its opening sentence, 'Le bon sens est la chose du monde la mieux partagée', is firmly based on the assumption that the mental processes of all men, if properly conducted, will lead to identical conclusions; and a similar assumption is implicit, as regards the psychology of the passions, in the same author's *Traité des passions* (1649). Much the same appeal to universal reason can be seen in the poetic treatises of La Mesnardière and D'Aubignac, as the foundation on which the *bienséances* as well as the 'rules' were based; while as regards creative writing, the poets of the mid-century come to distrust the promptings of the individual sensibility, and prefer to mould their imagination to the common denominator of a social group. So that whereas the typical baroque writer, however close his involvement with the society in which he lived, had been an individualist with regard to his artistic inspiration and his creative manner, the mid-century writer tends more and more to be a representative member of a social group, his own habits of thought and forms of expression corresponding closely to those of his readers.

The most striking example of this is to be found in the field of lyric poetry, where the linguistic and stylistic tendencies crystallized by the 'reforms' of Malherbe and Vaugelas combined with the favourite preoccupations of the habitués of the *salons* to produce a kind of writing that was often no more than intricate and mannered word-play. The principal theme of this poetry was love; but in the voluminous *poésie galante* of the period, sensuous imagery has given way to witty conceits, and the poet uses his imagination to appeal, not to the individual reader's senses, but to a much more universal intelligence. Content, although sophisticated, was frequently trivial; and the interest lay more often in the ingenious use of set forms such as the sonnet or the *rondeau*, than in genuine originality of theme or treatment.

Vincent Voiture (1598–1648), the 'court poet' of the Hôtel de Rambouillet, was one of the most successful exponents of this agreeable, but essentially minor, form of poetry. Every poet had his partisans, and literary controversies in the salons (e.g. the one over the respective merits of Voiture's 'Sonnet à Uranie' and Benserade's 'Sonnet sur Job') were frequent and lively. Among the collections of *petits vers*, the most celebrated was the *Guirlande de Julie* (1641), presented to Madame de

Rambouillet's daughter, Julie d'Angennes; the work of a score of habitués of the Hôtel, it contained ninety-odd 'floral tributes' in madrigal form. Altogether, this *poésie galante* was a most fitting expression of a refined, leisured society, which sought its amusements in parlour-games and practical jokes as well as cultivating more serious literary pursuits.

Generally speaking, these tendencies away from baroque individualism towards a literature more expressive of the cultural and social values of a homogeneous society made their mark earlier with regard to form than in respect of content. For the self-centred aristocratic idealism which inspired the protagonists of the Frondes also finds expression in the literature of the period – and nowhere more clearly than in Corneille's tragedies. His self-reliant heroes, capable of meeting every challenge and of overcoming all obstacles, are motivated by the same *éthique de la gloire*, that highly self-conscious moral code peculiar to a princely élite, which animated the Cardinal de Retz, Madame de Longueville, and other real-life leaders of the heroic but futile resistance to Mazarin's policies. In neither case is devotion to a cause free from the impulse to self-glorification; in both, there is an ever-present regard for the approbation of others, the desire to leave a striking example for posterity. The subtitle of *Cinna* is *La Clémence d'Auguste*, and the emperor's true greatness asserts itself as he pardons the conspirators instead of punishing them:

> Je suis maître de moi, comme de l'univers;
> Je le suis; je veux l'être. Ô siècles, ô mémoire,
> Conservez à jamais ma dernière victoire.

In *Horace*, the hero, having surpassed all expectations in the service of the state, asserts that

> pour laisser une illustre mémoire
> La mort seule aujourd'hui peut conserver ma gloire

– and even the martyrdom of Polyeucte is strongly marked by a similar urge:

> J'ai de l'ambition, mais plus noble et plus belle:
> Cette grandeur périt, j'en veux une immortelle,
> Un bonheur assuré, sans mesure et sans fin,
> Au-dessus de l'envie, au-dessus du destin.

The success of Corneille's plays, up to his withdrawal from the theatre in 1652, was due, as a recent writer has said, 'to the fact that the audience was prepared to share the same heroic assumption as the author';[1] his public held the same optimistic view of the individual's place in the universe, the same feeling for the sublime, idealized Roman virtues as portrayed in Plutarch.

It may be felt that these heroic, optimistic attitudes are unsuited to a tragic view of the world; and indeed, many critics find it impossible to accept the typical Cornelian plays of this period as tragedies. At best, this is a highly idiosyncratic kind of tragedy; and Corneille himself provided the key to its originality in the *Examen* to *Nicomède*, by substituting for the traditional Aristotelian tragic emotions of pity and fear the goal of *l'admiration*. The 'admiration' that we are intended to feel for Corneille's heroes has very much the sense of the Latin *admirari*: it implies 'awe' and 'astonishment' rather than moral approval;[2] and though most of his heroes do earn approval – for instance Nicomède, in whom contemporaries saw a portrait of Le Grand Condé – it is difficult not to feel a certain alienation from some of them. What we are asked to 'admire' in Corneille is something larger than life, out of the ordinary; this is very much what his tragedies are about, and the best of them, such as *Polyeucte* or *Pompée*, are still capable of arousing such a response.

In a much less intense, less dramatic, and altogether more *romanesque* way, the same appetite for idealized, heroic subject-matter, and the same optimistic belief in the individual's power to mould his own fortune, are reflected in the novels which were popular in the middle years of the century. These 'heroic' novels resembled *L'Astrée* in that they were longwinded, multi-volume adventure stories with incredible complications of plot, but they have shifted from D'Urfé's pastoral setting to the world of acient history; the two most celebrated examples of the genre, *Le Grand Cyrus* (1649–53) and *Clélie* (1654–60), both by Madeleine de Scudéry (1607–1701), being set in Persia and Rome respectively. Mademoiselle de Scudéry was a distinguished bluestocking and salon hostess, whose ideas – and those of her milieu – on the place of women in society, education and the relations between the sexes occupy a prominent place, in the form of discussions, in her novels; *Clélie* contains the famous 'Carte de Tendre', or allegorical map of the passions, which charts the traveller's way from Nouvelle Amitié to the cities of

---

[1] A. J. Krailsheimer, *Studies in Self-Interest* (Oxford, 1962), p. 78.
[2] Just as, to take two key-words from the vocabulary of Corneille's tragedies, *vertu* has very much the force of Lat. *virtus*, Ital. *virtú*, 'courage'; and *générosité*, closely connected with Lat. *gens*, denotes the values of a social caste.

Tendre sur Inclination, Tendre sur Estime and Tendre sur Reconnais-sance, avoiding the Lac d'Indifférence and the Mer d'Inimitié. Made-moiselle de Scudéry's novels also reflect the developing *salon* fashion for the literary 'portrait': set-pieces combining a physical and moral description of a well-known individual. They are *romans à clef,* which offered the initiated reader the satisfaction of recognizing the originals (Condé as Cyrus, Madame de Longueville as Mandane, etc.). As in Corneille's heroic tragedies, the courage, magnanimity and persever-ance of these idealized characters are finally rewarded, and it is easy to see how the element of wish-fulfilment added to the pleasure of Mademoiselle de Scudéry's readers.

Such novels may be virtually unreadable nowadays, but they are of considerable interest as a reflection of the society of the time. And they do help to show how the public of the classical age was formed: for if the involved plots, depending so heavily on disguise and mistaken identity, are a mark of the second-rate in literature (though it is worth noting the similarity of the plots of some of Corneille's own plays, such as *Pertharite* or *Héraclius*), the minute and searching analysis of the passions, when divorced from this superficial *romanesque,* can be seen to look forward to the greater psychological subtlety of Racine.

There were other writers at the same period, however, who made a more individual use of the novel form. Cyrano de Bergerac (1619–55), for instance, harks back to the Renaissance tradition of fictional voyages as a framework for social and political satire, and indeed may be regarded as an early exponent of science fiction. But so bold and provocative were the social ideas expressed in his *États et empires de la lune* and *États et empires du soleil* – based on the new Copernican system, they constitute an attack on the Aristotelian explanation of the universe – that neither work was published until after his death (in 1657 and 1661 respectively, the former in much expurgated form). Paul Scarron (1610–60) is much more down-to-earth as regards both his purpose and his literary manner: in his *Roman comique* (1651–7) he sets out to parody the heroic novel. Charles Sorel's *Francion* (1622) is Scarron's most obvious model in what is often called the 'realist' tradition in the seventeenth-century novel; but we are a long way here from the techniques of nineteenth-century realism, and in any case the contrived nature of the plot, with its sequence of brawls, fights, abductions and rescues, makes it clear that the author's prime purpose was to transpose the fictional structure of the heroic novel into a comic key. As the title indicates, this is a novel about the theatre: the reader follows the fortunes of an itinerant troupe of actors in 'la basse Normandie'. From this point of view, it has some real documentary value, but in his portrayal of provincial society Scarron yields to his penchant for good-humoured burlesque; and for an example of a novelist whose manner really does approach the documentary realism of the modern novel, we must turn to Furetière's *Roman bourgeois* (1668). Here, plot is minimal, and though Furetière also had a comic and satirical purpose, this does not prevent him from creating a convincingly authentic record of the day-to-day life of the Parisian bourgeoisie.

Scarron's gifts as a comic writer were not confined to the novel. There was quite a flowering of burlesque verse around 1650, of which his *Virgile travesti* (1648–52) is the best-known example. Charles Perrault was later to distinguish two ways of writing in burlesque style: 'L'une en parlant bassement des choses les plus relevées, et l'autre en parlant magnifiquement des choses les plus basses'. The latter, which we normally call the mock-heroic style (*l'héroï-comique*), is that of *Le Roman comique* (and later of Boileau's *Lutrin*); whereas in the true 'burlesque' of *Virgile travesti* the gods, goddesses and heroes of tragedy and the *romans héroïques* talk like market-porters and fishwives. It was not a very subtle form of entertainment, but it had its own sophistication, and was a cultured way of not taking one's culture too seriously.

Classicism: the Creative Years 1660–1680

Partly owing to the influence of the *salons*, and partly to the spread of those other civilizing forces which had been at work in society since the beginning of the century; also no doubt partly as a result of the failure of the Frondes and the collapse of so many heroic illusions, the *éthique de la gloire* was gradually replaced as a social ideal between about 1650 and 1660 by the concept of the *honnête homme*. The *honnête homme*, unlike the aspirant after *la gloire*, cultivated the social graces, and valued above all the pleasures of conversation and social intercourse. He was a cultured amateur, modest and self-effacing: 'Le vrai honnête homme est celui qui ne se pique de rien', to quote La Rochefoucauld's well-known *maxime*. Yet this was no pedestrian ideal. It was as demanding in its way as the Renaissance concept of the *uomo universale*, and the true *honnête homme* was a complete all-rounder: 'Cette science est proprement celle de l'homme, parce qu'elle consiste à vivre et à se communiquer d'une manière humaine et raisonnable', in Méré's words.

The day of the Hôtel de Rambouillet was now over, but other

salons, notably those of Mademoiselle de Scudéry and of Madeleine, Marquise de Sablé (*c.* 1599–1678), had taken its place. And under the personal rule of the young king the capital became, from 1660 onwards, more than ever the focal point of the cultural life of the country. The policy of attracting the nobility to court, and keeping them there to fulfil purely nominal ceremonial functions, created and maintained a large social group with few other interests but hunting, intrigue and the pleasures of the mind. The transfer of the court to Versailles in the early years of Louis XIV's reign gave a new precision to the formula 'la Cour et la Ville': here were the two milieux, not mutually exclusive but overlapping and interlocking, which were to provide the public for the new generation of writers, themselves for the most part courtiers and *honnêtes gens*.

François de La Rochefoucauld (1613–80) provides an interesting illustration of the transition between the two ages. An aristocrat who had played a leading part in the Frondes, he had been motivated in his early years by ambition and family pride – in other words by the quest for *la gloire*; but after the Frondes, defeated and badly wounded, as well as older and more experienced, he retired to private life, began a new career as a man of letters, and confessed, in a self-portrait, to 'une si forte envie d'être tout à fait honnête homme que mes amis ne me sauraient faire un plus grand plaisir que de m'avertir sincèrement de mes défauts'. The *Maximes* (1665), his principal literary achievement, owed a great deal both in form and content to critical analysis and discussion in Madame de Sablé's *salon*. They are a collection of 500 highly polished reflections on human behaviour, expressed in the most universal terms ('Le refus des louanges est un désir d'être loué deux fois'); the general tone is cynical, and self-interest is presented as the mainspring of all our actions ('Les vertus se perdent dans l'intérêt comme les fleuves se perdent dans la mer'). If there is a more positive message to be read into the work, it is the recognition of *l'honnêteté* as a code which preserves society as a viable institution ('S'il y a beaucoup d'art à savoir parler à propos, il n'y en a pas moins à savoir se taire'). Even *honnêteté*, however, is touched with cynicism in the *Maximes*; La Rochefoucauld's view of it is a pragmatic one, falling a long way short of the ideal defined by Antoine de Gombaud, Chevalier de Méré (1610–85), in his *Discours de la vraie honnêteté* and other essays, where it is presented as a real *art de vivre*.

The Frenchman who by the common consent of his contemporaries most nearly lived up to such an ideal was Charles de Saint-Denis, Sieur de Saint-Évremond (c. 1616–1703), who, after being active in politics and the army, was exiled and spent the last forty years of his life in England. Here he cultivated the pleasures of the mind, while not neglecting those of the senses: he was a true Epicurean, rejecting excess in all things, but believing, as he wrote, that 'nous avons plus d'intérêt à jouir du monde qu'à le connaître'. One of the most independent thinkers of his time, Saint-Évremond was also one of the most versatile writers; he wrote satire, comedy, philosophical verse, and above all was known as a letter-writer and essayist. He took a stand against religious intolerance, anticipating the deists of the following century; his exile from France gave him a valuable detachment as a commentator on public affairs; and, above all, his taste and discernment in literary matters make him, as has been said, 'probably the most interesting literary critic of the seventeenth century . . . we are not far from the later conception of criticism as the criticism of beauties, not faults'.[1]

Few honnêtes gens had the culture, the taste and the temperament to practise the art of living in such an exemplary way as Saint-Évremond; but it was this same ideal of tolerant, cultured Epicureanism which, whatever its limitations as a source of spiritual inspiration, for a spell of twenty years or so set the tone of the social life of the capital.

If this period saw the perfecting of the masculine ideal of honnêteté, it also saw the fullest development of the predominantly feminine cult of préciosité. The two phenomena are often regarded as opposites, and to the extent that honnêteté stands for moderation in all things, and preciosity for affectation and extravagance, this is obviously the case. However, it should be remembered that the 'précieuses ridicules' satirized by Molière and others were far from representing the whole picture, and that while the term précieuse itself may have been used as a pejorative label, the women to whom it was applied (Mademoiselle de Scudéry was the most celebrated, and the most influential, of the précieuses) were responsible for introducing a new subtlety and precision into the language, for establishing exacting standards of delicacy and refinement in matters of taste, and for propagating advanced social ideas about the equality of the sexes in marriage. In all these things, the aims of the précieuses ran parallel to those of the honnête homme, and the ideal of the educated, emancipated woman was very like a female counterpart of the masculine ideal defined above. But the natural desire of these early feminists to assert themselves meant that their ideas were often taken to

[1] P. J. Yarrow, A Literary History of France, Vol. II: The Seventeenth century (London, 1967), p. 333.

extremes, so that in practice the educated all-rounder tended to become a pedantic bluestocking, the civilized notion of 'honnête amitié' between the sexes sometimes became a prudish revulsion from the facts of life, and the *précieux* style in language and literature too easily degenerated into the affected jargon of a coterie.

The most complete representation of the *honnête homme* in the imaginative literature of the period is without a doubt to be found in the theatre of Jean-Baptiste Poquelin (1622–73), known as Molière. It was for a long time a commonplace of Molière criticism to identify him with the Cléantes, the Philintes and the Clitandres of his theatrical world, and to see such characters as representing his own philosophy of life. However, recent criticism has tended to emphasize the fact that as well as being a bourgeois by birth and upbringing, a courtier and an *honnête homme*, Molière was also an actor-manager and an entertainer. More completely a man of the theatre than any dramatist since Hardy, he was brought up on the *farceurs* of the Hôtel de Bourgogne, the leading comic actors of his youth, and the improvised acting of the Italian players in Paris. Departing to tour the provinces with his troupe in the mid-forties because of financial difficulties, he returned in 1658, and soon succeeded in imposing on audiences a completely new brand of comedy. While his early plays may be divided into full-length *comédies littéraires* in verse (e.g. *L'Étourdi*, 1658; *Dom Garcie de Navarre*, 1661) and one-act farces (e.g. *Les Précieuses ridicules*, 1659), from *L'École des maris* (1661) and particularly *L'École des femmes* (1662) onwards these two strains are fused. Molière's originality is thus to have created a formula which combined the 'classical' structure, the linguistic refinement and the portrayal of manners belonging to the accepted conventions of 'comedy', with the heightened, even caricatural, characterization proper to farce. Even in polished verse comedies, therefore, such as *L'École des femmes*, *Le Misanthrope* (1666), *Tartuffe* (1669) or *Les Femmes savantes* (1672), the comedy of manners – that is, the realistic representation of certain features of contemporary society – merely provides a framework for a comic portrayal of a central character or characters, in which exaggeration and fantasy play a considerable part. This mixture was hardly to the taste of highbrows and traditionalists; but Molière's spokesman Dorante in the *Critique de l'École des femmes* (1663) explicitly reconciles the two styles of comic writing in his defence of the new formula: 'Il n'est pas incompatible qu'une personne soit ridicule en de certaines choses et honnête homme en d'autres.' And indeed, Molière's comic characters, as well as being the object of our critical laughter, are also rounded personalities: we can accept them as plausible, representative members of society even though each is endowed with a particular obsession or *idée fixe* which renders him vulnerable to the comic process. An extreme case is that of Alceste in *Le Misanthrope*, in whom sympathetic and comic traits are so delicately balanced that they have provided a perennial subject for differences of interpretation, both inside and outside the theatre.

Le Misanthrope is the only play set in aristocratic circles; other plays mentioned, as well as prose comedies such as *L'Avare* (1668), *Le Bourgeois Gentilhomme* (1670) and *Le Malade imaginaire* (1673), portray the comfortable bourgeois milieu that was Molière's own. The central figures represent a variety of comic obsessions, some of universal relevance (miserliness, hypochondria), others of specifically contemporary significance (women's emancipation, social climbing, religious bigotry); but however topical the subject, and however prominent the satirical content, Molière's characters always possess a common denominator of humanity which makes them permanently acceptable as being like ourselves. Most plays contain, alongside the comic character, one or more examples of the *honnête homme*, either as active protagonists or as lay figures; whether or not we choose to identify the author himself with these 'raisonneurs' (and it would certainly be wrong to place too much emphasis on the didactic element in his plays), in a more general sense we can easily recognize the social norm against which his comic characters offend as that of a tolerant, humane exponent of *honnêteté*.

In *Tartuffe*, and in *Dom Juan* (1665), topical references and satirical implications were so provocative, since both plays dealt with the delicate subject of religious belief and feigned *dévotion*, that there were strong reactions from ecclesiastical quarters; while even *L'École des femmes* had given rise to a vigorous and sustained controversy with rival actors and men of letters. But from an early stage in his Paris career Molière could count on the support of the king, who became an active patron of his troupe. A number of plays were in fact written for performance at Versailles or other courts; and besides his *hautes comédies* and more traditional farces, both in the French and the Italian manner (e.g. *Le Médecin malgré lui* (1666) and *Les Fourberies de Scapin* (1671), both still highly popular), Molière also wrote several *comédies-ballets*, and collaborated in other *divertissements* which brought together the arts of poetry, music and dance in something not unlike the English court masque.

Such mixed entertainments – including the new genre of opera, and the *pièces à machines* with spectacular scenic effects due to the expertise of the Italian designer Torelli – were always favourites with the public. The biggest 'box-office' success of the century, however, judged by length of first run, was the *Timocrate* (1656) of Pierre Corneille's younger brother Thomas (1625–1709), a prolific playwright who was adept at gauging the public taste. *Timocrate* was exactly contemporary with the *précieux* novels of Mademoiselle de Scudéry; and like Philippe Quinault (1635–88) in his *tragédies galantes*, the author reproduced those *romanesque* features of disguise and amorous intrigue which the habitués of the *salons* so much admired.

However, the 1660s were to see the rivalry between the century's two acknowledged masters of serious drama. Corneille, returning to the theatre in 1659, wrote ten more plays in the next fifteen years; but though certain of these – *Sertorius* (1662), or his last play *Suréna* (1674) – will bear comparison with the plays of his middle period, the heroic idealism has now almost completely lost its conviction. His heroes have become much more materialistic and self-seeking in their aspirations; or else, like both Sertorius and Suréna, tragically aware that ideals are doomed to defeat. While Corneille retained his partisans among play-goers of an older generation, it was Jean Racine (1639–99) who appealed to the new audiences of the 1660s, for they were no longer so idealistic-ally minded in their attitude to psychology; there was a new realism, in tune with La Rochefoucauld's *Maximes* rather than with Descartes's *Traité des passions*. Of all the numerous 'parallèles' between the two great dramatists, none expresses this difference better than that written by Fontenelle, Corneille's nephew, with its cynical implication:

> Quand on a le cœur noble, on voudrait ressembler aux héros de Corneille; et quand on a le cœur petit, on est bien aise que les héros de Racine nous ressemblent.[1]

Whether, as has often been maintained, Racine's Jansenist upbringing was responsible for his view of human nature as perverse and wilful, controlled by the passions, or whether his knowledge of Greek tragedy, and the choice of Sophocles and Euripides as models, is sufficient to account for the fatalism of his own tragedies, it is certain that the imaginary world inhabited by his heroes is very different from that which we have analysed in the case of Corneille. Tragedy is for Racine

---

[1] Quoted in R. J. Nelson (ed.), *Corneille and Racine: Parallels and Contrasts* (Engle-wood Cliffs, N.J., 1966), p. 23.

the working-out of an inexorable series of events leading to a foreseeable catastrophe: plot is of the simplest; the action is already at crisis point when the play opens; and once the inexorable first step is taken, tension mounts between the incompatible protagonists until one or more of them is destroyed. Racine's career began in 1664 with *La Thébaïde*, a grim study of the mutual hatred of Oedipus' sons; this was followed by *Alexandre le grand* (1665), his only attempt at the manner of Thomas Corneille and Quinault. His masterpieces date from the highly successful *Andromaque* (1667), another tragedy based on Greek legend; after which, for *Britannicus* (1669) and *Bérénice* (1670), he turned to subjects from Roman history. *Bajazet* (1672) is based on an episode from modern Turkish history; *Mithridate* (1673) has as its hero the legendary enemy of Rome; and finally there followed two plays based on Greek mythological subjects: *Iphigénie* (1674) and *Phèdre* (1677), before Racine renounced the theatre, becoming reconciled with Port-Royal, marrying, and accepting a court office as *historiographe du Roi*. Even leaving aside his two later biblical plays, therefore, those based on Greek sources form a minority among his tragedies; if, nevertheless, one thinks of Racine as 'Greek' in comparison with the 'Roman' Corneille, this is because he endows the historical themes, like the legendary ones, with the same tragic fatalism: the downfall of Mithridate, or the shaping of the career of Néron, the 'monstre naissant' of *Britannicus*, are due not so much to some combination of historical contingencies, as to the corrupt human nature that these characters embody.

But dramatically powerful as his Roman plays are (even *Bérénice*, a tragedy with no bloodshed, and almost no action – merely the parting of a pair of lovers, in obedience to a 'raison d'État'), it is in his Greek plays that Racine reaches his greatest heights; and for many readers and playgoers, *Phèdre* in particular is one of the greatest tragedies of any literature. Construction of the play is exemplary: the unities are faultlessly, yet unobtrusively, observed, and each stage of the action accelerates the downfall of this perfect Aristotelian heroine, whom her creator saw as 'ni tout à fait coupable, ni tout à fait innocente, . . . engagée par sa destinée, et par la colère des Dieux, dans une passion illégitime dont elle a horreur toute la première'. Mythological allusions are aided by powerfully evocative imagery; and Racine makes of the classical alexandrine, and of the restricted vocabulary of *le style noble*, a medium so flexible in its range, and so marvellously expressive of tragic emotion that the 'poésie tragique' of *Phèdre* has never been equalled. Altogether, this play is the perfect example of that 'creative imitation' which was central to the theory of seventeenth-century classicism: Euripides' *Hippolytus*, and the versions of Seneca and other imitators, are left far behind, and from the moment of Racine's creation onwards, *Phèdre* stands as a truly French masterpiece.

In addition to comedy and tragedy, other poetic genres still enjoyed a traditional prestige – as can be seen from *L'Art poétique* (1674) of Nicolas Boileau-Despréaux (1636–1711), where the genres most highly regarded are the epic (ironically, since no epic of distinction was written during the whole classical period in France), the ode (of which Boileau himself, Racine and others wrote rather formal examples to commemorate official occasions) and satire. It was in his own *Satires* (1660 onwards) that Boileau had made his mark with contemporaries, using the form principally as a vehicle for literary criticism. As in the *Art poétique* (modelled on Horace's *Ars poetica*) and his *Épîtres* (1674 onwards), Boileau took his stand on formal perfection, and on the paramount importance of *la raison, le bon sens* in matters of literary taste. However, he recognized the inability of 'rules' on their own to produce poetry; and though he was himself a clever versifier rather than an inspired poet, what he looked for in the works of other poets was that intangible element of *le sublime* which defies definition – indeed, which perceptive critics throughout the century had referred to as *le je ne sais quoi*. The most attractive side of Boileau's talents as an original writer is shown in *Le Lutrin* (1674–83), the mock-heroic poem in six cantos based on personal rivalries in clerical circles in Paris, which provided a model for Pope's *Rape of the Lock*. Wit, fantasy, satirical purpose are all controlled by an urbane sense of form and style, which make of *Le Lutrin* a masterpiece of comic writing in the classical manner.

The other major non-dramatic poet of the classical age, Jean de La Fontaine (1621–95), surely suffers from the fact that the fable is usually associated with didactic writing for juvenile readers. However, in his *Fables* (1668; 1678; 1694), La Fontaine completely transcends the limitations of his chosen form; and though an earlier critical tradition concentrated excessively on the ethical teaching to be derived from them, we are perhaps better able today to appreciate, beneath the apparent naïvety of these traditional tales about animals, or these simple parables about stylized allegorical figures, the mature literary skills of a highly imaginative writer. The mock-heroic is one of the many elements which go towards making up La Fontaine's inimitable manner; but though he is often thought of primarily as a comic poet, deflating the vain and the pretentious, his range also includes the tender and the intimate, as well as the lyrical expression of a feeling for nature rare among his contemporaries. His vocabulary breaks the confines of *le style noble* – indeed, he derives great effect from the humorous juxta-position of the stylized and stately with the homely, the concrete and the picturesque – and as regards metre, while he can handle the noble alexandrine very impressively, his most characteristic manner depends on the virtuosity with which he manipulates the irregular rhythms of his favourite *vers libres*.

The novel was meanwhile being adapted to suit a new generation of readers; and although contemporaries still regarded it as a secondary genre, it produced at least one masterpiece which is an excellent em-bodiment of the essential classical manner. This is *La Princesse de Clèves* (1678) by Marie-Madeleine de La Fayette (1634–93), which may have owed something to collaboration with La Rochefoucauld and others, and certainly reflects ways of thinking, as well as linguistic habits, current in the *salons*. The novel has now turned its back on the fanciful *romanesque* settings of its pastoral and heroic predecessors, in order to explore the relationship between various kinds of love and the demands of society, in a sober, realistic context. (Indeed, the first novel to demonstrate such acute perception in a similarly realistic setting, *Les Lettres portugaises* (1669), was so convincing that for generations this remarkable little work – a collection of five letters written by a nun to her faithless lover – was thought to be authentic; its attribution, as a work of fiction, to Gabriel-Joseph de Guilleragues (1628–85), is now generally accepted.) Although Madame de La Fayette's novel is set in the French court of the sixteenth century, this is a transparent disguise for the manners and preoccupations of her own times; and her heroine, who rejects the chance of an apparently 'happy' marriage, because she is aware that few men are capable of preserving their love after marriage, and fears to sacrifice her own peace of mind, represents a mature blend of 'Cornelian' idealism with 'Racinian' realism. The language of the novel is very much of its time, achieving its effects by understatement and subtle nuance rather than by rhetorical flourish; and it is entirely fitting that a woman novelist should have created the most distinguished literary monument to that feminine influence which, in the *salons*, was largely responsible for making of the French classical language such an expressive medium for the lucid analysis of the affairs of the heart.

When we turn to Marie de Rabutin-Chantal, Marquise de Sévigné (1626–96), the other outstanding woman writer of this generation, we find someone who though very much of her time, is – not unlike La

Fontaine – too idiosyncratic in her manner to be truly representative. Her correspondence (published in the eighteenth century) gives a marvellously rich picture of the social scene, at court and in private, as well as a charmingly intimate portrait of the writer herself. Yet even when her letters are humorous, inconsequential and informal, they are written with a careful eye to literary effect, products of that art which consists in concealing artifice. Madame de Sévigné is not only an admirable example of the cultured, educated, critical reader for whom the *grands classiques* themselves wrote, but one of the most skilful – and one of the most engaging – prose-writers of her day.

But perhaps the most distinguished prose-writer of the period was a man who stood completely apart, and who, if he does reflect the society in which he lived, reflects it in a highly critical light. The *Pensées* of Blaise Pascal (1623–62) represent an uncompromising reminder of the spiritual values of the Christian faith. This work remained incomplete at Pascal's death, so that in place of the dialectical cogency of the *Lettres provinciales* (1656–7), his masterly satire directed against the casuistry and the 'morale relâchée' of the Jesuits, the *Pensées* possess a certain enigmatic quality and lack of structural coherence, in spite of the aphoristic brilliance of many individual fragments. However, the central theme – human weakness, and the futility of worldly life – is clear enough: Pascal's view of human nature has much in common with that of La Rochefoucauld or Madame de La Fayette, but in his case 'la misère de l'homme sans Dieu' is contrasted with man's potential greatness, which can be achieved through divine grace. It seems reasonably certain that the structure of the completed work would have focused on a persuasive appeal to the *honnête homme* to forgo the transitory delights and *divertissements* of this world, staking everything on winning the more lasting rewards of an after-life.[1]

Pascal is the first master of a really modern prose style, and a comparison with a writer like Descartes is most revealing in this respect. While Descartes's prose is full of tortuous Latinisms, Pascal uses a short sentence, and is sparing with subordinate clauses; and the ease, clarity and precision which result are equally appropriate to the penetrating analysis of human nature in the *Pensées* and to the irony and comic force of the *Provinciales*.

[1] Pascal's celebrated 'wager' is formulated in *pensée* no. 343 (ed. L. Lafuma, Paris, 1960).

Classicism: the Imitative Years 1680–1715

Something of what Pascal had hoped to effect with the *Pensées* was brought about by other means after his death. The example of the *solitaires* at Port-Royal, and the influence of Jansenist teaching generally; the pulpit oratory of Bossuet and others; the widespread work of lay *directeurs de conscience* in aristocratic and bourgeois households; and at court the personal example of Madame de Maintenon: through a combination of these factors, a new climate of *dévotion* begins to become apparent towards 1680 throughout French intellectual and cultural life. The consequences are numerous and varied. A new premium on orthodoxy led to a wave of 'conversions' among notabilities, some certainly genuine, many no doubt feigned – for to quote La Bruyère, 'un dévot est celui qui, sous un roi athée, serait athée'; renewed clerical opposition to the theatre led to persecution of actors (who were not to enjoy full civil rights in France until the Revolution); while at Versailles there was a new moral earnestness, even austerity, which contrasted oddly with the elaborate pomp and ceremony.

However outspoken some of his criticisms of the king, as well as of his subjects, for their falling-off from religious duties, it is impossible not to see in Jacques-Bénigne Bossuet (1627–1704) one of the principal pillars of the régime of 'le Roi Soleil'. For Bossuet, Louis represented the ideal of kingship, as God's representative on earth, the divinely ordained head of a society in which he saw the culmination of a providential historical process leading from the beginnings of Judaeo-Christian civilization to this magnificent climax. This theory of history, and of the Divine Right of Kings, was set out in the *Discours sur l'histoire universelle* (1681) and the *Politique tirée de l'Écriture sainte* (published posthumously in 1709), both written in Bossuet's capacity as tutor to the dauphin. But influential though this office was, he exerted a much wider influence through his sermons (up to 1669) and more particularly his funeral orations (up to 1687), which represent probably the highest level of classical oratory known in modern times. Bossuet, like Pascal, uses simple constructions; he makes little use of affective vocabulary, and his appeal is to the rational faculty of his hearers; but his sober, intellectual vocabulary is powerfully aided by rhetorical rhythms and patterns. For example, see how compellingly, in the *Oraison funèbre d'Henriette d'Angleterre* (1670), his message – a simplified version of Pascal's theme of the duality of man, the *grandeur* alongside the *misère* – is reinforced by an oratory whose power stands out even on the printed page.

Another royal preceptor (to the Duc de Bourgogne, the king's grandson) was François de Salignac de la Mothe-Fénelon (1651–1715). Fénelon was cast in a different mould from Bossuet: gentler and more inclined to mysticism in religion (his involvement with quietism, the doctrine of passive submission to the divine will, caused him to fall foul of Bossuet), yet readier to see faults in the system of absolute monarchy. The political reforms advocated by Fénelon and other liberals grouped round the Duke were principally expressed in a series of pamphlets and treatises; but the Archbishop also used fictional narrative as a vehicle for moral instruction to a young prince, in the allegorical novel *Télémaque* (1699). This purports to be a continuation of the fourth book of the *Odyssey*, and tells of Telemachus' wanderings in search of his father; instruction is chiefly provided by the goddess Minerva, in the guise of his wise companion Mentor, while the episodic structure permits of frequent portraits, exemplary or cautionary, of good and bad kings. *Télémaque* is more dated than most works of its time; but obeying, as it did, the precept of *instruire et plaire*, and combining pagan mythology with Christian ethical teaching, it is an excellent embodiment of the classical aesthetic. Rather marginal to the main development of the modern novel, it nevertheless represents a link between such seventeenth-century novels as those of Mademoiselle de Scudéry and the use of the novel form, for didactic purposes, by Voltaire and others a generation or two later.

Like Fénelon with Homer (and we may compare Boileau's relationship with Horace, Racine's with Sophocles and Euripides, and La Fontaine's with Phaedrus or Aesop), Jean de La Bruyère (1645–96) showed himself to be thoroughly 'classical' in placing himself under the patronage of a writer of antiquity; indeed, his *Caractères* (1688) began modestly as a translation of Theophrastus' *Characters*, amplified with some original 'portraits' of his own. However, compared with his Greek original (and with La Rochefoucauld, with whom he is often coupled), La Bruyère is less interested in generalized psychological abstractions common to all ages than in the specific follies and failings of seventeenth-century France (as the full title of the work, *Caractères de Théophraste traduits du grec, avec les Caractères ou les Mœurs de ce siècle*, indicates). Successive editions, up to 1694, added more material, and a very personal point of view emerges, critical of the king's warmongering and of extravagance at Versailles, and scornful of the vanities and pretensions of a status-conscious society. The final impression is of a humane, ironical view of mankind, sharpened in places into a trenchant criticism of his own age. If at times La Bruyère can write like La Rochefoucauld, and at others like Theophrastus, his more characteristic manner is one of graphic description; as has been said, he had the makings of a naturalist novelist.

A gift for description, allied to a very personal critical view of the court of the Sun King, also characterizes the *Mémoires* (covering the period from 1692 onwards, published in the nineteenth century) of Louis de Rouvroy, Duc de Saint-Simon (1675–1755). The approach is a somewhat jaundiced one: Saint-Simon shows the haughty prejudice of a *duc et pair* against what he calls a 'règne de vile bourgeoisie' (in other words, one in which administrative power had passed from the hereditary nobility into the hands of Louis's Ministers); but here is an enormously rich canvas, painted with a remarkable eye for detail.

Concentration on significant differences between individuals (as opposed to the preference for generalized abstractions about human behaviour, shown by Pascal, La Rochefoucauld, Madame de La Fayette – or even Racine) was still rare in imaginative literature; but such an approach is, of course, very much that of comedy. In prose comedy, writers like Edmé Boursault (1638–1701), Molière's colleague Michel Baron (1653–1729), Charles Dufresny (1648–1724) and Florent Carton Dancourt (1666–1725) developed a profitable vein of social satire. Baron's *Homme à bonnes fortunes* (1686) and Dancourt's *Chevalier à la mode* (1687) focus on the same social type, the *petit-maître*, while a number of Dancourt's other plays deal with the phenomenon of social climbing among wealthy *bourgeoises*, female counterparts of Molière's Monsieur Jourdain. The masterpiece of the genre is *Turcaret* (1709) by Alain-René Lesage (1668–1747), in which the central comic figure is a rich tax-farmer whose social climbing leads to his undoing. Lesage's view of society is thoroughly cynical, and the plot produces a 'ricochet de fourberies', as each confidence-trickster is in turn duped by another.

However, pride of place was still claimed, in the hierarchy of comic genres, by five-act verse comedy, and for another century playwrights were to continue composing very derivative *comédies de caractère* in this medium, in imitation of Molière; though one author to impose his own characteristic formula was Jean-François Regnard (1655–1709), who introduced into *haute comédie* destined for the Théâtre-Français the comic devices he had learned in writing for the less hidebound 'Italiens'.

His plays, of which *Le Légataire universel* (1708) is the best, contain a large measure of gay fantasy and literary parody; like the Italian actors, Regnard exploits theatrical illusion instead of trying to conceal it, and he is completely lacking in the sententious moralizing that was to affect his successors.

Otherwise, the general impression is of a period in which 'pure' literature remains derivative and uninspired. Exception must be made in tragedy for Racine's own last plays, *Esther* (1689) and *Athalie* (1691), in which creative dramatic writing was skilfully reconciled with the new climate of puritanical *dévotion* at Versailles; both plays were written, not for the professional theatre, but for the young ladies of a college at Saint-Cyr. Returning to the biblical subjects popular in the previous century, Racine also introduces a chorus of young women; in both plays, the choral passages were set to music. *Esther* hardly transcends the range of elegiac oratorio, but in *Athalie* the powerful characterization of the Queen of Judah, and the savage revenge executed by the prophet Joad in Jehovah's name, have caused many connoisseurs to see this as the peak of Racinian tragedy. Other writers of tragedy were as much overawed by the reputation of Corneille and Racine as comic playwrights were by that of Molière. Racine's outstanding successor was Prosper Jolyot de Crébillon (1674-1762), who in the early years of the century wrote a series of tragedies (e.g. *Atrée et Thyeste*, 1707; *Rhadamiste et Zénobie*, 1711), in which the subtler emotions of pity and fear are replaced by the pathetic and the terrifying. Crébillon is said to have declared: 'Corneille avait pris le ciel, Racine la terre; il ne me restait que l'enfer'; the spectator's sensibility is assaulted by scenes intended to shock, and by an abuse of emotive vocabulary.

Perhaps one sign of the lack of inventiveness in imaginative literature is the amount of attention given to theory and criticism: this period saw the outbreak of the 'Querelle des Anciens et des Modernes', in which the perennial controversy about the possibility of 'progress' in the arts came to a head in the Academy and elsewhere. While Boileau and others saw the best literature of antiquity as embodying permanent standards of excellence (and advocated imitation of such models as the means of attaining similar excellence), the 'Modernes' such as Charles Perrault (1628-1703) in his *Parallèle des anciens et des modernes* (1688-97) and Bernard Le Bovier de Fontenelle (1657-1757) in his *Digression sur les anciens et les modernes* (1688) claimed that the best of contemporary literature was inevitably superior, because of the greater maturity of the human mind. It was a sterile and inconclusive debate – paradoxically, the 'Modernes' illustrated their case by pointing to the excellence as creative writers of those who, as theorists, championed the superiority of ancient literature – but the underlying issue was a most important one. For the 'Modernes' indirectly, if not explicitly, anticipated those eighteenth-century thinkers whose rejection of the notion of a single universal aesthetic, valid for all time and place, in favour of a relativist approach, was to bring about the end of the neo-classical age.

For the time being, however, such ideas lay dormant, and creative writing remains largely derivative. If we turn to the literature of ideas, however, we find Pierre Bayle (1647–1706) and Fontenelle much more forward-looking. Besides his *Digressions* . . ., Fontenelle wrote an important work popularizing science in his *Entretiens sur la pluralité des mondes* (1686), an exposé of the Copernican system in the form of an urbane dialogue between the author and an intelligent, but uninformed, noblewoman; and in the *Histoire des oracles* (1687) he surveys pagan belief in oracular prediction in the spirit of Cartesian rationalism. Bayle, whose life-work was to be the erudite *Dictionnaire historique et critique* (first edition 1697), showed himself equally sceptical towards religious superstitions in his *Pensées diverses sur la comète* (1682). The seeds are here of that rationalist critique of tradition and authority in all spheres of intellectual activity, which was to characterize eighteenth-century thought. But if such signs of what was to come are already visible in the period which has been given the label of *la crise de la conscience*,[1] French culture still remained too insular for the crisis to become a general one; in particular, it lacked that contact with the outside world which was to prove the necessary catalyst.

The Age of Reason 1715–1750

After Louis XIV's death, the relaxed atmosphere of the Regency brought about certain tangible changes (for instance, the return of the Italian players who had been expelled in 1697 for a satire on Madame de Maintenon). There was a gradual increase in foreign contacts, and as the century progressed, intellectual life became more and more cosmopolitan. English influences became particularly important – it is common, indeed, to speak of eighteenth-century 'anglomania' – though in the first half of the century, such influences chiefly concern the literature of ideas rather than imaginative writing. The rapid growth of periodical literature produced many new journals which both reflected

[1] Cf. P. Hazard, *La Crise de la conscience européenne (1680–1715)* (Paris, 1935).

English influence – e.g. the *Spectateur français*, launched by Marivaux in 1722 in imitation of Addison's *Spectator* – and disseminated knowledge about England, e.g. Prévost's *Le Pour et contre*, begun in 1733. In Prévost's case this followed a visit to England, and other major writers who visited this country at a decisive point in their careers were Montesquieu and Voltaire.

Charles Secondat, Baron de Montesquieu (1689–1755), owed to the example of English life and letters several important features of his major work, *L'Esprit des lois* (1748): the notion of the separation of the three powers (executive, legislative and judiciary), and the ideal of a 'mixed', or constitutional, monarchy. But however widely read, and however influential (e.g. on the shaping of the American constitution), this was a work for specialists, which lies outside the province of imaginative literature – as does Montesquieu's historical work *Considérations sur les causes de la grandeur des Romains et de leur décadence* (1734). The work which best illustrates the spirit of the age, *Lettres persanes* (1721), was written before Montesquieu's English visit. Purporting to be a collection of letters written by two Persian travellers in Europe, with enough replies from the seraglio to sustain a flimsy plot, this volume appeals to the Regency taste for the licentious in literature, and also to the vogue for the exotic, which had been stimulated by the translation of the *Arabian Nights* (1704) and the publication of several authentic travellers' tales. But more important, its *romanesque* framework and episodic structure allow the author to range over a wide range of social, economic, political and religious practices; the naïve reactions of the Oriental travellers provide a means of submitting the customs of Western civilization to the critique of Cartesian rationalism; and Montesquieu is able, under a fictional cloak, to preach a message of tolerance, deism and social justice.

François-Marie Arouet (1694–1778), known as Voltaire, made direct use of his stay in England from 1726 to 1729 to compose an even more striking indictment of French society; indeed, his *Lettres philosophiques* (1734) were seized by order of the Parlement de Paris and publicly burnt. The *Lettres* contain a comprehensive survey of English political, religious, intellectual and cultural life; at each stage there is an implied comparison with France, almost everywhere to the advantage of the English. What Voltaire admires in English life is the evidence of a pragmatic, empirical outlook, resulting in religious tolerance, a constitutional monarchy, respect for the individual, and social and economic progress. The *Lettres* are most agreeably written: Voltaire covers his tracks by the use of irony, and by feigning to criticize English 'abuses' (as in the opening letters on the Quakers); though hardly subtle, this approach is very effective, and Voltaire's allusive, ironical manner is the one the *philosophes* were to favour throughout the century.

But we must remember that although to us Voltaire is principally remembered as a *conteur*, a *philosophe* and a campaigner for justice and truth, to his contemporaries – at least up to 1750 – he was first and foremost a writer of tragedy, to be spoken of in the same terms as Corneille and Racine. And if he was a 'Moderne' in intellectual matters generally, Voltaire was the most reactionary of 'Anciens' in matters of taste, never swerving from an uncompromising belief in a universally applicable aesthetic. His attitude to Shakespeare illustrates this. In the *Lettres philosophiques* he finds it possible to praise the English dramatist as a creator of 'belles scènes'; but judged as a whole, he finds him 'sans la moindre étincelle de bon goût et sans la moindre connaissance des règles'. And though on his return from England he appears not un-willing to commend certain features of Shakespearian tragedy to his readers, towards the end of his life (by which time other, much more sympathetic, interpreters were at work) he dismisses him scornfully as 'un sauvage ivre'. Other dramatists, even at the beginning of our period, were more openminded; for instance, Voltaire carried on a controversy with Antoine Houdar de la Motte (1672–1731), a friend of Fontenelle and champion of the Moderns, who argued for the use of prose as a medium for tragedy. However, in practice even La Motte lacked the courage of his convictions, and the real originality of his highly successful *Inès de Castro* (1723) was that it catered so well for the new wave of sensibility, concentrating on the pathetic sufferings of an innocent victim. Inès is persecuted because she has contracted a morgan-atic marriage with the Infante of Portugal, and the appearance of their young children on stage represents a *locus classicus* of that *pathétique moralisateur* which is found in so much of the imaginative writing of the century, based on the belief that display of the emotions must be salutary, and that readiness to be moved is proof of moral worth.

Even Voltaire himself made concessions to the *sensibilité* he affected to scorn. For instance, a completely inappropriate love plot is introduced into his first tragedy *Oedipe* (1718); and in *Zaïre* (1732), his finest play, the 'Aristotelian' tragic hero Orosmane takes second place to the pathetic heroine, killed as a result of her jealous lover's unfounded suspicion. But this updating of the Othello theme is only one aspect of *Zaïre*: the play is also an excellent example of the way in which Voltaire introduced ideological issues into tragedy, for Orosmane is a Moslem prince, and Zaïre a Christian; and the catastrophe is at least partly due to the fanatical zealotry of the Crusaders. In other early tragedies Voltaire introduced borrowings from Shakespeare: a crowd-scene in *La Mort de César* (1731), Hamlet's ghost into *Ériphile* (1732) and *Sémiramis* (1748); but the essential formula remains derivative and uninspired. If anything, there is a tendency for tragedy to degenerate into melodrama; and the only redeeming feature is the vigorous portrayal of a thesis, when Voltaire uses the theatre to preach his gospel of humanitarian tolerance (e.g. in *Alzire* (1736), which portrays the inhuman Spanish conquest of Peru in the name of Christianity; or in *Mahomet* (1742), in which the unscrupulous tyrant stands for all political oppression practised under cover of religion).

It was not only in tragedy that *le pathétique* made its appeal to theatre audiences. Among the oustanding *hautes comédies* of the period, there are few which are frankly *comic: La Métromanie* (1738) by Alexis Piron (1689–1773) is a refreshing exception. More typical are the heavily moralizing comedies of Philippe Néricault Destouches (1680–1754) such as *Le Curieux impertinent* (1709) or *Le Glorieux* (1732), and *Le Méchant* (1745) by Jean-Baptiste-Louis Gresset (1709–77). But Pierre-Claude Nivelle de La Chaussée (1692–1754) went much further, and created a new genre, *la comédie larmoyante*, which achieved its edifying effect above all by a pathetic appeal to the spectator's sensibility. *Le Préjugé à la mode* (1735) portrays the plight of a wife, unjustly neglected by her husband in obedience to the fashionable idea that to love one's wife is old-fashioned; but more typical is *Mélanide* (1741), in which the central character is a long-suffering unmarried mother (for the 'mariage secret' which was such a cliché of the sentimental literature of the age was merely a euphemism for a liaison). Virtue inevitably triumphs, but not before every pathetic possibility has been exploited, including the recognition-scene, the *scène à faire* of all these tearful dramas. Although Voltaire dismissed *comédie larmoyante* as 'la tragédie des femmes de chambre' he himself wrote one or two examples, his *Nanine* (1749) being inspired, like La Chaussée's *Paméla* (1743), by Richardson's novel.

An altogether subtler form of comedy had in the meantime been developed by Pierre Carlet de Chamblain de Marivaux (1688–1763). Marivaux began writing for the Italians, and although he never reproduced the stereotype 'Italian' comedy with its buffoonery and slapstick, he did take over stock characters such as the colourless lovers and the stylized valets. Freed from the need to develop 'character', he could exploit to the full his talent for light, graceful, inconsequential dialogue; similarly, his plots are of the simplest, and the conventional parents, guardians and rivals are never important in Marivaux's comedy: indeed, they are often dispensed with altogether, and what matters is the psychological 'obstacle' in the characters' minds. So, in the most characteristic of his plays, *La Surprise de l'amour* (1722), *La Double Inconstance* (1723), *Le Jeu de l'amour et du hasard* (1730) – generally considered his masterpiece – or *Les Fausses Confidences* (1737), dialogue acquires a real autonomy. It is from the very fact of two persons being together and conversing that the significant developments in his plots come about: they meet, each wishes to attract the other, but neither wishes to be caught; they fall in love; they become aware of their feelings; they resist; they yield. This sort of dramatic writing has been given the name *marivaudage*; the term is often used pejoratively of other writers, but applied to Marivaux himself it denotes a style which may be mannered and affected, but is full of psychological penetration. Marivaux is, with Beaumarchais, one of the two really original dramatic writers of the century; his plays have lasted better than most of the imaginative writing of the time, and have had a remarkable success in the theatre in our own day.

Something of the same delicacy of touch, particularly in the exploration of the feminine mind, marks Marivaux's two novels, *La Vie de Marianne* (1731–41) and *Le Paysan parvenu* (1735–6). These are both 'memoir-novels', written in the first person; and rather than a 'realist' picture of a social scene, they provide a very personal record of the reactions of an individual temperament to the places and persons surrounding the writer. The particular contribution of Marivaux to the novel is his sensitivity to nuances of behaviour and especially speech, as indices of character; but like most of his contemporaries, he paid little attention to form and structure in the novel, and both *Marianne* and *Le Paysan* are unfinished.

It was still common at this time to draw a distinction between a *roman* (a self-confessed work of fiction) and an *histoire* (a short story or 'memoir' which at least claimed to be authentic).[1] Marivaux may be said to represent a fusion of these two traditions; the other two major novelists of the time can be situated more easily with regard to existing categories. Lesage wrote two novels, *Le Diable boiteux* (1707), a fantasy in which a friendly demon lifts the roofs of houses in Madrid and reveals life as it is lived; and *Gil Blas* (1715–35), which adopts the

[1] Cf. F. Deloffre, *La Nouvelle en France à l'âge classique* (Paris, 1967).

episodic form of the Spanish picaresque novel. Both contain a series of good-humoured satirical sketches: though more down-to-earth than the *romans héroïques* of the previous century, they are less earthy than for example Scarron, and Lesage represents the equivalent in the novel of an urbane *comédie de mœurs*. Antoine-François Prévost (1687–1763) adopts a different sort of framework for his *Mémoires d'un homme de qualité* (1728–31) and *Le Philosophe anglais, ou les Mémoires de Cleveland* (1732–9): a first-person narrative, into which can be interpolated shorter autobiographical 'memoirs'. One of these, 'L'Histoire du chevalier des Grieux et de Manon Lescaut' (originally forming volume VII of the *Homme de qualité*), so transcends the limitations of its framework, and of the tradition to which this belongs, that it stands as a self-contained masterpiece among the great French novels. In view of Prévost's habitual prolixity, *Manon Lescaut* possesses a truly remarkable economy; the 'confessional' first-person narrative makes the idealization of the faithless Manon by her lover completely plausible, and the account of Des Grieux's degradation as a result of his passion for her has such a compelling fatalism and mythic power that the novel has understandably been called both 'Jansenist' and 'Racinian'.

The two kinds of novel – the autobiographical 'memoir' and the 'romance' – are further represented by Claude-Prosper Jolyot de Crébillon *fils* (1707–77) in *Les Égarements du cœur et de l'esprit* (1736) and *Le Sopha* (1745), the one catering for contemporary taste by offering the exemplary lesson of a 'case-history', the other by titillating the imagination. Prévost's later novels (e.g. *L'Histoire d'une Grecque moderne*, 1740) fulfil both aims; they are very much of their time, and have not survived the age in which they were written. Only in *Manon Lescaut* did Prévost capture a more universal appeal; with *La Princesse de Clèves, Manon* represents the expression of the French classical ideal in novel form.

Manon Lescaut is often compared with Defoe's *Moll Flanders*. Almost contemporary, and dealing with similar milieux, the two novels are nevertheless totally unlike in literary flavour. While Defoe the realist offers at every point material proof of Moll's poverty, Prévost is content to establish credibility by the autobiographical memoir form, and otherwise makes few concessions to 'realism'. In fact, he uses the same elevated, highly abstract *style noble* as usage decreed for poetic genres, and this is the key to the essential literary quality of his novel: Des Grieux's lament over the body of his dead mistress, for instance, constitutes an elegiac prose-poem. But however successful in such rare instances in raising the prosaic to the level of the sublime, *le style noble* was to cripple poetic expression, and inhibit imagination, throughout the century.

The most celebrated poet of this generation, Jean-Baptiste Rousseau (1671–1741), remained derivative as regards form and subject-matter, as well as expression; and perhaps the genre which best suited the stylized poetic diction, with its limited vocabulary, its abstractions, its colourless epithets and its heritage of clichés, was the philosophical ode developed by Voltaire. Voltaire's poetic output was considerable, one of his first literary achievements being the epic *La Henriade* (1723); but neither this nor his mock-epic *La Pucelle* (1755) equals poems such as his *Discours sur l'homme* (1738), modelled on Pope, *Le Mondain* (1736), a panegyric of modern civilization and a vindication of luxury, or the eloquent and moving *Poème sur le désastre de Lisbonne* (1756). In tragedy, the limitations of the impoverished vocabulary become more apparent as Voltaire and other playwrights turn from ancient history and mythology to modern subjects; cf. Voltaire's tragedies based on medieval French history (e.g. *Adélaïde du Guesclin*, 1734; *Tancrède*, 1760) and on Oriental civilizations (*Mahomet; L'Orphelin de la Chine*, 1755). Although the emphasis in such tragedies remains ideological, and local colour is not stressed, the shortcomings of *le style noble* are revealed when cannon and firearms have to be called 'foudres mugissantes' or 'longs tubes d'airain'.

Among prose-writers, the classical style continued to serve those who were concerned to generalize about human behaviour, such as Montesquieu in *L'Esprit des lois*, or Luc de Clapiers, Marquis de Vauvenargues (1715–47), whose *Introduction à la connaissance de l'esprit humain, suivie de réflexions et maximes* (1746) continues the manner of La Rochefoucauld, though without the latter's characteristic cynicism. It was not so suitable to the purpose of those – novelists, psychologists, lyric poets – who were less concerned with such general truths than with the exploration of the individual personality in relation to its surroundings. Such writers needed a more varied, concrete, colourful vocabulary, and the enrichment of the affective resources of the language; this is a development that we associate above all with the generation of 1830, but it was a continuous process, and the language of Diderot and Rousseau is no longer that of Montesquieu and Voltaire. In this sense, if in no other, there is some truth in Goethe's remark, 'One world finishes with Voltaire, another begins with Rousseau'.

In spite of his conservatism in literary matters, Voltaire created, or at least made his own, the genre which best represents the spirit of the closing decades of our period. *Gulliver's Travels* is perhaps the nearest antecedent to Voltaire's *contes philosophiques*; indeed, *Micromégas* (1752), in which the Earth is visited by giants from Sirius and Saturn, clearly owes a good deal to Swift. More characteristic, however, are those *contes* in which the central character is a human traveller whose reactions to the vicissitudes of life make him wiser and if not happier, at least more resigned to his lot. Social satire abounds – from passing digs at rival philosophers or men of letters, and caricatural portraits of priests or politicians, to a much more sustained attack on various aspects of French life in *L'Ingénu* (1767). But Voltaire's chief subject in the *contes* is metaphysical speculation, and he uses this narrative form for the imaginative treatment of those philosophical issues which concerned him all his life: the question of a benevolent Providence (*Zadig*, 1747); the problem of evil (*Candide*, 1759; *Le Blanc et le noir*, 1764). Characterization remains rudimentary: the 'rounded' characters of the novel would not have suited the author's purpose, and Voltaire's ideal traveller is a simple, passive figure – the names Candide and l'Ingénu are indicative of the quality shared by most of his heroes – surrounded by caricatural puppets who respond in a predictable way to every new experience. In fact, this is the world of the comic strip cartoon – or would be, were it not for Voltaire's mastery of the literary language; for here we have the supreme example of classical French as the language of reason: crisp, economical sentences constructed with an eye to balance and antithesis, and gaining the maximum effect from irony and understatement.

Candide is the richest of the *contes*, and one of the acknowledged masterpieces of eighteenth-century literature. This is a devastating attack on the optimism professed by Leibniz and Pope, sparked off by the facile religious and philosophical explanations of the Lisbon earthquake. As one nightmarish experience succeeds another, Candide progresses from parrot-like repetition of Pangloss's 'Tout est au mieux' to a reasoned acceptance of the message of the wise old Turk, 'Il faut cultiver notre jardin'. An avoidance of futile speculation; the acceptance of life as it is; a practical endeavour to improve one's lot and that of others: such is the positive conclusion offered in *Candide* by one who was to write as his own epitaph:

J'ai fait un peu de bien; c'est mon meilleur ouvrage.

Bibliography

GENERAL STUDIES

As regards comprehensive literary histories of the period, A. Adam, *Histoire de la littérature française au XVIIe siècle*, 5 vols (Paris, 1948–56), is in a class by itself, combining as it does detailed information over a very wide range with an individual (and often original) point of view. This period is also covered in such single volumes as J. Vier, *Histoire de la littérature française, XVIe–XVIIe siècles* (Paris, 1959), and P. J. Yarrow, *A Literary History of France, II: Seventeenth Century* (London, 1967), as well as in a volume of essays by several hands, J. Cruickshank (ed.), *French Literature and its Background, II: Seventeenth Century* (London, 1969). An excellent series of volumes by various authors, still in course of publication (*Littérature française*, published by Arthaud), includes J. Morel, *La Renaissance, III: 1570–1624* (Paris, 1973), A. Adam, *L'Âge classique, I: 1624–1660* (Paris, 1968), P. Clarac, *L'Âge classique, II: 1660–1680* (Paris, 1969), and R. Pomeau, *L'Âge classique, III: 1680–1720* (Paris, 1971). The volume in this series devoted to the period 1720–1750 (J. Ehrard, *Le XVIIIe Siècle, I*) has still to appear; but the eighteenth century has been treated in J. Vier, *Histoire de la littérature française, XVIIIe siècle*, 2 vols (Paris, 1971), R. Niklaus, *A Literary History of France, III: Eighteenth Century* (London, 1970), and J. Cruickshank (ed.), *French Literature and its Background, III: Eighteenth Century* (London, 1970).

Two volumes by J. Lough, *An Introduction to Seventeenth-Century France* (London, 1954) and *An Introduction to Eighteenth-Century France* (London, 1960), survey the historical and social background against which the literature of the respective periods was written; while a rather more specialized background is treated in each of two works by G. Mongrédien, *La Vie de société aux XVIIe et XVIIIe siècles* (Paris, 1950), and *La Vie littéraire au XVIIe siècle* (Paris, 1947). The two volumes by W. D. Howarth, *Life and Letters in France, I: The Seventeenth Century* (London, 1965), and R. Fargher, *Life and Letters in France, II: The Eighteenth Century* (London, 1970), portray the social and intellectual world of selected authors of these two centuries and of the public for whom they wrote. G. Reynier, *La Femme au XVIIe siècle* (Paris, 1929); M. Magendie, *La Politesse mondaine et les théories de l'honnêteté en France de 1600 à 1660* (Paris, 1925); A. Adam (ed.), *Les Libertins au XVIIe siècle* (Paris, 1964); R. Lathuillière, *La Préciosité*, vol. 1 (Geneva, 1966); and G. Mongrédien (ed.), *Les Précieux et les précieuses* (Paris, 1963), between them give a very informative account of various social movements which were intimately connected with the literature of the century. For the detailed picture of an immensely wide range of the intellectual life of the seventeenth century, there is no modern work to equal C. A. Sainte-Beuve, *Port-Royal*, 3 vols (Paris, 1953–5; first published 1840–59); though J. C. Tournand, *Introduction à la vie littéraire du XVIIe siècle* (Paris, 1970), offers a brief but helpful survey of the intellectual and moral climate of the time. Stimulating interpretative studies of the moral climate of the seventeenth century from a personal point of view are offered by P. Bénichou, *Morales du Grand Siècle* (Paris, 1948), and A. J. Krailsheimer, *Studies in Self-Interest* (Oxford, 1962). The first two volumes of P. Trahard, *Les Maîtres de la sensibilité française au XVIIIe siècle*, 4 vols (Paris, 1931), deal with the moral and intellectual atmosphere of the period 1700-50.

Within the seventeenth century, there was until quite recently a tendency to concentrate excessively on the generation of 1660-85 (together with such other 'classical' phenomena as the early tragedies of Corneille). However, the post-war years have seen a remarkable widening of this interest, with the development of an important new focus of critical attention in the literature of the 'preclassical' or 'baroque' generation, and in the contrast between this and classical literature itself. Among critical works reflecting this new orientation are R. Morçay and P. Sage, *Le Préclassicisme* (Paris, 1962); J. Rousset, *La Littérature de l'âge baroque en France* (Paris, 1954); M. Raymond, *Baroque et renaissance poétique* (Paris, 1955); I. Buffum, *Studies in the Baroque from Montaigne to Rotrou* (Yale, 1957). G. de Reynold, *Synthèse du XVIIe siècle: France classique et Europe baroque* (Paris, 1962), and V. L. Tapié, *Baroque et classicisme* (Paris, 1957), explore the relationship between the two critical concepts, relating the literary context to the intellectual background and the context of the visual arts respectively.

Among the wealth of secondary literature devoted to French classicism, the following will be found particularly useful. R. Bray, *La Formation de la doctrine classique en France* (Lausanne, 1931), deals with the background of theory, while G. Highet, *The Classical Tradition* (Oxford, 1949), relates French (and European) neo-classicism to the literature of classical antiquity. D. Mornet, *Histoire de la littérature française classique, 1660-1700* (Paris, 1947), studies the relationship between the masterpieces of the 'grands classiques' and the more general development of the genres within which they worked; and H. Busson, *La Religion des classiques* (Paris, 1948), investigates the religious beliefs reflected in the works of the major writers of the period 1660-85. W. G. Moore, *French Classical Literature: An Essay* (Oxford, 1962), and P. H. Nurse, *Classical Voices* (London, 1971), present critical studies of the acknowledged masterpieces of the period; while M. Turnell, *The Classical Moment: Studies of Corneille, Molière and Racine* (London, 1947), studies the three major representatives of classicism in the theatre. J. Brody (ed.), *French Classicism: A Critical Miscellany* (Englewood Cliffs, N. J., 1966), is an anthology of critical views on the subject from the seventeenth century to the present day; and among the most important interpretative essays published in recent years are H. Peyre, *Qu'est-ce que le classicisme? Essai de mise au point* (Paris, 1942), and E. B. O. Borgerhoff, *The Freedom of French Classicism* (Princeton, 1950).

Turning to works dealing with the post-classical generations, we find fewer general studies. A. Tilley, *The Decline of the Age of Louis XIV* (Cambridge, 1929), treats the literature of the period 1687-1715, while G. Atkinson and A. C. Keller, *Prelude to the Enlightenment* (London, 1971), choose for their survey the period 1690-1740. F. C. Green, *Minuet* (London, 1935), approaches the imaginative literature of the eighteenth century by means of a comparison with its English counterpart.

DRAMA

Modern historical scholarship has produced an invaluable reference-work in H. C. Lancaster, *A Study of French Dramatic Literature in the Seventeenth Century*, 9 vols (vol. 9 *Recapitulation*) (Baltimore, 1929-42): while offering little critical evaluation, this gives exhaustive information about troupes, stage conditions, authors and plays. For material conditions in the theatre, the acting profession, etc., W. L. Wiley, *The Early Public Theater in France* (Cambridge, Mass., 1960), constitutes an excellent introduction; this can be supplemented by more specialist works such as S. W. Deierkauf-Holsboer, *L'Histoire de la mise en scène dans le théâtre français à Paris de 1600 à 1673* (Paris, 1960); T. E. Lawrenson, *The French Stage in the Seventeenth Century* (Manchester, 1957); J. Lough, *Paris Theatre Audiences in the Seventeenth and Eighteenth Centuries* (London, 1957); G. Mongrédien, *La Vie quotidienne des comédiens au temps de Molière* (Paris, 1966). J. Scherer, *La Dramaturgie classique en France* (Paris, 1950), is an important work analysing the conventions within which the seventeenth-century dramatist worked.

The dramatic literature of the seventeenth century is surveyed, briefly and in a highly personal manner, by W. G. Moore in *The Classical Drama of France* (Oxford, 1971); and that of the later period, unimaginatively but quite informatively, in E. F. Jourdain, *Dramatic Theory and Practice in France, 1690–1808* (London, 1921).

Tragedy is dealt with, economically but suggestively, in G. Lanson, *Esquisse d'une histoire de la tragédie française* (New York, 1920), and in J. Morel, *La Tragédie* (Paris, 1969). Its more detailed history during various parts of our period is covered in E. Forsyth, *La Tragédie française de Jodelle à Corneille (1553–1640)* (Paris, 1962); G. Brereton, *French Tragic Drama in the Sixteenth and Seventeenth Centuries* (London, 1973); and H. C. Lancaster, *French Tragedy in the Time of Louis XV and Voltaire* (Baltimore, 1950). As regards tragicomedy, the standard work is H. C. Lancaster, *The French Tragicomedy; its Origin and Development from 1552 to 1628* (Baltimore, 1907), while the other popular dramatic form of the early seventeenth century is dealt with in J. Marsan, *La Pastorale dramatique en France à la fin du XVIe et au commencement du XVIIe siècle* (Paris, 1905). The hybrid sentimental comedy which flourished in the 1730s is the subject of G. Lanson, *Nivelle de La Chaussée et la comédie larmoyante* (Paris, rev. ed. 1903). General works on comedy during the period include E. Lintilhac, *Histoire générale du théâtre, III: La Comédie, XVIIe siècle* (Paris, 1908); *IV: La Comédie, XVIIIe siècle* (Paris, 1909); R. Guichemerre, *La Comédie avant Molière, 1640–1660* (Paris, 1972); P. Kohler, *L'Esprit classique et la comédie* (Paris, 1925); J. Lemaître, *La Comédie après Molière et le théâtre de Dancourt* (Paris, 1882).

However, most of the critical writing on classical drama has been concerned, not with the development of genres, but with the work of particular authors; and the volume of writing devoted to Corneille, Molière and Racine bears abundant witness to their pre-eminence.

Corneille criticism has taken on a new character since the war. G. Lanson, *Corneille* (Paris, 1898), is the most valuable early study; but a new approach may already be seen in V. Vedel, *Deux classiques français vus par un étranger* (Paris, 1935), while O. Nadal, *Le Sentiment de l'amour dans l'œuvre de P. Corneille* (Paris, 1948), remains the most influential revaluation. L. Rivaille, *Les Débuts de P. Corneille* (Paris, 1936), and G. Couton, *La Vieillesse de Corneille* (Paris, 1949), helped to turn critical attention away from a handful of 'major' plays by focusing on the beginning and end of the playwright's career respectively. G. Couton, *Corneille* (Paris, 1958), is a workmanlike general introduction, while other recent studies of value include S. Doubrovsky, *Corneille et la dialectique du héros* (Paris, 1963); R. J. Nelson,

Corneille, His Heroes and their Worlds (Philadelphia, 1963); P. J. Yarrow, *Corneille* (London, 1963); and J. Maurens, *La Tragédie sans tragique: le néo-stoïcisme dans l'œuvre de P. Corneille* (Paris, 1966).

The long-standing critical comparison between Corneille and Racine, which forms the subject of an anthology, R. J. Nelson (ed.), *Corneille and Racine: Parallels and Contrasts* (Englewood Cliffs, N. J., 1966), has been brought up to date by G. May, *Tragédie cornélienne, tragédie racinienne* (Urbana, 1948), and G. Pocock, *Corneille and Racine: Problems of Tragic Form* (Cambridge, 1973); while the contrast between Racinian and Shakespearean tragedy has perhaps nowhere been better handled than in L. Strachey, *Landmarks in French Literature* (London, 1912). Among recent critical works on Racine, an excellent introduction would be J. C. Lapp, *Aspects of Racinian Tragedy* (Toronto, 1955), or O. de Mourgues's sound and balanced *Racine, or the Triumph of Relevance* (Cambridge, 1967). T. Maulnier, *Racine* (Paris, 1935), still offers a very stimulating interpretation. P. France, *Racine's Rhetoric* (Oxford, 1965), and G. Cahen, *Le Vocabulaire de Racine* (Paris, 1946), provide the best guide to a critical assessment of Racine's literary technique; and E. Vinaver, *Racine et la poésie tragique* (Paris, 1951), stresses the part played by the poetry in the make-up of Racinian tragedy. The sociological interpretation of L. Goldmann, *Le Dieu caché* (Paris, 1955), has been influential, as has the structuralist interpretation of R. Barthes, *Sur Racine* (Paris, 1963). In the 1960s Racine became the subject of a sharp critical controversy between the 'nouveaux critiques' represented by Barthes and others, and their more conservative opponents led by R. Picard,whose *La Carrière de J. Racine* (Paris, 1956), is a valuable source of detailed documentation. A. Bonzon, *La Nouvelle Critique et Racine* (Paris, 1970), gives an account of this controversy; while R. C. Knight (ed.), *Racine (Modern Judgements)* (London, 1969), provides a more general selection of modern critical views.

In Molière's case, post-war criticism shows a turning away from earlier preoccupation with the 'meaning' of the plays towards a more objective aesthetic approach. Two works in particular stimulated this change: W. G. Moore, *Molière: A New Criticism* (Oxford, 1949), and R. Bray, *Molière, homme de théâtre* (Paris, 1954). The best recent interpretations include D. Romano, *Essai sur le comique de Molière* (Berne, 1950); J. Guicharnaud, *Molière, une aventure théâtrale* (Paris, 1963); J. D. Hubert, *Molière and the Comedy of Intellect* (Berkeley and Los Angeles, 1962); and M. Gutwirth, *Molière ou l'Invention comique* (Paris, 1966); though H. Bergson, *Le Rire* (Paris, 1900), still remains one of the most stimulating brief introductions to the essential character of Molière's comedy. A conspectus of modern critical views is presented in J. Guicharnaud (ed.), *Molière (Twentieth-Century Views)* (Englewood Cliffs, N. J., 1964). Readers interested in the interpretation of classical drama in the theatre by various actors should consult M. Descotes, *Les Grands Rôles du théâtre de Molière* (Paris, 1960) (cf. Descotes's companion volumes on *Racine* and *Corneille*, published in 1957 and 1962 respectively).

Turning to the post-classical period, Regnard's comedy is dealt with in A. Calame, *Regnard, sa vie et son œuvre* (Paris, 1960); Marivaux's dramatic writings are the subject of K. N. McKee, *The Theater of Marivaux* (New York, 1958), and are also dealt with at length in E. J. H. Greene, *Marivaux* (Toronto, 1965), and P. Gazagne, *Marivaux par lui-même* (Paris, 1954); and Voltaire's tragedy is studied in H. Lion, *Les Tragédies et les théories dramatiques de Voltaire* (Paris, 1896), and R. S. Ridgway, *La Propagande philosophique dans les tragédies de Voltaire* (Geneva, 1961).

POETRY

The works indicated above as dealing with baroque literature nearly all pay considerable attention to the poetry of the early seventeenth century. These should be supplemented by R. Winegarten, *French Lyric Poetry in the Age of Malherbe* (Manchester, 1954); J. Rousset, *L'Intérieur et l'extérieur* (Paris, 1968); and O. de Mourgues, *Metaphysical, Baroque and Précieux Poetry* (Oxford, 1953). For the second half of the century, J. Brody, *Boileau and Longinus* (Geneva, 1958), provides an important revaluation; while with regard to La Fontaine, O. de Mourgues, *La Fontaine: Fables* (London, 1960), is the best short introduction; H. Taine, *La Fontaine et ses fables* (Paris, 1853), is still useful despite a rather old-fashioned approach; and J. D. Biard, *The Style of La Fontaine's Fables* (Oxford, 1966), presents a detailed analysis of the poet's technique.

Anthologies of verse covering the period under review include A. J. Steele (ed.), *Three Centuries of French Verse, 1511–1819* (Edinburgh, rev. ed. 1961); J. Rousset (ed.), *Anthologie de la poésie baroque française*, 2 vols (Paris, 1961); O. de Mourgues, *An Anthology of French Seventeenth-Century Lyric Poetry* (Oxford, 1966); and M. Raymond and A. J. Steele (eds), *La Poésie française et le maniérisme, 1546–1610* (Geneva, 1971).

PROSE FICTION

The standard account of the novel in the early and middle years of the seventeenth century is M. Magendie, *Le Roman français au XVIIe siècle, de l'Astrée au Grand Cyrus* (Paris, 1932); E. Showalter, *The Evolution of the French Novel, 1641–1782* (Princeton, 1972), deals competently with the development of this genre over the remainder of the period under review; A. Le Breton, *Le Roman au dix-septième siècle* (Paris, 1890), is workmanlike but old-fashioned. F. Deloffre, *La Nouvelle en France à l'âge classique* (Paris, 1967), surveys the short story throughout the seventeenth century and up to 1735.

M. Magendie, *L'Astrée d'Honoré d'Urfé* (Paris, 1929), situates this novel in its period and assesses its influence; and Mme de La Fayette's work is studied by H. Ashton, *Mme de La Fayette, sa vie et ses œuvres* (Cambridge, 1922); C. Dédéyan, *Mme de La Fayette* (Paris, 1956); and J. Raitt, *Mme de La Fayette and 'La Princesse de Clèves'* (London, 1971).

For the period 1700–50, A. Le Breton, *Le Roman français au XVIIIe siècle* (Paris, 1898), has been superseded by V. G. Mylne, *The Eighteenth-Century French Novel* (Manchester, 1965), and G. May, *Le Dilemme du roman au XVIIIe siècle* (Paris, 1963). Individual novelists of this period are studied in H. Roddier, *L'Abbé Prévost, l'homme et l'œuvre* (Paris, 1955); P. Brooks, *The Novel of Worldliness: Crébillon, Marivaux, Laclos, Stendhal* (Princeton, 1969); and in the works on Marivaux by Greene and Gazagne referred to above.

For the philosophical *conte* as created by Voltaire, see J. Van den Heuvel, *Voltaire dans ses contes* (Paris, 1967), and V. Schick, *Zur Erzähltechnik in Voltaires 'Contes'* (Munich, 1968).

NON-FICTIONAL PROSE

From the profuse Pascal bibliography, J. Mesnard, *Pascal, l'homme et l'œuvre* (Paris,

1951), stands out as a useful brief introduction. Another general study is J. H. Broome, *Pascal* (London, 1965); while Pascal is treated in a stimulating but idiosyncratic way in L. Goldmann, *Le Dieu caché* (see above). On Pascal's style, see P. Topliss, *The Rhetoric of Pascal* (Leicester, 1966). La Rochefoucauld is presented succinctly in W. G. Moore, *La Rochefoucauld, his Mind and Art* (Oxford, 1969); Saint-Évremond is treated in Q. M. Hope, *Saint-Évremond, the 'honnête homme' as Critic* (Bloomington, Ind., 1962); and La Bruyère in the very compact P. Richard, *La Bruyère et ses 'Caractères'* (Paris, 1946). Mme de Sévigné may best be approached through A. Tilley, *Mme de Sévigné, Some Aspects of her Life and Character* (Cambridge, 1936), or A. Bailly, *Mme de Sévigné* (Paris, 1955); and E. Carcassonne, *Fénelon, l'homme et l'œuvre* (Paris, 1946), and J. Calvet, *Bossuet, l'homme et l'œuvre* (Paris, 1941), provide good introductory guides to their respective subjects.

For the literary aspect of the 'ancient *v.* modern' controversy, the comprehensive studies of H. Rigault, *Histoire de la querelle des anciens et des modernes* (Paris, 1856), and H. Gillot, *La Querelle des anciens et des modernes en France* (Paris, 1914), may be supplemented by T. A. Litman, *Le Sublime en France (1660–1714)* (Paris, 1971). For the literature of ideas at the turn of the century, P. Hazard, *La Crise de la conscience européenne (1680–1715)*, provides a most valuable introduction.

A suitable brief guide to Montesquieu is J. Dedieu, *Montesquieu, l'homme et l'œuvre* (Paris, 1943); and R. Naves, *Voltaire, l'homme et l'œuvre* (Paris, 1942), and N. Torrey, *The Spirit of Voltaire* (New York, 1938), provide a sound general introduction to Voltaire as a thinker and as a writer. A. Noyes, *Voltaire* (London, 1936), is readable but controversial.

THE CLASSICAL LANGUAGE

The language of the period 1600–1750 is often deceptive in its resemblance to twentieth-century French. Where texts cannot be read in scholarly editions which provide linguistic assistance, it may be useful to refer to specialist dictionaries such as the *Dictionnaire de l'Académie française* (fascimile reprint of the 1694 edition) (Lille, 1901); G. Cayrou, *Le Français classique* (Paris, 1924); or J. Dubois and R. Lagane, *Dictionnaire de la langue française classique* (Paris, 1960). A. Haase, *Syntaxe française du XVIIe siècle* (Paris, 1914), gives an authoritative account of the linguistic usage of the period; and F. Brunot, *Histoire de la langue française des origines à 1900*, vols 3–6 (Paris, 1909–33), provides a thorough analysis of all aspects of the classical language.

BIBLIOGRAPHICAL AIDS

Suggestions for further reading may be found in A. Cioranescu, *Bibliographie de la littérature française du XVIIe siècle*, 3 vols (Paris, 1965–6); *Bibliographie de la littérature française du XVIIIe siècle*, 3 vols (Paris, 1969); and in *A Critical Bibliography of French Literature, III: Seventeenth Century*, ed. N. Edelman (Syracuse, N.Y., 1961); *IV: Eighteenth Century*, ed. G. R. Havens and D. F. Bond (Syracuse, 1951); *IVA: Eighteenth Century, Supplement*, ed. R. A. Brooks (Syracuse, 1968). O. Klapp, *Bibliographie d'histoire littéraire française* (Frankfurt-am-Main, 1956–), continues as an annual publication.

FRENCH LITERATURE
FROM 1750 TO 1870
Henri M. Peyre

General Characteristics of the New Age

No century in the history or in the literature of France constitutes a
harmonious whole, and the eighteenth century least of all. By 1750 or
thereabouts, some profound changes had occurred. The literary
prestige of the age of Louis XIV had declined. Even in the theatre,
where Voltaire continued to proclaim his admiration for Racine, a
new trend was leading away from classical tragedy toward bourgeois
drama and toward plays with the political and ideological bias. Comedy
was no longer following in the wake of Molière. The novel of manners
was becoming the true heir to the moralists of the seventeenth century
who had satirically portrayed the ridicules and the types of 'la cour et
la ville'. The heroic fiction of the age of *préciosité* and the conventional
idealization of love were making way for the search for sensations and
for a strange combination of eroticism and of sentimentality. The
philosophical spirit which Bayle, Montesquieu and the early Voltaire
had done much to foster grew more bellicose after 1750: it had become
clear that, in France at least, improving things through despotism was
a forlorn hope. Louis XV was not to be converted to reforms and
would not heed the advice proffered by philosophers. The cultural
prestige of France throughout continental Europe had never been
greater; but neither the diplomacy nor the armies of the French king
deserved much admiration. In France itself, the fashionable society and
the men of letters were more and more sensitive to the novelties
imported from Great Britain. Voltaire might recant his youthful
enthusiasm for Shakespeare; but Shakespeare, dressed up in French garb,
Milton, Richardson, Sterne, the English constitution as presented (and
often distorted) by Montesquieu provided new models for Diderot and

Rousseau; and the *Encyclopédie* itself originated from a British forerunner, *Chamber's Cyclopedia*.

Montesquieu had published his great work, *L'Esprit des lois*, in 1748
and was to die seven years after. The novelist Lesage disappeared
before the middle of the century, in 1747. Fontenelle survived to reach
in 1757 the age of a hundred years; Marivaux, no longer active as a
playwright or as a novelist, died in 1763. The new spirit of the age
was asserting itself as Buffon, in 1749, brought out the beginning of
his *Histoire naturelle*, Diderot, also in 1749, his *Lettre sur les aveugles*,
to be followed in 1751 by his *Lettre sur les sourds et les muets*, Rousseau
his first *Discours sur les sciences et les arts* and Turgot the second of his
Discours sur le développement de l'esprit humain in 1750, exactly a century
after Descartes's death. In 1750 also, Voltaire left for the court of
Frederick II of Prussia, convinced that the reign of the Enlightenment
would be ushered in by his stay in Berlin, where he would bask in the
admiration of a liberal and philosophical king. His *Siècle de Louis XIV*
(1751) reflected his glowing optimism. His illusion was short-lived;
two years later he left, embittered, to exercise his sovereignty over
literature closer to France, in his residence near Geneva. In 1751, the
first volume of the *Encyclopédie*, of which Diderot was the indefatigable
master mind, started the organized campaign of the *philosophes* for the
ideas of freedom, toleration, progress, applied science bringing greater
happiness to the masses and helping to vanquish the age-old control
of the Church over the minds of men.

Several works of lasting beauty appeared during the second half of
the century; but the aim of most men of letters then was no longer to
produce carefully elaborated, sedulously polished works of art. They
were determined to act upon their countrymen, and their fellow beings
in other lands, 'here and now'. Hence the multiplicity of short pamphlets, of aggressive and satirical pieces touching on religion, philosophy,
politics. New ideas were sprouting everywhere. The style aimed at
alertness, often at levity, and was used to arouse the readers from their
complacency and to impel them to action. At no time probably had
literature thus strained every nerve to change man through changing
institutions and redressing the wrongs caused by superstition, ignorance
and passivity. If De Quincey's famous distinction between the literature
of knowledge and the literature of power may be resorted to, the immense and varied knowledge of the French thinkers of the Age of
Reason was of the kind which also brings power. The studies on the
eighteenth century initiated by Gustave Lanson in a memorable series

of Sorbonne lectures (1907–10), followed up by his disciples in France
and elsewhere, have altogether routed the previous assertions of historians like Tocqueville and Taine who had declared the *philosophes*
to be but dreamers building a heavenly city and reasoning on man in
the abstract. On the contrary, they were persons who travelled outside
their own country; who observed all kinds of men under all social
conditions; who devised empirical remedies for specific woes which
aroused their pity and shocked their reason. Several of them had
attempted administrative tasks and had been confronted by prejudices
and selfishness. Rousseau himself, as self-centred as any sensitive,
suffering Romantic ever was to be, informed himself carefully on
local conditions and moods in Poland or in Corsica, before he agreed
to offer projects of constitutions for those countries. Religious polemics,
philosophical speculation and theology had, during the previous two
centuries, been treated by, and as, literature. The second half of the
eighteenth century did not deem it unworthy of literature to deal with
constitutional and administrative questions, with inequities, privileges,
social misery, and to offer new hopes for improvement of their fates
to suffering creatures. The social sciences, as we have come to call
them, were the creation of the Encyclopedists and of their friends.
Ethics was by them divorced from any revealed religion and linked
with reason. A writer of small talent, Toussaint, proclaimed the total
severance of ethics from religion in a book, *Des mœurs* (1748), which
was condemned to be burned, but widely read throughout the second
half of the century. La Mettrie and d'Holbach warmly argued that
the atheist can be the most moral of creatures.

At the same time as the thought of the age was directed to devising
empirical solutions for problems which should no longer be tolerated
in their present state, outrageous to reason and goodwill, it also rose
above the immediacy of the practical. The decades which preceded,
and to some extent prepared, the French Revolution offered to men
throughout Europe the lineaments of a new faith. If Christianity was
indeed on its decline, new myths, that is to say, great visionary concepts presented as passionately desirable because opening the gates of a
new Garden of Eden, had to be forged, from which the religion of
humanity would evolve. They were chiefly the myth of progress; the
notion of the unity of mankind, resting on mutual toleration and
peace, substituted for fanaticism and national hatreds; the search for
happiness in this world, 'a new idea in Europe', announced triumphantly the revolutionary Saint-Just; the innate goodness of nature

and the rightful claims of instinctive forces; and the reliance upon sensibility and upon the dynamic power which accrues to ideas when they are felt and lived as well as thought. Most socialist and communist movements of the nineteenth and twentieth centuries, most revolutionary trends and reforms stressing more well-being for men of all conditions have looked back to that nursery of ideas and of myths which the second half of the eighteenth century was in Britain, Germany, Italy and, above all, France.

Voltaire, Diderot and the Encyclopedists

The concentration on a better future to be prepared for mankind in no way precluded a clearer vision of the past. History, as distinct from chronicles and memoirs, had reappeared, after a long eclipse, with the new sense of relativism which accompanied the breakdown of dogmatist complacency around 1700. Voltaire had a vivid imagination which enabled him to conjure up figures of individuals, details of daily life, the concerns of the men who had lived in bygone eras. He was not altogether impartial and avoided above all else being lifeless. He realized, as many of his successors in our midst have acknowledged, that ultimately all history is contemporary history, that is to say, written from the vantage point of a present to which the historian cannot help being committed. And he also realized the immense power of history, which can be a dynamite, exploding prejudices, overturning mental habits of inertia and even institutions, impelling men to evolve from the contemplation of the past the guidelines towards a better future.

The earliest attempt at historical writing by Voltaire was his lively narrative of the meteoric rise and of the tragic fall of a contemporary king, Charles XII of Sweden. *L'Histoire de Charles XII* had appeared in 1731, thirteen years after the actual death of a king who had been an adventurer and a warrior of genius. Voltaire's analytical clarity and the sprightliness of his narrative style endowed that early volume with all the attractions of a novel, and few novels then existing could be compared with it. Soon after, Voltaire set to accumulating notes, ransacking documents, questioning older people in preparation for *Le Siècle de Louis XIV*, published in 1751 and corrected and revised until 1768 when it received its final form. It is a work of dazzling intelligence and of very thorough and rich documentation. Voltaire condemned the greatest errors of the long reign during which he himself had been born: Louis XIV's bungling of religious affairs, his blindness in expelling from his kingdom the Protestants who would not be converted to Catholicism when he revoked the Edict of Nantes in 1685, his lack of tolerance. He did not condone the follies of endless and fruitless wars which ruined the country. But he was rightly fascinated by the excellence of Colbert's administration, by the dignity and the achievements of the monarch, and especially by the flowering of letters, arts and the adornments of life under the reign of Louis XIV. That volume imposed for over a century on posterity the image which it was to retain of the so-called 'classical' age of France.

At the same time, however, impatient to overturn the narrow philosophy of history proposed by theological historians like Bossuet, who saw in world history the unfolding of a providential plan and the Judaeo-Christian tradition as alone concerning modern men, Voltaire had undertaken a radically new attempt: a history of civilization. Kings, great personages, warriors, would be relegated to a secondary place. History would cease being a dismal record of fights, banditries, love affairs or greedy rapines of sovereigns; it would tumble down from their pedestals those who had passed for traditional heroes and often were mere plunderers. True great men would be those who have served civilization and contributed to the increase of human happiness. The title of the new work, a milestone in the writing of history, first published in 1756, then in its definitive shape in 1769, is *Essai sur les mœurs et l'esprit des nations*. It surveyed some eight centuries of world history with brilliance. The implicit assumption was that the Jewish and Christian nations and those of Graeco-Roman antiquity should cease to be central in world history. Peoples of Africa, America and Asia in particular, and above all the Chinese dear to Voltaire, had counted also in the development of manners, commerce, art; the concept of a chosen people or of a superior race was derided. The progress of reason had been halting and difficult; but it offered mankind the one glimmer of hope for the future. From that book dates the modern conception of history.

Voltaire's activity during the last twenty-five years of his life was prodigious. His light verse would be enough to win immortality for any poet, in playful genres, neither lyrical nor epic, which are the most difficult of all to practice. His *Mélanges*, some personal memoirs on his ill-starred sojourn at the court of Frederick II of Prussia, other scathing expositions of the gross improbabilities in the Old Testament and sarcasms at the claims of the Scriptures to be God's revealed word, stand among the most entertaining as well as the most impudent pieces of literature. Voltaire's huge correspondence is generally regarded as his masterpiece, and the greatest ensemble of letters in the whole range of world literature. There are treasures of mordant wit, of raillery against superstition and fanaticism in many of the articles of the *Dictionnaire philosophique* (1764), but also much solid information and not a little deep as well as courageous philosophical speculation on religion, ethics, laws, politics, tolerance. At the same time, Voltaire ceaselessly indulged in polemics against institutions and men that denied equality and toleration to those individuals who suffered in a society founded upon privileges. He proved to be a man of action, taking risks, pleading earnestly for freedom of conscience, for freedom of speech, for individual liberty and for a minimum of economic security. Some high-brow historians of philosophy have denied him the title of philosopher, because he never attempted to erect a comprehensive system and to imprison himself in it. On the essential articles of his generous humanitarian faith, however, Voltaire never wavered. He would not accept Christianity, on account of the monstrous crimes committed by the Churches which called themselves Christian; but was always a deist, fairly close to pantheism, believing in a deity that was the guarantor of justice and charity but who could not work miracles or be moved by prayers. There was much in the world, in Voltaire's eyes, which displayed fanaticism, cruelty, hatred; but through work, hope, generosity to others, the burden of those evils might some day be lightened for Voltaire's successors.

Voltaire's glory eclipsed that of many of his contemporaries. Yet Diderot (1713–84) was at least as great as he as an initiator of new ideas, as a bold philosophical speculator, and as a practitioner of genres of writing (the modern novel, the drama, art criticism) which were to develop and to endure, while the epic, tragedy and even the philosophical tale were to die with Voltaire. But Diderot published only a portion of his multifarious writings in his lifetime. He disseminated paradoxes, brilliant considerations on nature, on evolution, on language, psychology, the techniques of arts and crafts throughout ephemeral articles or in the pages of the *Encyclopédie*. He suffered in the eyes of posterity from not having summed himself up in two or three masterpieces or in systematic treatises which could be quoted conveniently in anthologies. The middle of the twentieth century has fully rehabilitated him. With his unevenness, the swiftness of his touch, his impatience and his versatility, he is, of all the eighteenth-century authors, the one who most completely gives the impression of a genius: of achieving with ease what the most assiduous talent can never hope to accomplish.

Diderot's intuitive and impatient manner of thinking did not allow him to compose an elaborate novel with a contrived structure and characters depicted as independent from the author. He accumulated anecdotes, intervened with philosophical digressions, favoured an oral style which mirrored the verve and the ebullient richness of his own conversation. Yet *La Religieuse*, an epistolary novel portraying the torments of a nun in an eighteenth-century convent, and *Le Neveu de Rameau*, a superbly animated dialogue and the portrayal of a Bohemian individualist, count among the best novels of the age; both were published long after Diderot's death. Diderot's dramas, substituting the portrayal of social conditions for the analysis of characters and sentimental middle-class families for princely or aristocratic heroes, are too didactic; they lack the imaginative grip on the audience (*Le Père de famille*, published in 1758; *Le Fils naturel*, 1757). But Diderot's fertile mind teemed with brilliant ideas on the drama, which were to influence much of the French mid-nineteenth-century un-Romantic comedies. His *Paradoxe sur le comédien* (published only in 1830), contending that self-mastery and deliberate histrionics, not sincere and overpowering emotion, should hold the key to the actor's success, is a brilliant and provoking piece of sophistry. In his *Salons*, and in a number of occasional writings on aesthetics and on ancient and modern literature, Diderot poured out penetrating remarks: he wanted to be the advocate of truth, naturalness, balance, wisdom and moderation. But there were always two men in him, waging an intestine struggle. He confessed his rage at being shackled by a philosophy of which his mind could not but approve, but which his heart belied. More even than Montaigne or Gide, he always was to remain a creature of dialogue. He never reached a harmonious system of serene conclusions on any great issue, aesthetic, ethical, political or philosophical. He oscillated, threw illuminating flashes, fighting tirelessly as a committed man who ran risks and persecution, and anticipating the future.

His letters to his mistress, Sophie Volland, are less witty and acrid than Voltaire's, but more passionate and, along with some of Rousseau's, the most exaltedly lyrical in French. Almost alone, he inspired, directed, stubbornly defended the gigantic undertaking of the *Encyclopédie*, a systematic dictionary of ideas, arts, techniques, in thirty-three volumes. The great mathematician d'Alembert wrote the preliminary

Discourse which, in 1751, expounded the philosophy underlying the work. The Catholic parties and the royal authority did all they could to have the work condemned and came near to success more than once. For the whole enterprise was to be a tribute to reason, hence also to toleration, to science helping mould a new ethic; tradition was disregarded and, in spite of many precautions and shows of submission to the ecclesiastical authorities, religion was ridiculed and attacked.

Diderot was not alone in that labour of fifteen years. He drew little effective assistance from Voltaire, from Rousseau who soon broke away from the group of Encyclopedists. He had secretaries, poly-graphists who borrowed second-hand information here and there. Among his friends were a dozen great and active minds, who, each in his own right, some retaining an allegiance to traditional religion, others assaulting it frontally, fought for the victory of knowledge, science, toleration, enlightenment through education, over the forces of darkness. None had the profundity and the originality of touch of Diderot; several wrote a turgid prose and had little sense of form. But they helped spread abroad the new ideas. Helvétius (1715–71), with whom Diderot often disagreed, upheld a materialistic doctrine in his book *De l'esprit* (1758) which the censors had burned; he negated innate ideas and set much store by education. D'Holbach (1723–89), a German baron and, like Helvétius, a man of immense wealth, although verbose and repetitious, expounded a consistent materialistic view of the universe in his *Système de la nature* (1770), borrowing some of Diderot's views. Condillac (1714–80), an *abbé* and apparently a man of faith to the end, is one of the earliest original speculators on language and an empiricist, explaining all of the child's development through sen-sations and denying, with Locke, that any innate ideas could exist which did not spring from sense-experience. D'Alembert (1717–83), a mathematician of genius, lent his prestige to the Encyclopedists. Several other priests, Abbé Morellet (1727–1819), a skilled polemicist, Abbé Raynal (1713–96), who indicted the behaviour of Western Europeans in their colonies of Asia and of America and a bitter foe of the Church, drew suggestions from Diderot's universally curious mind. Less well-known polemicists went over to atheism and even to advo-cating a form of communism in politics. La Mettrie (1709–51), a medical man and a scientist of note, attempted to dissect and to study man as a pure mechanism. Diderot, who stood in need of a more imaginative and more human view of things, balked at the mechanistic materialism of his friends.

He might have felt closer to Buffon (1707–88), whose vision of the early ages of the earth and of the slow development of man was both poetical and philosophical. He observed facts, studied first-hand reports of explorers; but his bent was toward systematization and broad and bold generalizations. He wrote with great care, with an excessive and starched dignity. But he married literature and science, as was the wish of his century, and he opened up majestic vistas on the origins of the world and of man.

Diderot's imagination was even bolder: it was fired by the study of medicine and of biology. It was attracted by a materialism which was then a more poetical, and even a more spiritual and organic explanation of natural phenomena, than the desiccated orthodoxy of the tradition-alists. To the moderns, the most prophetic intuitions of Diderot are to be found in a very few booklets published in his lifetime (*Pensées sur l'interprétation de la nature*, 1754; *Entretien d'un philosophe avec la maréchale de . . .*, 1776) and in others which only appeared posthum-ously (*Dialogue avec d'Alembert, Rêve de d'Alembert*). Diderot daunt-lessly came to grips with the problem of how matter can become life and eventually spirit. He introduced into philosophical thinking, before Hegel, the momentous notion of development, and he stands as the direct forerunner of Lamarck's transformism and even of Darwinian evolutionism. God (on whom Diderot never quite made up his mind in order flatly to deny His existence or to consider it as a possibility) is not, for him, the creator of the universe. Rather is He an ideal notion, created by man, which will assume more reality as man acquires more consciousness and a more generous sense of his solidarity with other men. 'Élargissez Dieu!' exclaimed Diderot to his contemporaries, if you wish me to believe in Him. 'Tout ce qui blesse l'espèce humaine me blesse,' he added, in sentences which anticipate Hegel, Marx and even the twentieth-century existentialists. The quest for happiness is legitimate; but happiness is most securely reached if, through edu-cation and through altruism, we also work for the general happiness of our fellow beings.

Jean-Jacques Rousseau

There was a fundamental contradiction in Diderot's thought governed by his sensibility, as there was in much of the second half of the eighteenth century, torn between negativism and the wish to propose a new faith, between the cold data of modern science making it well nigh impossible to believe in the soul and in an immortal life, and the desire to salvage the best which religion had once embodied for man. Diderot admitted those contradictions with honesty. Jean-Jacques Rousseau (1712–78), under an appearance of more implacable logic, was no less of a Proteus and lived his ideas passionately not mistaking consistency for truth. Hence unresolved contradictions and a tension in his writings which have constantly puzzled and moved the generations which came after him. Hence also the secret of his enormous influence on the world, on ideas, on sensibility, on the manner in which men have looked into their inner selves, on politics, on ethics and on religion. The British historian Lord Acton asserted one day that Rousseau had achieved more with his pen than perhaps any man who ever wrote.

He was an outsider to the French, having been born in Geneva of Swiss parents, and he understood the French all the more acutely from feeling both as an alienated man among them and yet as one of them. He hardly knew his mother, who died soon after his birth; his father took little care of his education. He was for all practical purposes a self-made man who wandered across Savoy, then on the roads of France until, in 1742, at the age of thirty, he reached Paris. The varied incidents of his youth, and even more the impressions left in him by that strange and hardly regular life, are well known to us through the *Confessions* which he wrote late in his life. That self-taught man succeeded in acquiring a vast knowledge and in developing a style remarkable for its terse rigour, its cogent rhetoric and, often, its poetical beauty. He was perhaps a sick man, afflicted with nervous troubles and probably also with physical ills which made him very shy with women. He had known poverty, years of anxious wandering in solitude, the humiliation of living as a servant scorned by persons whose intellect and taste he could not esteem. He was ready to turn into a rebel against much that struck him as unjust and corrupt in the existing order. His capacity for enthusiasm, his warmth, his concern with his own ego which he cherished as unspoiled by intellectual disquisitions and by the quibblings of sophists, were soon to oppose him also to the *philosophes* of his day. He found a congenial spirit in Diderot and was dazzled by the fireworks of his intuitions. They later diverged in their views and their temperaments clashed. Rousseau's extreme touchiness doomed him to solitude and even to the self-inflicted torment of anxiety. He held little hope in the ability of reason to improve man's fate or even to discover a truth which might satisfy him. 'Si c'est la raison qui fait l'homme, c'est le sentiment qui le conduit.' All his assertions were to be passionate denials of the claim that knowledge truly coincides with life. Kierkegaard, Nietzsche, Tolstoy and a great number of Romantic poets of Germany, Britain and France were to be, in that respect, Rousseau's spiritual heirs.

Rousseau leapt into the limelight in 1750 with his first *Discours*, probably set in motion by a brilliant flash of Diderot's conversation, in which he contended that no moral or social improvement had resulted from the progress of the arts and the sciences. There is rhetorical declamation in the development, but there is also an ardent conviction that society life and the cultivation of letters and arts carry with them the seeds of corruption. In 1754, an even more thundering 'Second Discours', *Sur l'origine et les fondements de l'inégalité parmi les hommes*, denounced inequality, and men's passive acceptance of it, as an unmitigated evil: it attacked property, which until then had been treated by Locke and other political thinkers as a sacrosanct right. Wealth was regarded by him as being almost synonymous with evil and with the exploitation of others. Rousseau reasoned in the abstract: so little was then known about primitive men that all that could be done was to imagine what may reasonably have happened in the beginnings of human history. Rousseau's thought was later distorted and caricatured; he was depicted as advocating a return to primitivism and even to savagery. He always knew better, and that his *Discours* was a Utopia: human nature, he repeated, does not retrace its steps backward. But he introduced into modern sensibility a very powerful feeling of nostalgia for the past and the no less epoch-making theme of Western man's profound dissatisfaction with modern civilization.

Rousseau had suddenly become one of the most famous men in Europe: the upstart that he had been and the former lackey had turned into a haughty moralist who advised and chided mundane Parisians. He indicted the theatre in an eloquent *Lettre à d'Alembert sur les spectacles* in 1758, contending that the portrayal of passions, often of crimes, in tragedy and the laughter at the expense of innocuous fools in comedy are incompatible with morality. Far from acting as a purgation of passions, literature, and especially dramatic literature, envenoms them and instils them into audiences.

Soon after, in a feverish crisis of creativity, Rousseau composed, between 1756 and 1762, three works of great length and weight: a novel, *La Nouvelle Héloïse*, which appeared in 1761, a treatise on education which is also a novel in its own way and the embodiment of a myth like those of Plato, *Émile, ou De l'éducation* (1762), then the most momentous work of political philosophy in the French language, *Le Contrat social* (1762). Soon after, from 1764 on, in a state of nervous upset and of exasperated sensibility, Rousseau began his *Confessions*, to be published posthumously.

La Nouvelle Héloïse, composed feverishly while Rousseau was in love with Madame d'Houdetot, seduced by her coquettish charm but warned beforehand that his exalted desire of her would never be rewarded, is a great love novel; when all is said and in spite of much didacticism in it and of many artful digressions, one of the greatest love novels in literature. Rousseau portrayed in it the dissociation between desire and possession, the lover's attempt to reach the whole being, or the soul, of his partner through the senses, the ecstasies of imagination transfiguring the loved one and far preferable to the cold and cerebral calculations through which Laclos or Sade then reviled love. In several respects, Stendhal's idealization of women and Proust's delineation of love as created by imagination are prefigured in the novel. Julie, clear-headed, naïvely calculating, evolving from the temptations of the flesh to the placid happiness of married life but tempted again when her elaborately acquired wisdom is near collapse, is a very real and appealing woman: she has few equals in the whole range of nineteenth-century French fiction.

Émile is by definition more didactic and more schematic. Rousseau, having shown in his novel how, through repentance and acceptance of one's fate, adults can again become natural and true beings, wished to provide an ideal model of a child preserved from the evils of bookish conventional education and from the corrupting influence of society. To this very day, some of the lessons offered in that fictional treatise have inspired reformers of education in several countries. The book is instinct with nostalgia and warmth, for Émile is the child that Rousseau would have wished to be. The latter sections of *Émile* illustrate Rousseau's view of religion. They were condemned by the authorities, the book was banned and the author persecuted. For it founded religion solely on the heart and its immediate certainty. The divinity of Christ and the authority of the Scriptures were left out of Rousseau's theology. Still, more than in the writings of the *philosophes*, Rousseau's treatise, like his moving letters to Monsieur de Malesherbes, breathed a need for the divine and conveyed a direct religious experience. Some of its exclamations are unforgettable: 'J'étouffe dans l'univers' or 'Que d'hommes entre Dieu et moi!'

The *Contrat social*, strangely, failed to impress and to disturb the contemporaries. It only came into its own with the French Revolution, and through its influence over Robespierre and Saint-Just. It proposed an ambitious reorganization of society, founded upon the consent of the governed who alienate part of their autonomy in order to strengthen the State. The scheme is ingenious, delicately balanced, unworkable in practice. But Rousseau acutely perceived the vices of political society as it existed in his time: built-in privileges and inequality; the artificial arousing of new needs which end in enslaving us; the stifling of the personality under the weight of selfishness. To Rousseau, happiness should lie in the art of concentrating one's feelings around one's heart and in the preservation of freedom. Might can never establish right. Inequality cannot be complacently tolerated. Through Rousseau's ideal contract, natural inequality is corrected through civic equality; men, born unequal in strength and talent, become equals in their rights. Political science had been chiefly descriptive with Locke and Montesquieu; with Rousseau it became normative. What exists in no way stands justified because it does exist. Society must be reformed just as man can be made better.

The *Confessions*, then the *Rêveries d'un promeneur solitaire* composed in part in 1776 and left unfinished at Rousseau's death in July 1778, are his masterpieces as a writer of prose, not yet musical and colourful, but delicately sensuous, vibrating with warmth and sincerity. Those volumes opened up the sluices of romantic confessional literature (in Goethe, Wordsworth, Hazlitt, Stendhal, Nerval). The cult of Rousseau began soon after his death. Kant, Hölderlin, Fichte, Hegel and Schiller celebrated him in Germany. Shelley excepted Rousseau alone from his condemnation of most French authors and appealed to him as his guide, as Dante had done Virgil, in his last poem, *The Triumph of Life*. Tolstoy venerated Rousseau as a saint all his life. The threefold stages of Rousseauistic philosophy, pristine innocence of man in the instinctive state, fall through greed and selfishness, redemption through repentance and spiritual rebirth, parallel to Christian theology, have since been found to haunt many a utopian and socialist system. The spirit of revolt which animated the Genevan reformer lies at the source of the many movements of discontent which, in the twentieth and twenty-first centuries, are likely to impel several continents to seek for more justice, for a greater harmony with nature, a closer communion with our environment and more fraternity. Whether Rousseau, or any eighteenth-century thinker, would have welcomed the Revolution is doubtful. To some extent at least, Rousseau and others inspired it, through suggesting to the people that things should and might be better and that society as it existed then was rotten at the core. Their influence in that sense has been a revolutionary and a constructive one.

Literature from the Later Eighteenth Century to Chateaubriand

There was a rich fictional production throughout the second half of the eighteenth century – probably not quite equal in works of towering eminence to what it had been in the England of Richardson, Fielding, Sterne and Goldsmith, but extraordinarily varied. The novel of feeling, often preposterously sentimental, lachrymose, mawkish, replete with complaints about the inanity of life and about *ennui*, paved the way for the romantic outbursts of the succeeding eras. Its best work is *Paul et Virginie* (1785) by a strange neurotic adventurer, Bernardin de Saint-Pierre (1737–1814), who was endowed with a powerful descriptive talent and introduced a new sense of colour in literature. The story, on the innocent and touching loves of two children grown up on a French island off the coast of eastern Africa, enjoyed a world-wide fame. It is told with delicacy and with no fear of ridicule. But the novel of sensuousness and of eroticism, which also appeared in the same era, is the one in which the sophisticated modern readers delight. Restif de la Bretonne (1734–1806) is both an eroticist, multiplying imaginary love adventures, and a sentimentalist; he wrote as many novels as he had, or so would he want us to believe, love affairs: close to 250. The best owe their value to his acute gift of realistic observation of farmers and artisans (*La Vie de mon père, Monsieur Nicholas*) and to his visionary evocation of Paris as the city of feminine adventures and of vice. Choderlos de Laclos (1741–1803), an army officer, intent on being a moralist and in truth a fervent admirer of Rousseau's sentimentality, composed one of the most astonishing volumes in the whole range of French fiction: *Les Liaisons dangereuses* (1782). It is an epistolary novel, like *La Nouvelle Héloïse*, but in no way one of confession or of respect for the eternal or for the ephemeral feminine. Valmont, a calculating seducer, undertakes to win the physical love of a girl just out of her convent education; then, through appealing to her pity, to her wish to reform a corrupt man, through surrounding her with insidious attacks like a fortress to be stormed, he convinces a respectable and pious woman to yield to him. He conspires all the while with another woman, bent like him upon destroying virtuous and chaste people. The plotting seducers are punished in the end, as in a good moral tale. But few delineations of pure evil, set free in a society where moral values had broken down, can match that cerebral, pitiless, powerfully and tersely written master-piece. The Marquis de Sade (1740–1814) in comparison seems coarse in his devices and effects, repetitious, verbose and unreal in his naïve invention of impossible cruelty. He enjoyed a secret popularity with a few throughout the nineteenth century, when it was hardly possible to read him openly. Ever since the middle of the twentieth century, when all censorship of his tedious stories was given up, the fame of Sade as a novelist, as distinct from the curiosity which may go to a pathological case, is in danger of being exploded. His talent is mediocre.

The Parisian stage during the reign of Louis XVI was lively; trans-lations (or more properly adaptations) of Shakespeare suddenly caught the imagination of the public; the melodrama tended to replace mori-bund tragedy, and did so almost completely during the Revolutionary years. Pastoral comedies flourished, often interspersed with pretty musical pieces. The one important writer for the stage, who impressed his contemporaries and has lost none of his vitality and forcefulness to this day, is the strange, self-taught adventurer Beaumarchais (1732–99). His life was incredibly full of dubious undertakings, speculations, histrionism. With *Le Barbier de Séville* (1775) and even more *Le Mariage de Figaro* (1784), he wrote plays which are neither profoundly analytical nor didactic, but which carry the audience along through their verve, their inventiveness and their gift of life. Insolently, Beaumarchais attacked the inequalities in society and the greed of courtiers. The character of Figaro, which soon became an immortal type, raised to an even more poetical plane by Mozart's opera (1786), stands among the unforgettable creations of universal drama.

Poetic diction, the lack of boldness in breaking away from old-fashioned moulds and discredited formal conventions, had hampered the renewal of poetry in France, while Blake, Cowper, then Words-worth and Coleridge in England, Goethe and Schiller in Germany were already treating renewed themes in a fresh language and asserting the rights of imagination. A great deal of verse was written in the eighteenth century in France, but the only poet who survives today is André Chénier (1762–96). He had a keen sense for the beauty and simplicity of ancient Greek poetry. He imitated with rare felicitous-ness the poets of the Palatine anthology and Theocritus. He also composed tender elegies, and ranks among the most delicately sen-suous poets in the French language. He attempted scientific poetry and he had the courage to break the rigid mould of French versification. When his poems were made accessible to the general public in 1819, the Romantics at once hailed him as a renovator of verse. There is however nothing Romantic about him, no passionate nostalgia for Greece as in Hölderlin or Keats, no reliving of the myths and symbols of Hellas; but he is an exemplary artist. And the verse which he composed, in a vengeful mood when imprisoned by the Revolution or in a tender note of protest attributed to a woman prisoner against an untimely death ('La Jeune Captive') reaches an intensity of emotion unmatched by the poetry of his age. He was guillotined under the Terror, two days before the fall of Robespierre which would have brought him his release from prison.

Literature has often flourished in the midst of social and political unrest and lagged in periods of prosperity and peace. The age of Euripides and of Aristophanes, that of Lucretius and Cicero, the blossoming of poetry and philosophy in Germany when she was oppressed by foreign conquerors testify that violence and uncertainty as to the future can foster original creation. But the era of the French Revolution (1789-99) and of the Napoleonic wars which followed until 1815 stand as an exception. Too many of the potential talents were drawn to political action, to military campaigns and to administering conquered territories all over Europe. The public which might have welcomed literary innovations in the wake of Diderot and Rousseau was scattered by emigration, threatened by the guillotine or engrossed in revolutionary eloquence when clubs and groups multiplied in Paris; journalism, aiming at immediate and often brutal effects, prospered at the expense of finished novels and of elaborate moralists' essays. Melodrama appealed to an enlarged and less fastidious public and helped relegate to a bygone era many of the classical theatrical conventions. Patriotic odes and military songs were more in honour than polished madrigals and sentimental elegies. Philosophy continued to be cultivated, chiefly in a dry, analytical vein, by a group of theoreticians called the *idéologues*, much admired later by Stendhal. Science knew an extraordinary development, with Monge, Lamarck, Bichat, Lagrange, Laplace and Ampère, but left no enduring literary monument; it did impress the literary imagination of the Romantics.

The outstanding writers of the first fifteen years of the nineteenth century lived in majority outside France: Madame de Staël (1766–1817) suffered much when, exiled by Napoleon, she had to remain near

Geneva; she was Swiss, but Parisian at heart. Her tumultuous love affairs and her imperious character brought her rich material for fiction or even for the probing analysis of herself. But her two novels (*Delphine*, 1802; *Corinne*, 1807) are cold and unimaginative. She was at her best in manipulating ideas, often borrowed from others, at times original with her. *De la littérature* (1800) and even more *De l'Allemagne* (composed in 1810, published in London in 1813) offer confused but occasionally illuminating views on the relations between letters and society and on the need to create a renovated and 'Romantic' literature, answering the needs of the moderns. Unlike other émigrés, she understood and praised the positive legacy of the French Revolution.

One of her intimate friends, Swiss also and even more cosmopolitan than her, was Benjamin Constant (1767–1830). He wrote some powerful pamphlets on politics and philosophy of history, assailing Napoleon's thirst for conquest and advocating liberal causes. But his chief claim to fame is his contradictory, vacillating, often pathetically abject but lucid *Journal intime*, which displayed his lack of will, and his novel *Adolphe* (1816). In *Adolphe*, in a splendidly economic style, he told of his romantic longings, soon followed, once they have reached their object, by pitiless cruelty. It is a masterpiece in cerebral dissection and in exposing the stages of slow *désamour*, or falling out of love; long before Proust, the lovers may be said to discover there that love is a mutually inflicted torture, but the woman is the pathetic, sorrowful victim. Another Swiss, Senancour (1770–1846), published in 1804 a touching series of imaginary letters, *Obermann*, displaying the same inflexible gift for searching analysis of oneself as does Constant, but a more poetical leaning to reverie and a voluptuous enjoyment of melancholy. The French Romantics after 1833 when they rediscovered *Obermann*, and Matthew Arnold in Britain, were to hail the book as a mirror to their own disenchantment.

Napoleon was himself one of the great writers of his time, in the burning love letters of his youth, in his proclamations to his soldiers, in the hundreds of articles which he dictated to sway the public opinion of his subjects. His early interest lay in literature and he had nurtured the ambition to be a writer. Indeed, without the *Mémorial de Sainte-Hélène* written by his companion Las Cases, his figure and his thought would not have dominated nineteenth-century history as they came to do. Literature made and perpetuated his legend. Chateaubriand (1768–1848), born one year before him, first praised by the emperor when he attempted to bring the French back to the Christian fold, then

Napoleon's political opponent, never ceased being fascinated by him. He is the one supreme French writer between Rousseau and Hugo. After a brief trip to America in 1791, from which he derived images and reminiscences which enriched all his work, then a stay with the émigrés fighting the French Revolution, and years of poverty as a teacher in England, he became famous with a short novel, *Atala* (1801), with a long, uneven, chaotic praise of Christianity as providing writers and artists with original themes and feelings, *Le Génie du christianisme* (1802), and an autobiographical and sombre *récit*, *René* (1802). His thought lacked consistency, his information was chiefly acquired at second hand; his favourite theme of the religious faith of two lovers (one Christian, the other pagan or Moorish), impeding their happiness, became a trite cliché. But he had an unequalled gift as a writer of musical, voluptuous prose. His arguments in defence of religion are often childish; he hardly lived a life of piety himself, he was an indefatigable lover of married women, and loved by them even more ardently than he could love. He did not succeed in politics when, after the fall of Napoleon, he became Ambassador to London and Minister of Foreign Affairs. He was aghast at the young Romantics who looked up to him as a revolutionary, while he always remained faithful to the 'glory that was Greece'. But he had, in *René*, then in his *Mémoires*, offered a poetical analysis of the *mal du siècle* with which most of his followers were afflicted: the realization of the gap between man's yearnings and his possibilities, between idealized woman and real ones, and a gloomy obsession with *ennui*. Musset and Baudelaire were to echo his plaintive moan. His masterpiece, one of the great works in French literature, is his *Mémoires d'outre-tombe*, composed over forty years and published, as the title stipulated, after his death. The book is as filled with his dominating personality as Rousseau's *Confessions*; the portrait he draws of himself is not accurate in many details; facts are transposed or transfigured; the fear of old age and of death echoes through it like an obsessive anthem. But the splendour of the prose, seldom purely decorative, more often terse, evocative and always unerringly felicitous, never ceases to hold the reader under its spell.

Romanticism

The Romantic movement, which Diderot and Rousseau had heralded as early as 1760, and which had permeated the sensibility of the young in France under the reign of Louis XVI, was then delayed in its full outburst through a number of causes, some historical and the product of chance, others deep-seated. Its true flowering is often assigned, for French literature, to the years 1818–22, when at last poetry seemed to shake itself free from classical trappings and to express personal moods in more musical verse. By 1818–22, the German Romantic movement, in poetry and in philosophy, had spent itself: Goethe alone survived and stood serenely above all literary controversies, contemptuous of the eccentricities and follies of the young Romantics who had not learned, as he had, the lesson of wise resignation and replaced the Wertherian longing for suicide with acceptance of one's fate and the consolation to be found in beauty. The first great generation of English Romantics, that of Wordsworth and Coleridge, had by 1820 spent its inspiration and certainly its spirit of rebellion. Their successors, Keats, Shelley and Byron, were all cut off in their prime between 1821 and 1824. Walter Scott's novels of chivalry had already become more popular on the Continent than they were in Britain, where a new mood of realistic portrayal of society was dawning. As Romanticism seemed to be waning elsewhere, it stormed literature, the arts, even society in France. It had grown slowly and against many odds; but it also had struck sturdier roots. In spite of appearances to the contrary and of glib assertions in manuals of literary history, Romanticism refused to bury itself after its glorious outburst of 1820–45. It revived, often with more impetuous, more morbid vigour; first with the generation of Flaubert, Leconte de Lisle and Baudelaire, then with Taine, Zola, Verlaine and Rimbaud; then again with the symbolists, with the surrealists. It is hard to mention a writer of the twentieth century who has not relived Romanticism in one or other of its facets, be it Huysmans, Apollinaire, Claudel, Aragon, Bernanos, Mauriac, Giono, Cocteau or Céline. In technique, in style, in restraint, those modern Romantics differ from Balzac, Michelet and Hugo. Their blend of pose and of sincerity is more expertly contrived. But their discontent with the present and with the human condition, their spirit of revolt, their concern with their own ego reconstructing the world from the microcosm of the self, their poetical vision of life – these are the expressions of a deep Romantic sensibility.

Romanticism in France, more so than in other Western countries, affected, and even invaded, fiction, drama, the writing of history and of criticism, philosophical speculation, political theorizing, the fine arts and, naturally, poetry. It long was the custom to stress the theories, manifestos and doctrines which accompanied, and occasionally preceded, the appearance of the works themselves. Literary debates have indeed always been a favourite pastime of the French writers, who are fond of elaborating theories in order to justify their practice and to convert followers. In truth, the discussions around Romanticism, which ranged from Madame de Staël's writings to the final victory of the new school or group, after 1830, were confused, contradictory, chaotic. Magazines were founded which soon perished. Newcomers to the world of letters shifted from one circle or *cénacle* to another. As always in France, politics and religion intruded into the literary feuds: most of the young Romantic poets, including Lamartine, Vigny and Hugo, began by being royalist and Catholic. But the political regime which followed the fall of Napoleon and the clerical reaction which so angered the hero of Stendhal's *Le Rouge et le noir* soon disappointed them. In poetry, they wanted to suggest rather than to state, to appeal to the reader's imagination and not so much to his rational intellect, and to rival the soft and languorous effects of music.

As elsewhere in Europe, the Romantic mood in France was an assertion of the rights of imagination against the primarily analytical function assigned to the intellect in some aspects of eighteenth-century thought. It stressed each individual's uniqueness, as manifested in his sensibility and in the cherished treasure of childhood memories; the self, in its originality and even in its idiosyncracies, counted for more than man envisaged in his generality and in attempting to reach truths valid for all men in general. The social and political upheavals of the Revolutionary and Napoleonic period had left young people frustrated, ill-adapted to a reality which suddenly appeared prosaic and inglorious to them. Their discontent expressed itself in politics; in literature, against the constricting theories inherited from arid neoclassical legislators; it spread to the whole of life and lamented the finiteness of man's fate and the impossibility of reality ever to come up to the desires or the dreams of those sons of the new century. *Le mal du siècle* is the name they gave to their grief and to the enjoyment of that anxious sorrow paraded as a badge of superiority. Werther, René, Byron's mysterious criminals, Musset's characters were in part literary types and soon degenerated into conventional ones. But many of the young, in books and in life, modelled themselves on those heroes. Classicism had seldom been lived in actual daily existence, or been an ideal of conduct mirrored in the letters and memoirs of seventeenth-century people; Romanticism was. Neurotics, insane artists, suicides, hunted men pursued by their own passions or yearnings abound in the literary works, but also among the men and women who actually lived in the years 1820–60.

A peculiar feature of French Romanticism is that the innovators encountered a revered and built-in classicism, taught in the schools and established officially in the salons, the academies, the State-subsidized theatres, such as no other country in Europe had. That classical tradition, once inspired by the examples of Greece and Rome, had come to be regarded by the French as having sprung from their soil and as somehow in harmony with the land and the character of the country. It stressed the values of order, of restraint, of clarity, and the Romantics soon realized that they could only win against the classical forces by borrowing much from them. More important still, along with an elaborate concern with form and recourse to rhetoric, the French classical writers (from Montaigne to Pascal and Bossuet, from Corneille to Racine and Madame de la Fayette) had displayed a rare insight into the inner life of man. The Romantics who first assumed an attitude of opposition to the partisans of the classics had resorted to vituperation and insult; but they soon realized that ultimately they would have to be judged according to their success in probing the innermost secrets of men (in their moments of passion, ambition and tragic stress, or in their lyrical and elegiac moods) as penetratingly as the classical moralists and dramatists had done. Hence a considerable element of what may be called 'classicism', or 'le classicisme des romantiques', in Stendhal, Mérimée, Lamartine, Hugo, Musset and Nerval.

Finally, literature has long been far more institutionalized in France than in other countries. It enters into the daily lives of people, occupies a prominent place in their conversations and in the daily press and is a means of acceding to honours and even to political power. The stakes in literary controversies are therefore high. The more resistant to change the literary institutions are (academies, universities, Ministries of Education), the more exacerbated and violent their young opponents become; hence the violence of the struggles around questions of versification, matters of style, the dramatic unities, mixing the tragic and the comic genres or, as Hugo advocated, the grotesque and the sublime. The Romantics had to wage far more stubborn fights in Paris than in London, Milan, Jena or Weimar; but their victory, when at last it came, proved also more lasting. French Romanticism was no longer a small clique of innovators grouped around a banner and a manifesto; it incorporated into itself the best of the legacy of classicism. It became the lasting new French tradition.

Romantic Poetry

Poetry was the literary genre that had lagged behind for decades, and it was in the realm of lyrical poetry that the renovators were most eagerly awaited and could achieve most. Romanticism has often, in consequence, been equated with lyricism and with a new freedom in the treatment of diction and verse. For a long time, literary historians traditionally singled out Lamartine, Vigny, Hugo and Musset as the giants of Romanticism. Our perspective is different today. Hugo may well be regarded as the Romantic poet *par excellence*, although he really came into his own as an original visionary and symbolic genius long after the heat of the Romantic debates had cooled off. But the other giants of French Romanticism were not poets in verse: rather Delacroix the painter, Berlioz the musician, Balzac the novelist and Michelet the historian.

Lamartine (1790–1869) had immense natural gifts as a poet: a rich, responsive sensibility, a unique, if perilous, facility, the talent of a soft, melodious musician in verse. His *Méditations poétiques*, in 1820, filled the public with rapture. In truth, many of the poems were rhetorical developments on immortality or on man seeking consolation for his love sorrows or his oppressive solitude in a divine presence; the nature poems and the elegies expressed in verse what Rousseau and others had earlier expressed in prose. But they included at least one poem, 'Le Lac', which has lost none of its freshness and cogency as a masterpiece. There are love poems even more feverish, such as 'Ischia', in the *Nouvelles Méditations* (1823); or longer, more ambitious hymns to nature, love and death in the *Harmonies poétiques et religieuses* (1830), the poet's greatest lyrical achievement. Then, having reflected deeply and with much vigour on politics and society, having revolted bitterly against religion after his daughter died in the East, Lamartine composed some of the bitterest and most virile poems in the French language: 'Les Révolutions', 'Gethsémani ou la mort de Julia'. In 1835, he published a strange, modern, profoundly moving epic, set in a rustic background, *Jocelyn*, perhaps the most successful long poem in French. Politics, fiction, history and essays then attracted him and he only rarely returned to his poetical inspiration.

Alfred de Vigny (1797–1863) came, like Lamartine, from an aristocratic and royalist family, but his imagination always bore the imprint of the Napoleonic influence and suffered from the mediocrity of French army life (he was an army officer for fourteen years) and of the materialistic ambitions of the middle class during the Romantic era. He wrote only two slim volumes of verse, *Poèmes antiques et modernes* (1826), of which 'Moïse', on the theme of the solitude to which genius is doomed, is unforgettable, and *Les Destinées* (1864, but published in reviews twenty years earlier). Vigny also wrote plays and novels of merit, if not of the very first order, and left some of the most pregnant reflections of a philosophical moralist since Pascal. His poetry was long and profoundly thought, it is expressed with condensation and at times illuminated, especially in 'La Maison du berger', with the most grandiose and evocative images in French poetry before Baudelaire. It is an indirect lyricism; the poet seldom says 'I'; he prefers to impersonate himself as Moses, Samson cursing womanhood because he has been betrayed by Delila, or Christ on the Mount of Olives urging God to enlighten and guide the forlorn world of men.

Hugo had all the talents and he attempted all the genres of poetry. Born in 1802, he survived until 1885 and composed verse almost to the very end. His very early verse is picturesque, scintillating, rich in metrical experiments; with *Les Orientales* (1829), he displayed the dazzling gifts of a virtuoso and flooded French poetry with colour. Between 1831 and 1840, having lost some of his early royalist fervour and while uninterruptedly composing plays and novels, he published four volumes of poetry: *Les Feuilles d'automne* (1831), tinged with melancholy and already tempted by the invisible lurking behind the visible tapestry of shapes and colours; *Les Chants du crépuscule* (1835); *Les Voix intérieures* (1837); *Les Rayons et les ombres* (1840), in which nature, reverie, love, Napoleon's epic figure haunting the poet, politics, social pity and art serve as themes for Hugo's extraordinary facility. Political ambitions, an active and complicated series of affairs of the heart, the overwhelming grief caused in 1843 by the accidental drowning of his daughter and of her young husband at Villequier and then the revolution of 1848 brought a respite to Hugo's production. Only in 1853 did he come out with the most impassioned and vengeful satirical poetry written in French since Agrippa d'Aubigné: *Les Châtiments*. Some pieces are still splendidly lyrical, but less personal: they herald the ultimate triumph of justice and of democracy over the tyranny of Napoleon III, whom Hugo hated all the more for having himself through his verse contributed to spreading the Napoleonic legend which was to help elect the 'petit Napoléon' as a caricature of the great one. Hugo condemned himself to exile in Jersey, then in Guernsey, in the Channel Islands: for eighteen years, he lived in that gloomy, tempestuous landscape, meditating on the watery abysses which had engulfed his daughter, on death, on the meaning with which life should be endowed in order to be livable, on mystical philosophies and strange religions. The great volumes of poetry composed by Hugo, often in a state of trance, appeared in 1856 and in 1859 (for the first series): *Les Contemplations* and *La Légende des siècles*. None, not even *Les Fleurs du mal*, equals them in variety, depth and forcefulness. Romantic they are, in so far as they are passionate, personal, anguished by all the questions asked by a religious sensibility which came near to identifying itself with the divine. Lyrical they are also, through the exaltation of their impassioned tone, the musical riches of the verse and the prominence of the poet's personality questioning the cosmos in order to unravel the secrets of life after death. But in the long meta-physical developments of 'Ce que dit la bouche d'ombre', more con-cisely in 'Paroles sur la dune', in the sublime evocation of Adam and Eve mourning, in the early days of creation, the death of Abel and the fate of Cain ('Les Malheureux'), finally in the grandiose epic fragments of *La Légende des siècles*, reaching its most grandiose and wildest beauty in 'Le Satyre', Hugo pushed back the limits which had until then circumscribed French poetry. Later still, in grave hymns collected in *Toute la lyre* (published only in 1888), in the one French epic which can be compared to Milton's *Paradise Lost*, *La Fin de Satan* (published in 1886), Hugo showed that he was far more than a virtuoso of metrics and an orator in verse: an original thinker and a decipherer of the unknown.

It had been fashionable for a time, after Hugo's death and as a petty revenge against the enormous place he had occupied in his century, to belittle his dramas, his novels and his essays. Twentieth-century critical opinion has reversed that verdict. The psychology of Hugo's dramas is rudimentary; the dramatic devices used are crude. But, in the best of them (*Hernani*, 1830; *Ruy Blas*, 1838) the bold marriage of comic and melodramatic elements and the splendour of the lyrical passages carry audiences along. Neither Vigny (in his more austere but also tense and unconvincing play with a purpose, *Chatterton*, in 1835), nor Alexandre Dumas the elder in his hastily contrived plots, came so near as Hugo to creating the theatre of the new era. Hugo had reflected with independence on the means by which the drama of the moderns might be less stylized, less pure and also less aloof from ever diverse and chaotic life, of wider appeal to the masses, than the classical theatre of old. He illuminatingly envisaged the grotesque (in his eyes as necessary as the sublime *élans* of lyricism in the drama) as a moment of pause, a springboard from which to leap towards the beautiful with a fresher and intenser perceptiveness. His many novels, likewise, cannot be set beside those of Stendhal for psychological acuteness or discreet poetry or beside those of Balzac for convincing creation of characters. But their merits lie elsewhere. *Notre-Dame de Paris* (1831) is one of the powerful historical novels in the world; *Les Misérables* (1862) combines sentimental idylls, mystery thrillers, vivid evocations of Paris and pictures of social evils and of misery which are to this day much admired by social historians. In 1866 and in 1868, during his exile, Hugo completed two of the most powerful visionary novels, as hallucinating as anything in Dostoevsky, Emily Brontë or Melville, *Les Travailleurs de la mer* and *L'Homme qui rit*. Even when he stood at the peak of his popularity and revered by the masses as no poet had ever been in France, Hugo continued experimenting with new forms, striking new paths, taking immense risks. He filled his volumes of prose essays, such as *William Shakespeare* (1864) and *Post-Scriptum de ma vie* (posthumously published in 1901) alternately with declamatory platitudes and with lucid insights. 'Poètes!' he exclaimed, 'voilà la loi mystérieuse: aller au delà.'

Alfred de Musset (1810–57) was ten or twenty years younger than the three poets who ruled over the poetical domain between 1820 and 1835, when Romanticism was triumphant. He had neither the powerful creative imagination of his elders nor their concern with expressing philosophical or cosmological thoughts in his verse. Like other poets who were almost exactly his contemporaries, Aloysius Bertrand, Gérard de Nerval, Maurice de Guérin and Théophile Gautier, all born between 1807 and 1811, he felt frustrated at reaching the literary stage too late. 'Je suis venu trop tard dans un monde trop vieux,' he lamented in one of his oft-quoted lines. It was necessary for these men to strike new paths. They attempted the poem in prose: Aloysius Bertrand (1807–41) in the vivid, colourful and quaint descriptions of *Gaspard de la nuit*, which Baudelaire considered as the inspiration for the new language of his own prose vignettes; Maurice de Guérin (1810–39) with more passionate pantheistic warmth and a pagan fervour which he blended strangely with his Christian faith, in 'Le Centaure' and 'La Bacchante'. Théophile Gautier (1811–72) became, later, a respected literary figure and the champion of art for art's sake. His lifelong fight for the purity of literature and his passionate acts of faith in art as alone deserving and bestowing immortality, while gods and men, philosophies and political regimes come and go, won him the admiring friendship of Flaubert, Baudelaire and Mallarmé. His place in French poetry, however, rests on his much earlier, and far from impassive and serene achievement. *Albertus* (1833), *La Comédie de la mort* (1838) and even *España* (1845) are obsessed by religious symbols and the melancholy regret of lost faith, and even more by death in its most macabre shapes. Hugo later, and Baudelaire in particular, who both admired Gautier, were impressed by that vision of skeletons, of corruption of the flesh, worms gnawing at vigour and beauty. Gautier's stress on artistry and his insistence upon finding in the cult of art a substitute for all the other lost absolutes have left a deep imprint upon the poets of other nations, among them Ezra Pound.

The two poets from that second Romantic generation who appear most significant to us after a century and a half are Musset and Nerval. Musset's nature was highly nervous, indeed almost morbidly so, capricious, eager for pleasure and doomed to fits of despair: he was, as much as Baudelaire, Nerval or Verlaine, one of the 'accursed poets' of the last century. Success had very early hailed his dazzling talent and his insolent *joie de vivre*. He made fun of the Romantics' poses and of their sentimental affectations with wit and a cheerful, well-meant irony. He had a rare gift for dividing himself into dual personalities and for dramatic dialogue. He needed passion, however, and the understanding of patient, loving women who would nurse his whimsical moods and perhaps hold him on the slope which ultimately led him to drinking and to the drying-up of his talent. His Venetian adventure with the novelist George Sand, a few years older than he, in 1833, is famous. He emerged from it embittered, tortured by jealousy, prone to cursing womankind as a whole, but also a more sincere poet of love. Four lyrical dialogues between his muse and himself, and in truth between the two facets of his nature, his *Nuits*, are his supreme poetical achievement. The tone of anger, the unrestrained display of sentiment, the rhetoric of those *Nuits* have been criticized by the poets succeeding Musset who had more sanity and more self-control than he. But there is another side to Musset's poetry: a concrete, humorous, lucid and intelligent form of lyricism, the original charm of which has not vanished. Musset is moreover a master of vivid, witty prose, reminiscent of the eighteenth century in its economy and swiftness. He is the author of stories and tales scarcely less effective than those of Mérimée, and of the best plays left by the nineteenth-century theatre: *Les Caprices de Marianne* (1833), *On ne badine pas avec l'amour* (1834) and the enigmatic and tragic *Lorenzaccio* (1834) were not acted when they appeared; but they have held the stage ever since. The marriage of Romantic passion and of classical insight into the secrets of the human heart, of the instinct for self-destruction and of the Hamlet-like analysis of that destruction by its very victim, is most felicitously concluded in Musset's plays.

Gérard de Nerval also attempted the dramatic genre, but he could not dramatize his own inner conflicts to carry an audience along with him. He lived, miserably, by his pen and he had to write much ephemeral criticism, like his friend Gautier. But he revealed in some delicate, dreamy tales, the best-known of which is *Sylvie* (1854), the talent of a deft, poetical story-teller, and a vision of life which melts reality into dreams and symbols. The symbolists and the surrealists alike, Alain-Fournier, Marcel Proust and Jean Giraudoux have sensed, and proclaimed, their affinities with that writer of the purest prose of any Romantic who, although he went through four crises of insanity and probably hanged himself in a wretched alley in Paris in 1855, never forsook his attachment to a classical clarity. His most vibrating prose, tormented, discontinuous, mysteriously moving, is in an unfinished half-mystical record of one of his descents into the inferno of madness, *Aurélia* (1855), probably the most faithfully poetical document on the state of dream which Nerval calls 'a second existence'. In the last ten years of his brief life, Nerval also composed some six or eight very mysterious sonnets, alluding to his very personal experiences as a worshipper of women, as a religious seeker who tried to marry paganism and Christianity, as a dreamer of dreams formerly dreamt and as an explorer of the realm which lies beneath and beyond reason: 'El Desdichado' (the disconsolate one), 'Delfica' and 'Artémis' are the finest of them. Their very obscurity, which defies all explanation, and their allusiveness, as well as their weird evocative power, have immortalized Nerval among the French poets.

Romantic Theatre and Fiction

The Romantic age, intent upon the liberation from all artistic constraints, had expanded the drama beyond all formal limits. In its rejection of the unities of time and place, which in truth had long degenerated into mere superstitions, Romantic drama also disregarded the need for concentration and for some unity of interest.

Yet the limitations in any audience's capacity for attention are not easily cast aside, and the drama stands in need of tension and of confrontation of adverse forces or individuals. Hugo's *Cromwell*, Goethe's *Faust*, the poetic dramas of several English Romantics, later those of several symbolists are too ambitious, too all-encompassing, too diverse to be brought down to the humble necessities of staging, interpretation and performance. The novel, on the contrary, lay open for the Romantics to experiment with to their hearts' content. It had inherited a relatively short tradition, scarcely two centuries old, and not yet venerable. It offered no models which might be called perfect, as drama and, to a lesser extent, poetry did. It was meant to reach new layers of the reading public, to whom powerful effects, even if crude, ebullient vitality, suspense and a reflection of the surrounding society mattered more than analytical subtlety. The eighteenth-century French fiction, with its stress upon aristocratic life and prejudices of class, on cerebral eroticism and on escape into lachrymose sensibility, no longer seemed attuned to the society which emerged from the Revolution and the Empire. Even when set beside the reforming zeal of the *philosophes* and their audacity as thinkers, that novel had appeared anachronistic or puny. The novel, after 1820 or so, underwent a rebirth in France, Britain and Russia. It caught up with the moods and the problems of the new age.

One of its aspects was the personal novel, which Chateaubriand, Constant, Nerval and several lesser Romantics renovated. It is one of the original creations of modern literature and, under diverse forms, it was to be attempted by Flaubert (in *Novembre* and others of his early works), Loti, Gide and Proust in France. The German Romantics had been fond of the *Bildungsroman*, or novel in which the old-fashioned and somewhat disconnected picaresque adventures were presented as moulding the personality of the young man and serving as his education, sentimental and intellectual. Thackeray's *Henry Esmond*, Meredith's *Harry Richmond* and subsequent portraits of the artist as a young man in the twentieth century are personal novels after a fashion. The genre is close to, yet different from, the autobiography or the memoirs, for the novelist does not survey his past experience from the vantage-point of the present and he does not attempt to vindicate his actions or to endow his existence with a meaning. The work remains a fiction, in no way enslaved to reality as it may have been lived or remembered. The novelist is all the freer to create half-imaginary characters with his own experience as he is aware of reaching thereby a higher or deeper truth. He endeavours to convey the feeling of time passing and slowly corroding adolescent dreams. Balzac's *Le Lys dans la vallée* (1835) and *Louis Lambert* (1833), even Stendhal's *Le Rouge et le noir* (1831) and most of the early novels of George Sand could be termed personal novels and owe much of their intensity to the close links between the author and the protagonist who is also the narrator.

A second characteristic innovation achieved by the Romantics in the realm of fiction was the blossoming of the historical novel. The new era had witnessed the introduction of the great concept of relativism in all branches of human thinking. Remote people, chronologically five, ten or more centuries distant (the Crusaders, the early French kings, the early Germanic or old Scottish heroes), geographically thousand of miles away (Orientals, Egyptians, African blacks, New World Indians) fascinated the once self-contained Western nations. Walter Scott enjoyed an immense fame in France and gave an impetus to the historical novel. Picturesque details, vivid descriptions, at times an excess of local colour marked those novels; the psychological delineation of characters was often sacrificed to this affluence of exterior details. Still Balzac, in *Les Chouans* (1829), an evocation of the Vendean wars, and in many other stories set in the Napoleonic past or earlier, Hugo in *Notre-Dame de Paris* (1831), Mérimée in his *Chronique du règne de Charles IX* (1829) and, in a more superficial way but with a fertility of imagination seldom equalled, Alexandre Dumas (1802–70), lover of the intricate conspiracies of the French court under Charles IX, Henri III and Louis XIII, remain as the chief representatives of that form of fiction.

The enormous importance of political and social factors, which had escaped the eighteenth-century novelists, had been projected forward by the Revolution and by the upheavals in French society. It could not be ignored by the fiction writers of the Romantic age. George Sand for several years wrote socialist and reformist novels; Balzac aimed at no less than depicting the whole social scene of Paris and the provinces; Stendhal's *Lucien Leuwen* (posthumously published) is, among several things, a novel on politics, and so is, in one at least of its facets, Flaubert's *L'Éducation sentimentale* (1869). The theme of the decadence of a society, and of the corresponding ascent of the speculators and upstarts and of the greedy and selfish middle class, was to be treated many times by the novelists of several countries after Balzac. Even more than the tragedy of old, the novel was to feed on the collapse of the great under the blows of fate and, like comedy, on the triumph of the mediocre ones.

The term Romantic often connotes an excess of the imaginative faculty and a concentration on the self which would seem to preclude the cool, realistic observation of things as they are. Flights of visionary imagination, metaphysical ambitions and the desire to reach the invisible behind the concrete characterize the fiction of Balzac, Hugo and even that of George Sand. Baudelaire did not err when, in a lucid passage in prose, he hailed Balzac, not as a realist, but as a rival of reality and as a visionary. Still there is a passionate view of the real which, instead of leading a novelist or a historian to copy it, to draw an enumerative catalogue of its parts, to analyse it scientifically, brings reality back to an intenser life. That imaginative realism (it has also been called 'magic realism' when its power of transforming and of purifying the real is granted free rein, or 'symbolic realism') is that of Dickens, of Gogol and, naturally and primarily, of Balzac. The Paris of *La Fille aux yeux d'or* (1835) or of *Le Père Goriot* (1834), the Touraine of *Eugénie Grandet* (1833) or the Normandy of *La Vieille Fille* (1837) are more mysterious, more hauntingly alive and, in a word, truer than truth. The vision of a passionate man, who identifies himself with what he perceives or contemplates, is often more acute than that of a detached and cool observer. There is a realism of the Romantics, to which Zola was to be the heir, far truer because it is selective and alive, than that of the few novelists of scant talent who brandished the banner of realism in France around 1855–65.

George Sand (1804–76) lived even more novels than she wrote. The story of her loves has delighted many a biographer. Great men (and not a few small ones) were drawn to her, as lovers (Mérimée, Musset, Chopin) or as friends (Delacroix, Sainte-Beuve). She failed to find much lasting happiness in those liaisons, and she had been wretchedly deprived of it in her unfortunate marriage. Her most moving, and weirdest, novel, *Lélia* (1833), hinted at some of the frustrations, physiological or psychological, to which her love life was doomed. It is doubtless the most high-pitched as well as the most declamatory of the French personal novels, and it offers the most clear-sighted analysis of the sexual, sentimental and social problems faced by woman in a society which does not grant her her due. After a number of social novels, vindicating the rights of the industrial workmen and of the economically oppressed in modern society against the conservative establishment, George Sand reached a vast audience through her stories of agrarian, and idealized and idyllic, life in the country: *La Mare au diable* (1846) and *François le Champi* (1850), eagerly read by Proust's Marcel and by many a French child. Their poeticization of country life strikes us today as artificial and insipid: the French peasantry has ceased to be lauded as pure, healthy and moral by French writers. However, the author's love for nature is genuine. In other respects, and while not one of her novels remains as a masterpiece of fiction, George Sand must be considered as one of the five or six great women writers of France. Like Lamartine, she did not learn how not to yield to her natural facility. She attempted almost every subject in the novel, including religious mysticism in her strange story of monastic life, *Spiridion* (1839).

Stendhal (1783–1842), fond of irony as he was, obsessively introspective but much too discreet to flaunt his ego unrestrainedly, compulsively fond of hiding under assumed names and of putting on sneering masks, stands at the opposite pole from George Sand. He studied mathematics with zeal, then the severe analytical methods of logicians and materialistic thinkers of the Napoleonic age; he served in the emperor's armies, adored Italy, while missing Paris as soon as he had crossed the Alps and well aware that his beloved Italy was a figment of his imagination crystallizing youthful memories. He wrote a great deal, borrowing unashamedly here and there; he launched into Romantic controversies in his very disappointing *Racine et Shakespeare* (1823–5), proved far more acute in his small and disconnected treatise *De l'amour* (1822), which was neglected by his contemporaries. He filled out pages with private jottings or heterogeneous fragments of a desultory, at times very perspicacious, diary. Almost as an amateur, he wrote a very curious novel, *Armance* (1827), on a theme then seldom broached in literature. The delineation of feelings has rare charm and mystery and the technique is ingenious in its lack of self-consciousness. He then published two of the most admired novels in the whole range of literature, but which it took Europe fifty years to assess with justice: *Le Rouge et le noir* (1831) and *La Chartreuse de Parme* (1839). *Lamiel*, left unfinished at the author's death, with a young woman as the heroine, almost deserves to be set beside those masterpieces and is less artificial and less incredible than *Lucien Leuwen* (also posthumous and unfinished), in which the woman adored by Lucien lacks all convincingness.

Stendhal's creation, like his personality, is replete with contradictions, and that complexity, which at times is merely a pose to cover the author's ingenuous naïvety, that apparent disregard, or unawareness, of

rules of composition, recipes, structural devices, accounts for much of
the originality of the Stendhalian fiction. Julien Sorel (in *Le Rouge et
le Noir*), the son of a poor carpenter who dreams of the warrior's glory,
attempts to make his way in a hypocritical society by turning into a
Tartuffe; he appears at first to be a cold, calculating character. He
analyses the mechanics of post-Napoleonic society and hopes to
assert his intellectual's superiority over the selfish and narrow-minded
nobles who too long had stifled talent. But his romantic sentimentality,
his shyness and his impulsiveness give the lie to Julien's will to remain
cool and calculating. He triumphs momentarily over his shyness to
win the love, tender and half-maternal, of Madame de Rênal. He moves
to Paris, trains himself to appear energetic and cold, succeeds in several
diplomatic missions and in elaborate schemes to seduce highly placed
ladies. The proud daughter of his aristocratic employer, Monsieur de
la Mole, falls in love with him; he is just as wildly in love with her, but
both play a game of haughty indifference in order the better to insure
the slow crystallization of feelings into passion, dear to Stendhal. An
amazing marriage is planned between the humiliated aristocrat and the
carpenter's son; but Julien is still in love with Madame de Rênal. He
shoots her in church, without killing her, with no apparent or logical
motive, and is condemned to death. Mademoiselle de la Mole, his
frustrated bride, will gruesomely treasure the head of her guillotined
husband-to-be, which she is allowed to carry away, in the proud
manner of her sixteenth-century ancestors. The delineation of a society
torn between the heirs to privilege and the men from the masses who
wish to unleash further the revolutionary forces makes the novel a
dramatic comment on the society of 1830: 'Chronique de 1830' was the
novel's subtitle. But the creation of characters, impossibly heroic and
capricious in their contradictory moods, like that of Mademoiselle
de la Mole, whose passion is chiefly what Stendhal had classified as
'amour de tête', maternally tender like Madame de Rênal, of half a
dozen secondary figures all sharply drawn and full of life, is what gives
its greatest price to the novel. The ambivalence of love and hatred,
of scorn and remorseful humility, is superbly depicted. The dénouement is illogical, as life often is; but it is in harmony with the character
of the hero, and of Stendhal's own romantic view that to be condemned to death is the only thing which cannot be bought and
which ennobles a man. The style is swift; it eschews pompous romantic
descriptions and lyrical élans. Yet, in a few evocations, the whole poetry
of sentiment surges forth, suggested with a superb economy of

words: Julien 'brûlant d'amour, mais la tête dominant le cœur', asks himself in the second part of the novel: 'Qui jamais m'aurait dit que je ressentirais de telles délices à pleurer?' or, listening to the sound of the vain words uttered by his own lips, Mademoiselle de la Mole's lover dreamingly remarks: 'Ah! . . . si je pouvais couvrir de baisers ces joues si pâles, et que tu ne le sentisses pas!'

The secret of Stendhal's appeal to the century which followed his own lies primarily in the poetical suggestiveness of his novels. An amateur among novelists, he confessed to Balzac, who had the generosity and the vision to hail him in 1839 in a fine article, that it had never occurred to him that there could exist laws for the art of fiction or rules how to fabricate a novel. He observed none. Physical description bored him; so did any realistic portrayal of the setting of his scenes, or of his characters. He did not build up his stories around a climax or a dramatic crisis. He followed his own rhythm, now nonchalant, now hurried. He smiled at his own heroes, Julien, Fabrice, Lucien, Lamiel, in part through shyness and for fear the reader would recognize too much of himself in them, in part through kindly irony. His love affairs are astonishingly pure; not a trace of eroticism in them, and even less of a stress upon crude physical contacts. In daily life, Stendhal's avowed purpose was to set out every morning on a hunt for happiness, and he would have liked to be a conqueror of beautiful ladies: he was ugly, shy, too imaginative and hence conscious in advance of the poor showing he would probably make. But he presented himself in Lucien Leuwen, understood and loved by an intelligent father (as Stendhal had not been), and especially in Fabrice, the hero of *La Chartreuse de Parme*, who is present at the Battle of Waterloo without realizing that a great battle is being fought, as radiant with charm, seductiveness and an insolent independence from all social shackles. That projection of what Stendhal would have wished to be is perhaps the most beloved by the moderns of all the heroes in French fiction; and the woman who loves Fabrice with devotion and intelligence, in an affair which remains platonic, may well be, along with one or two heroines of Tolstoy, the most attractive woman in the whole range of the European novel.

Mérimée (1803–70), more versatile and more expert in social life and in literary strategy, was a close friend of Stendhal, twenty years his elder; but he treated him somewhat condescendingly, as did Sainte-Beuve and many of his contemporaries. Mérimée enjoyed a greater fame much earlier; he has paid for it, rather unjustly, by being less eagerly read in our own time. His prose is more direct, slightly dry in its stress upon irony and in its affectation of remoteness from the reader. His art of story telling is more self-conscious, skilful at working up to a dramatic climax, fond of surprising and of slightly upsetting the public. In fact, there was much sentiment and tenderness also in Mérimée, and a profoundly romantic longing for all that is primitive, violent, even cruel. He had a keen eye for local colour, for spontaneous and unrestrained characters (the gypsy Carmen, the Corsican woman Colomba), for all that seemed to jolt the complacency of refined, worldly culture. There is much in common between Ernest Hemingway and him; but Mérimée's knowledge of literature, of art, of sophisticated people extended much further. In many fields he was a pioneer: as an archaeologist and art critic, who rediscovered romanesque architecture and frescoes and helped preserve them; as a specialist of Russian literature (Pushkin, Gogol), which he read in the original and translated; as the author of *récits* or long short-stories of which he left exquisite models to Flaubert, Maupassant and his other successors in English and American letters. *Carmen*, his most celebrated novel, appeared in 1845 and struck the Romantic public with its restraint, its hardness and its vitality. Bizet's opera (1875), which itself took several years to be accepted by the musical audiences, has popularized its theme but not matched the force of the original. *Le Vase étrusque*, *La Double méprise*, *La Vénus d'Ille* and *Tamango* (a heart-rending story on the slave trade from Africa to the New World) are masterpieces of economy and of vividness as well as of half-repressed pity for the follies and self-inflicted miseries of passionate creatures.

The range of Honoré de Balzac (1799–1850) is immeasurably wider. He has often been said to be the most prolific and powerful giver of life to other creatures, next to God and next to Shakespeare. Most critics would readily declare that he is second to none among the novelists of the world, except perhaps Tolstoy and Dostoevsky; and for the latter, Balzac's work served as a point of departure. He wrote incessantly, harassed by debts, by business undertakings which ruined him, by time- and energy-consuming love affairs. His first novels, of scant literary merit, appeared under pseudonyms. From 1830 on, Balzac became aware of his extraordinary powers of observation and imagination. Both faculties had in him a similar source: the memories of an unhappy youth and a prickly and vulnerable sensibility. 'Il n'y a que les âmes méconnues et les pauvres qui sachent observer, parce que tout les froisse et que l'observation résulte d'une souffrance. La mémoire n'enregistre bien que ce qui est douleur.' That avowal in one of his early letters to Madame Hanska, in 1833, is revealing. He pierced through objects, landscapes and people with a searching glance, plumbed them to their depths, and he at once reconstructed the inner life of the characters, or even the houses and towns thus seized by his lucid and intuitive sympathy. In 1833, he hit upon a new concept of creation which filled him with joy: to have the many characters of his series of varied novels reappear from one book to another. Thus they had a past, a well-rounded personality, more density than fictional creatures who briefly go across a story and vanish before the reader has been able to identify with them. Some monotony also is entailed by that device, which has probably been praised to an excess, and there is artificiality in linking those men and women from the four corners of France, all meeting in the slums or the salons of the metropolis. In 1842, boldly rivalling Dante, Balzac defined his aims in a preface to the *Comédie humaine,* which claimed to be nothing less than the huge fresco of a whole society in a state of flux, with a bulging inferno abandoned to greed and vice, and a shrunken paradise.

All aspects of life in France (Balzac who had travelled across Europe for his love encounters gave only scant place, and only in his short stories, to countries other than his own) are portrayed and generalized upon in Balzac's fiction: for he was determined to establish laws of society and even laws governing human passions. He insisted that it is not enough to be a man: one must be a system. Provincial life, army life and the Napoleonic epic in particular; the peasantry, to which he was not partial; shopkeepers and tradesmen; courtesans, convicts, lesbians, inverts; married couples, dissolute wives, husbands addicted to debauchery; philosophers, inventors, artists, monomaniacs of all sorts. The greatest of Balzac's novels are not those which are traditionally read by schoolchildren and students, but *Béatrix* (1839), *Les Illusions perdues* (1837–43), *Le Curé de village* (1839), *La Rabouilleuse* (1842). His short stories at their best cannot be matched in the French language: *L'Auberge rouge, Le Réquisitionnaire, El Verdugo, Le Chef-d'œuvre inconnu.* Faults abound in works which were hastily written, often to pay off urgent debts: lengthy descriptions which always play a function in the novel but which strike some readers as too slow-moving, an obsession with money, budgets, sordid calculations and generally an abundance which overwhelms the average reader. Henry James commented upon that virtue of saturation in Balzac, which is perhaps inseparable from genius at its most restlessly inventive. Many of the world's greatest novels are indeed long novels, through which we thread our way as through a confusing but tantalizing labyrinthine universe.

His grip upon reality is one of Balzac's outstanding gifts. But he never submits to things as they are. To him, as later for Balzac's admirer, Marcel Proust, reality truly begins in the mind of the artist who selects scattered and unconnected elements in nature and recomposes them into a living whole. Balzac unashamedly alluded to his gift of second sight and compared his glance into others' secrets to that of God: nothing remained hidden from him. Since Baudelaire first called him a visionary, the word has been used to designate him. He had been impressed by, even converted to, the mystical doctrines of Swedenborg. Man, he repeated, is capable of reaching the infinite. 'Nous sommes nés pour tendre au ciel', Balzac asserted in his strange Swedenborgian novel *Séraphita* (1835). Energy and will-power, the qualities which had been displayed to an unheard-of degree by the great men of the Revolution and by Napoleon, could, in his view, be multiplied in man by systematic cultivation. Such was the dream of *Louis Lambert* (1833), who died from an excess of happiness after attempting to multiply his, and man's, will-power. Balzac's characters are often criminals or half-insane individuals devoured by the evil forces in them. But the greatest of them are perhaps those who rashly leap forward to wrestle with fate: the inventor (in *La Recherche de l'absolu*, 1834), the gambler (in *La Peau de chagrin*, 1831), the artist redoing the work of God or forcing God to surrender some of his secrets (*Le Chef-d'œuvre inconnu, Gambara, Facino Cane*). 'Il s'agit', declared that supremely Romantic novelist eager to help man transcend himself, 'de donner des ailes pour pénétrer dans le sanctuaire où Dieu se cache à nos regards.' (*Les Proscrits*, 1831.) Romantic characters in drama and fiction had Cain, Lucifer himself, Mephistopheles and other adversaries of God as their prototypes or else, in their yearning to expand man's powers, they aimed at nothing less than becoming gods themselves.

Historians, Reformers and Critics

If the nineteenth century was in Western Europe the supreme age of fiction, it was also, and chiefly in France, the age of history. Dissatisfaction with the present was part of the Romantic mood: their dreams were too lofty, and too utopian, for them to be prosaically content with the *hic et nunc*. They either wanted to rush the oncoming of a better future by changing social and political conditions, or else they felt nostalgic for the past ages in which they wished they could have lived: primitive times, Greece, India, the Middle Ages, the times of the troubadours and of the cathedrals. The relativist trend already conspicuous in eighteenth-century thought afforded the Romantics a clearer perspective on manners, customs and outlooks on life other than their own. Unlike periods of contentment with the prevailing regime and way of life, the decades that followed the French Revolution, aghast at some of the upheavals through which their country had just gone, lavishly bestowed their sympathy on past ages. Few of the historians then aimed at an objectivity which, to them, would have been tantamount to indifference and coldness. It was an anguishing concern for the men of 1820–50 to attempt to explain to themselves why and how the Revolution had had to heap up ruins and to erect a new order by breaking away with much of the past. Were the Terror and the massacres of 1794, were the dead and wounded of the Napoleonic wars, necessary to a Providential scheme? Or were they an act of evil forces which God would not curb? Were they essential to the progress of enlightened society of which the eighteenth century had dreamt? The new age was haunted by the ambition to elicit, from the contemplation of the past, the probable course of the future and perhaps the over-reaching laws of history. In its imaginative *élan*, it also endeavoured to reduce multifarious, irrational events to one great underlying force: conflict of races, nationalism, the spread of humanitarian socialism, revolutionary urges blindly sweeping man along. Moreover, and the secret of the momentous importance of history for the nineteenth century lies primarily here, history was conceived as literature and even as poetry. Its appeal was taken to be imaginative and sentimental. Nations would discover in their history an exciting source of poetry and a spur to greatness. 'Every nation's true Bible is its history,' Carlyle was to declare. Michelet, Renan, Taine and others were all convinced that we can only understand, and perhaps control, the present if we know how that present has come to be what it is: in other words, its genesis and the rationale underlying its development.

The impact of that history which was also an integral part of literature was enormous, and has remained so to this day; because it contained vivid scenes, easily detached from their context and read in anthologies, and because, as elementary education spread, every child in France was exposed to extracts from French historians, on the Gauls, on Joan of Arc, on the splendour of the Renaissance, on the growth and spread of civilization, on the achievement of the Revolution. The epic of Napoleon, related by historians and conjured up in Balzac or Hugo's novels, spread a screen of glory between the feudal and monarchical past of France and the present. The clock would never again be moved back. Michelet, in that respect, is not only one of the two or three supreme prose writers of France; he has also been the architect of democratic France.

He had predecessors: austere, professorial Guizot (1787–1874) and clear, didactic, logical Thiers (1797–1877), both of them statesmen whom their historical talent catapulted to political power, as has often been the case in France. Augustin Thierry (1795–1856) had a more vivid power of recreative sympathy with the past and a more brilliant talent as a writer. He upheld theoretical views on race which are no longer considered as valid, but which dramatized his perspective on the past. In his *Histoire de la conquête de l'Angleterre par les Normands* (1825), he sided with the conquered Saxons, whose rights he vindicated, against the invaders from France. In French history, he likewise read a justification of the former serfs and oppressed classes revolting, thanks to the French Revolution, against the conquering 'race' of Germanic oppressors. He gave arguments for the resolute ascent of the Third Estate against the privileged aristocracy.

Michelet (1798–1874) is a more feverish and passionate temperament, along with Balzac and Hugo one of the three great visionaries of French literature. He had grown up in poverty and he always remained close to the poor, refusing to become the favourite and thereby the prisoner of the official circles or of the salons. His was a tense, neurotic temperament, obsessed by death, dramatically in need of feminine love and even prone, as his *Journal*, published only in 1965, has revealed, to idolizing the other sex. He felt with an almost morbid intensity, suffered with those whom history had crushed, passionately hated the oppressors. His sensations, when recalling or reimagining past events and reconstructing figures of history, were acute and intense. They were immediately rendered into images and magnified into symbols. His style is the most naturally, overpoweringly metaphorical of any prose writer. The past, studied in archives and old prints, sprang to life for him; and, like Homer's Ulysses visiting the nether world, he poured out his own life blood over heroes and forces of old to resurrect them. His definition of history has remained famous: 'la résurrection intégrale du passé'.

to find much comfort in traditional Christian faith, they took refuge in art as the only enduring value and a substitute for religion. Less concerned with their own individual, puny sufferings than the earlier Romantics had been, they were more objective and cooler in the sarcasms which they heaped on the conditions imposed by fate. They no longer moaned 'I suffer', but rather 'man suffers'; the circumstances meted out to him in the modern world render happiness an utter impossibility.

Matthew Arnold, the Tennyson of *In Memoriam*, Swinburne and others in Britain in prose and verse expressed that mood of discouragement. So did Heine, Wagner and several philosophers in Germany. In French poetry, the greatest of the poets who have been called Parnassians – for having collected samples of their verse in *Le Parnasse contemporain* (the first collection published in 1866) – Leconte de Lisle (1818–94), found fault with the sentimentality and the verbal facility of some at least of the Romantics, including Lamartine and Musset. Yet his condemnation of life recalls Vigny and his passion for colourful landscapes, for animals, heroes of primitive violence, reveals his affinities with Hugo, whom he succeeded in 1886 at the French Academy. In 1852, after several curious pieces inspired by Fourier's socialist utopias, Leconte de Lisle published his *Poèmes antiques* with a manifesto advocating more knowledge, more thought in poetry and a return to the vigour of the early ages of man's cultural history, those of ancient India and of Greece. He varied his inspiration further and perfected his form in his *Poèmes barbares* (1862), the theme and the scene of which are often in the tropics or in strange mythologies of northern Europe or of the New World. The poetry is haughty and, on first appearance, may seem impersonal and forbiddingly pedantic. The author sums up defunct cultures in their religion, their mythology and their artistic achievement. The form is monotonous: few rare images, many vague, abstract epithets. The descriptions of animals, attentive and evocative, have become popular more easily than the epic fragments which conjure up the sumptuous mythologies of remote lands. Yet, in his poems on the gods and heroes of Greece ('Khirôn'), on 'Hypatie', the priestess of pagan philosophy murdered by Christian fanatics, and even more in his evocations of his own romantic childhood ('Ultra Coelos', 'La Fontaine aux lianes', 'Le Manchy'), in his invectives against the materialistic ugliness of the modern world ('Dies irae', 'Solvet saeclum') and in a few graceful and musical pieces on young women ('La Fille aux cheveux de lin', 'Épiphanie'), Leconte de Lisle composed several of the noblest and richest pieces in the French language. His friend and disciple, the Cuban Heredia (1842–1905), collected his sonnets later in the century; but he had published some of the most majestic ones, like 'Les Conquérants', as early as 1869. Mallarmé, Verlaine, even the young Rimbaud, before 1870, looked up to the group of the Parnasse, in which Gautier and the fanciful, more humorous Banville (1823–91) were held in honour, as the fountainhead of poetical innovations in the years 1866–70.

The other great poet of that generation, Baudelaire (1821–67), belonged to no group. He did not look back to the past like the Parnassians or profess the cult of plastic, impassible beauty. He deliberately wanted to be modern and to elicit and convey the poetry of urban life. A very original section of his *Fleurs du mal*, his poems in prose curiously entitled *Le Spleen de Paris* and brilliant aesthetic essays in his *Curiosités esthétiques* (1868) are a plea for modernity in art and letters. Manet, Degas, Monet, Toulouse-Lautrec, and Daumier before them, were to reorient French painting away from mythological and historical subjects and towards the epic beauty of life around us. Baudelaire, unafraid of prosaism and eschewing the grandiloquence of some Romantics, brought poetry down to the evocation of silent, intimate tragedies of everyday life: 'Le Cygne', 'Les Petites Vieilles', the dramatic and mysterious sonnet 'A une passante', opened up a vein of poetry altogether different from the Parnassian stress upon remote and majestic beauty. They constituted an attempt to achieve in verse, much more tersely, what Balzac had accomplished in prose: to introduce the beauty and the mystery of modern urban life into literature.

Baudelaire had received other legacies from the Romantic movement, in which he saw the latest embodiment of beauty: the stress upon acute, rare, even morbid sensations; the substitution of strangeness (which he had especially admired in the stories of Edgar Allan Poe), of ugliness, of fear and even of hysteria, for the former aesthetic ideal placed in harmony, idealization and serenity; the exploration of the subconscious, erotic, at times sickly layers of our own beings, in which the flowers of evil are rooted. Some of his most original poems jolted the readers of 1857 and of 1861 (the dates of the first two editions of *Les Fleurs du mal*) who wanted security and prudent normalcy in literature: six pieces were condemned in court and had to be omitted from the volume. In truth, however, there is nothing obscene or even deliberately erotic in Baudelaire's poetry. Physical desire is always softened or offset either by tenderness and the treatment of the woman as a kind sister or motherly soothing presence or by spiritualization. 'Une Charogne', 'Une Martyre', even the long 'Femmes damnées' on the theme of lesbian women which had fascinated Baudelaire, end in Platonic exaltation of the spirit above and behind the flesh or in austere moral lessons. Elsewhere, as a remnant of an exasperated Romanticism, Baudelaire treats the loved and hated woman as a vampire or as an agent of the devil sent to torture the lover: there are banalities in *Les Fleurs du mal*, and there are artistic flaws also (excessive generality, monotony of the adjectives, halting inspiration and consequently poor endings of sonnets, the quatrains of which had opened triumphantly). When all is said, however, Baudelaire remains the greatest love-poet in the French language and (in 'L'Héautontimoroumenos', 'L'Irrémédiable', 'Spleen') the most relentless psychological and moral analyst of guilt, dread and remorse in poetry.

All other poets of the generations that grew to manhood in 1845–60 pale into insignificance when set beside Baudelaire, Leconte de Lisle and Hugo who was still in those years the chief poetical force. The newcomers, all impressed by the *Fleurs du mal*, Verlaine, Mallarmé, Corbière and Rimbaud, composed their greatest work after 1870. Lautréamont (1846–70), also an heir to the morbidly weird and, regrettably, to the declamatory rhetoric of the strangest of the Romantics, remained unknown to his contemporaries. The drama of the Second Empire era enjoyed great vogue as comedy, musical comedy, operetta and moral plays with a purpose (the latter chiefly attempted by Alexandre Dumas *fils*, 1824–95); but it had scant originality and hardly counts as literature. The novel and the philosophical, moral and critical essay are the two vital branches of literature, along with poetry. The age was one of startling prosperity, of material progress, of modernization of the houses, the cities, the countryside; but its literature, as often is the case in eras of prosperity (in America in 1920–30 or in 1960–70, and in France after World War II) turned its back against that reign of comfort and security. It criticized the society and portrayed the frustrations and failures of individuals.

A good many of the novels published between 1850 (when Balzac died) and 1870 (when the Goncourts, Daudet and Zola brought about the renewal of fiction through a more systematic realism) were platitudinous stories which, under the banner of realism brandished by Champfleury (1821–89), undertook to observe and to copy reality at its most commonplace. Most of that realism was woefully deficient in style, in power of organization and even in the gift of personality which alone can endow observation with significance and with life. Others were well-meant moral portrayals of the aristocratic and middle classes, insipid and timorous, which, for several decades, made up the reading allowed to French 'jeunes filles de bonne famille', until the emancipation or the revelation of marriage opened up to them tales of adultery. Fromentin (1820–76), a painter and an art critic of note, published in 1862 a personal novel, *Dominique*, which, while still lacking in boldness and recoiling before a silent tragedy of a young man's controlled passion for a married woman, was impregnated with the charm of rare delicacy in the analysis of feelings and in the rendering of nature poetry in the country of La Rochelle. Barbey d'Aurevilly (1808–89) was a more impetuous personality, fanatically Catholic and furiously romantic, who lived and wrote in solitude, convinced that his age had passed him by. He made himself famous through his original critical judgements, often altogether erratic, at times surprisingly discerning. He is also the author of novels in which his Catholic inspiration and his nostalgia for the past do not hamper the delineation of violent passion: *L'Ensorcelée* (1854), *Un Prêtre marié* (1865), *Les Diaboliques* (1874). Huysmans, Bourget himself and Bernanos belong to the same spiritual family.

The truly great novelist between Balzac and Zola, a Norman like Barbey d'Aurevilly, less of a visionary than he, but the supreme technician of the art of fiction and a powerful influence on the literatures of English-speaking countries, is Gustave Flaubert (1821–80). His early novels, the most revealing of which is *Novembre* (1842), and even the first version of *L'Éducation sentimentale* (1845) reveal the intensity with which he felt and lived all the excesses of romantic sensibility. There was a morbid strain in him as much as in Baudelaire, youthful dreams of suicide, a constant meditation on death. With rare determination, young Flaubert resolved to silence the almost hysterical romantic in him, to reserve his dreams of violence and of monstrous excesses for his historical fiction: *Salammbô* (1862) and the long, tedious series of apparitions which tempt, metaphysically and sensually, the saint in *La Tentation de Saint Antoine* (1874). These are such richly documented books, such pedantic reconstitutions of the ancient world in which Flaubert wished he had lived, that the virtue of life, of chance or passion upsetting the elaborately contrived structure, has been banished from them.

There lingers some coldness and probably an excess of self-awareness on the part of the novelist, too relentless a control of his inspiration in *Madame Bovary* (1857). 'Toute maîtrise jette le froid,' remarked Mallarmé, who was even more of a calculating artist, athirst for the perfection of an absolute, than Flaubert. Flaubert's supreme mastery over every episode, every page of his novel, every pronouncement, every gesture of his characters, does not actually throw a shiver down our spine. But at times, and the novelist was aware of it, his quest for a gradual progression from incident to incident, for the elimination of chance or the emergence of the unforeseen, satisfied the reader's intellect more than his urge to be moved or to dream. Flaubert wrote a revealing sentence in the notes of his trip to Carthage in 1858, as he realized that Parnassian beauty can mean the elimination of life and of the involuntary, unforeseen, destructive intrusion of truth in a work of art: 'Il faut faire, à travers le Beau, vivant et vrai quand même.' Still for the student and for the technician of fiction, no novel is more superb than *Madame Bovary* with its blend of pathos and of irony, of carefully observed country life and of all the chaotic impulses of average creatures in revolt against surrounding mediocrity but unable to escape from their own harassed selves.

Many devotees of Flaubert have preferred his first masterpiece *L'Éducation sentimentale* (1869). There is indeed even more of Flaubert himself in the dreams, the romantic idealization of woman, the melancholy resignation of the protagonist, an average man 'without qualities' and without serious faults, too weak either for crime or for heroism. But the book is more than a *Bildungsroman*: it is the portrayal of a whole generation, for which 1848 was the dividing line between illusions and reality, the idealists bent on reforming society and the shrewd pragmatic ones who knew how to profit from the collapse of many hopes and how to adapt themselves. The bankruptcy of a whole generation and of a chimerical romantic love is the subject of that slow-moving fresco. *Bouvard et Pécuchet* (published posthumously in 1881), left unfinished by the author, is an epic of human stupidity, sarcastic yet kindly; Flaubert's universal pessimism gave itself free play there. *Un Cœur simple* is a short masterpiece of tender irony, less tense than Flaubert's novels, and in his other *contes* (*Saint-Julien l'hospitalier*, *Hérodias*) the novelist returned to his romantic vein, his love for colourful violence. 'Je suis un vieux romantique enragé,' he wrote to his friends, and he remained one to the end.

In an oft-quoted article on *Madame Bovary*, Sainte-Beuve had detected, and appeared to denounce, the prevalence in the literature of

1850–65 of 'anatomists and physiologists', all observers and dissectors of the human brain and heart, and shatterers of many illusions. The scientific spirit of objective observation, historical impartiality, explanation through quantitative factors and through causes, invaded Europe after the middle of the nineteenth century. France counted an especially large number of scientists who were also excellent writers and, in several cases, who were close to men of letters: Pasteur (1822–95), Berthelot (1827–1907), Renan's lifelong friend, Claude Bernard (1813–78) and a medical man who was also an eminent lexicographer and a champion of positivism, Littré (1801–81). The most rapturous hymn to science, and especially to historical and philological sciences and the new vision of the human past they afforded, was written in 1848 (but published only in 1890) by Renan (1823–92). Trained for the priesthood, the young Breton scholar lost his faith when studying exegetically the Semitic languages and the evidence against accepting the Bible as a revealed book. He voraciously devoured several languages (Hebrew, Aramaic, Arabic, ancient classical and modern tongues), studied archaeology, epigraphy, comparative mythology and undertook the history of the most momentous phenomenon in human history: the replacement of the Greco-Roman culture by Christianity, the origins and slow unfolding of Christian religion and its preparation by the Jewish people. Tirelessly, and in spite of a violent outcry against him as a desecrator of faith and an Antichrist, Renan devoted twenty-five years of labour to his twelve-volume enterprise: the *Histoire des origines du christianisme*, from the *Vie de Jésus* (1863) to *Marc-Aurèle* (1881) and the *Histoire du peuple d'Israël* (1887–93). These learned volumes rest on an immense mass of precise research, but they are also written with art, often with grace; they aim, like Michelet's history, with less imaginative fire and in a softer, more allusive and insinuating manner, at resurrecting a remote past. The scenery in which the Hebrew prophets, Christ and St Paul lived, the collective moods of those ages when imaginative dreams, superstitions, *élans* of the heart and protests against social injustice counted for more than the observation of facts or the logical reasonings of philosophers are very skilfully brought back to life by Renan. Often he is led to conjecture and to reinvent, since precise documentation is not available. With a subtlety which sometimes displays itself too complacently, he practises what he called the art 'de solliciter doucement les textes'. These volumes exercised a far-reaching influence in France and elsewhere for decades: they instilled into many unbelievers a new sense for the poetry of Christianity and the eagerness, if dogmas, rites and theology are to be thrown overboard in our time, to preserve at least the sensibility and the idealism which Christian faith had for centuries embodied for the West.

Renan is also a master of the philosophical essay, urbane, mellow, written in elegant, mellifluous prose, fond of suggesting paradoxes and of indulging in dreams on the future of mankind. Several are written in the form of dialogues or of dramas, dear to the author who enjoyed the dialectical clash of ideas. His literary masterpieces are to be found in a remarkable series of historical, biographical and 'moral' studies – moral connoting the psychological meditations on the meaning of life and on the guidance of men by generous ideas, as the adjective often does in French. Those masterpieces of the genre of the essay, probably the finest in French since Montaigne, are scattered in *Études d'histoire religieuse* (1857), *Essais de morale et de critique* (1859), *Souvenirs d'enfance et de jeunesse* (1883) and *Feuilles détachées* (1892).

Renan encountered, in his reflections on the Jewish people, the notion of race, which puzzled or seduced every historian of the last century. He was for a time half-tempted by some of the speculations on the subject indulged by Arthur de Gobineau (1816–82), in his *Essai sur l'inégalité des races humaines* (1851–5). Gobineau's factual errors, his venturesome conclusions and his dogmatism on the subject soon repelled the subtler and more balanced mind of Renan. The utilization made, chiefly in Germany, of Gobineau's theory that there once existed a pure Aryan race, which racial mixture had brought to degeneracy, should not make us underestimate the dazzling intelligence and the terse, ironical style of the author. He has been praised by British connoisseurs of the East as the author of the most penetrating stories ever laid in Asia, *Nouvelles asiatiques* (1876); his reports and letters from Iran, where he served as a French diplomat, his stories on *La Renaissance* (1877) and his novel *Les Pléiades* (1874) are works of a very rare, perhaps of a very great, talent.

Taine (1828–93) exercised in the last decades of the nineteenth century, along with Renan, a profound influence on French psychologists, critics and novelists, such as Ribot, Barrès, Bourget, Brunetière and Maurras. After an early volume of comic and scathing irony on the superficial philosophers who had preceded him in France, *Les Philosophes français du XIXe siècle* (1857), and a rigidly dogmatic attempt to explain La Fontaine through his 'race' and his 'milieu', Taine published a remarkable series of essays entitled *Essais de critique et d'histoire*

(1858, 1866), few of which have lost their freshness and their force of conviction after a century, and the most famous of his critical achievements, his five-volume *Histoire de la littérature anglaise* (1864, completed in 1869). The chapters on Chaucer, Shakespeare, Swift and Byron, controversial as they are, are still thought-provoking today. The doctrine of its introduction is too rigorous and fails to make an allowance for the unpredictable originality of one brother in a family, of one author among a thousand who were moulded in the same 'race', environment and time. But it constituted a bold and coherent attempt to understand literary and artistic works and not merely to enjoy them in a dilettante way.

Taine subsequently turned to history. The defeat of France at the hands of Prussia in 1870 shattered many of his dreams, as it did those of Michelet and Renan. The sight of the Parisian mob, enraged by the defeat and the siege, seizing power with the 1871 Commune, destroying and burning buildings, then savagely punished by the reaction which defeated them, strengthened Taine's profound pessimism on human nature. He ceased to have any faith in democracy. He regretted the Revolution, the vain conquests of Napoleon and the political instability of the French. He envied the reforming and moderate spirit of the British monarchy. In order to understand his countrymen and his own age, Taine undertook to explore *Les Origines de la France contemporaine* (1875–93) in six brilliant, dogmatic and partial volumes. His generalizations on the regrettable consequences for France of the 'classical spirit', allegedly abstract, doctrinaire, unmindful of the empirical lessons of facts, have had a powerful appeal for the political thinkers of France who, in large numbers, have criticized parliamentary democracy. It was probably a misfortune for the country that, after Michelet's revolutionary enthusiasm, most of the eminent political thinkers of France were hostile, or implacably severe, to democracy.

The fall of Napoleon III in September 1870 marked for France the closing of an era which had experimented in a number of political regimes without finding stability but which had at last effected an industrial revolution and brought economic welfare to a larger number of citizens. But literature, as always, stood in opposition to the spread of those material forces and collective trends which strengthened the State and the administration and threatened to restrict the freedom of the creative individual. Literary and artistic works were either a means of escape from too crushing a reality or a bitter criticism of things as they were (in fiction, drama, history). With Hugo, Leconte de Lisle or Baudelaire as with Stendhal or Flaubert, the nobleness of the writer's profession lay in his calling everything in question and in protesting against the injustice (of the social order and more generally of the human condition) in the name of an ideal, however dimly conceived. Under a wide diversity of shapes, the revolt of the Romantics, first asserted by their predecessors such as Diderot and Rousseau, had echoed throughout the years 1800–70. It has hardly ever been silenced since.

Bibliography

The titles listed here are necessarily very few, in relation to the huge number of volumes which have, within the last fifty years, been devoted to the interpretation and criticism of French literature in its modern periods. Very specialized works and works not readily accessible, or not available in the two languages taken to be familiar to the users of this volume (English and French) have been left out. For the French titles for which no place of publication is mentioned, Paris is to be understood.

SECOND HALF OF THE EIGHTEENTH CENTURY: VOLTAIRE, DIDEROT, ROUSSEAU

The writers of the age of Enlightenment had suffered relative neglect during the century which followed, partly as a reaction against the French Revolution and the movement of ideas which had seemed to prepare it, partly because the seventeenth century had been set up by academic critics as the classical century *par excellence* and the one best fit to provide models for the youth. Historians of the Revolution like Michelet, historians of arts and manners like the Goncourt brothers, had started a rehabilitation of the literature of the Regency and of the reign of Louis XV. A new and more scientific study of the 'Philosophic Spirit' was started by G. Lanson on the eve of the First World War. The empirical spirit of that age, its admiring attitude toward English thinkers and novelists, its impact upon the American Founding Fathers, have since made it a favourite period of study for English-speaking scholars.

Among the general or inclusive works which have reappraised the thought of the eighteenth century (chiefly in its second half), the following are especially relevant: C. Becker, *The Heavenly City of the Eighteenth Century Philosophers* (New Haven, 1955); I. Berlin, *The Eighteenth Century Philosophers, The Age of Enlightenment* (London and New York, 1956); E. Cassirer, *The Philosophy of the Enlightenment* (Princeton, 1951; appeared in German in 1932); L. Crocker, *An Age of Crisis: Man and World in Eighteenth Century French Thought* (Baltimore, 1959) and *Nature and Culture: Ethical Thought in the French Enlightenment* (Baltimore, 1963); J. Ehrard, *L'Idée de nature en France à l'aube des Lumières* (Flammarion, 1970); J. Fabre,

Lumières et romantisme: Energie et nostalgie (Klincksieck, 1963); P. Gay, *The Enlightenment, an Interpretation*, 2 vols (New York, 1966 and 1969); F. C. Green, *Minuet, a Critical Survey of French and English Literary Ideas in the Eighteenth Century* (London, 1935); G. Havens, *The Age of Ideas: From Reaction to Revolution in Eighteenth Century France* (New York, 1955); G. Lanson, *Essais de méthode, de critique et d'histoire littéraire* (1965); R. Mauzi, *L'Idée du bonheur au XVIIIe siècle* (1960); R. Mortier, *Clartés et ombres au siècle des Lumières* (Geneva, 1969); R. Niklaus, *The Eighteenth Century: 1715–89* (London, 1970); J. Roger, *Les Sciences de la vie dans la pensée française du dix-huitième siècle* (1963); J. Starobinski, *L'Invention de la liberté* (Geneva, 1964); K. Mannheim, *Ideology and Utopia* (London, 1936, and New York, 1960); A. Viatte, *Les Sources occultes du romantisme, 1770–1820* (1938). On the idea of progress more particularly, C. Becker, *Progress and Power* (Stanford, 1936); J. B. Bury, *The Idea of Progress* (London and New York, 1955; first published 1932); C. Frankel, *The Faith of Reason* (New York, 1948); F. L. Tuveson, *Millennium and Utopia* (Berkeley, 1949).

On Voltaire, a number of the many volumes of *Studies on Voltaire and the Eighteenth Century*, published by T. Besterman in Geneva and subsequently in Banbury, Oxfordshire, have added greatly to our knowledge of the eighteenth century. Among the mass of significant works on Voltaire, the following will be found especially useful: H. N. Brailsford, *Voltaire and Reform in the Light of the French Revolution* (London and New York, 1959; first appeared 1935); P. Gay, *Voltaire's Politics* (Princeton, 1959); G. Lanson, *Voltaire* (1906), translated into English with substantial additions (New York, 1966); A. Maurois, *Voltaire* (1935); R. Naves, *Le Goût de Voltaire* (1938); R. Pomeau, *La Religion de Voltaire* (1969; first published 1956) and *Voltaire par lui-même* (1955); J. Sareil, *Voltaire et la critique* (Englewood Cliffs, N. J., 1966).

On Diderot, several volumes of *Diderot Studies*, edited by Otis Fellows and other Columbia University scholars, have appeared in Geneva since 1949. See also L. Crocker, *Two Diderot Studies: Ethics and Esthetics* (Baltimore, 1952); H. Dieckmann, *Cinq leçons sur Diderot* (Geneva, 1959); R. Pomeau, *Diderot, sa vie et son œuvre* (1967); J. Proust, *Diderot et l'Encyclopédie* (1962); A. M. Wilson, *Diderot* (New York, 1972, new ed.).

On Rousseau, biographical, political, ethical, literary and philosophical aspects of his controversial personality and writings have long been discussed in book after book. Among the recent titles: P. Burgelin, *La Philosophie de l'existence de Rousseau* (1952); E. H. Dobinson, *Rousseau: his Thought and its Relevance Today* (London, 1969); F. C. Green, *Rousseau: a Critical Study of his Life and Writings* (Cambridge, 1955); R. Grimsley, *Rousseau: a Critical Study of Self-Awareness* (Cardiff, 1961); R. D. Masters, *The Political Philosophy of Rousseau* (Princeton, 1968); M. Raymond, *Rousseau: la quête de soi et la rêverie* (1962); J. Starobinski, *La Transparence et l'obstacle* (1957); C. E. Vaughan, *The Political Writings of Rousseau* (Cambridge, 1915).

A few sundry titles on other thinkers and on novelists and dramatists are grouped here: J. Bouissounouse, *Julie de Lespinasse* (New York, 1962); R. Desné, *Les Matérialistes français* (1965); J. Fabre, *Chénier, l'homme et l'œuvre* (1951); R. Hubert, *Les Sciences sociales dans l'Encyclopédie* (Lille, 1923); R. Niklaus, *Beaumarchais, le Barbier de Séville* (London, 1968). On Condorcet, J. Schapiro, *Condorcet and the Rise of Liberalism* (New York, 1934); on Turgot, D. Dakin, *Turgot and the Ancien*

Régime (London, 1939); On the eighteenth century novelists: M. Blanchot, *Lautreámont et Sade* (1949); P. Brooks, *The Novel of Worldliness* (Princeton, 1969); G. Gorer, *The Life and Ideas of the Marquis de Sade* (London, 1953, new ed.), and G. Lély, *Sade: étude sur sa vie et ses œuvres* (1967); A. Malraux, *Le Triangle noir* (1970); G. May, *Le Dilemme du roman au dix-huitième siècle* (New Haven, 1963); V. Mylne, *The Eighteenth Century French Novel: Techniques of Illusion* (Manchester, 1965); E. Showalter, *The Evolution of the French Novel, 1641–1782* (Princeton, 1972); P. Stewart, *Imitation and Make-Believe in the French Novel, 1700–50* (New Haven, 1969); E. Sturm, *Crébillon fils et le libertinage au XVIIIe siècle* (Nizet, 1970).

ROMANTICISM

There exists a whole library on the Romantic movement in France and in other countries of Europe. Romanticism can be variously conceived as starting in the middle of the previous century (with Rousseau, Diderot, Goethe, Ossian and others), as a movement culminating in 1820–45, or as a revolution of sensibility and of thought whose impact was felt over the whole nineteenth century and is still powerful today. The following titles are selected as the most relevant: M. H. Abrams, *The Mirror and the Lamp, Romantic Theory and the Critical Tradition* (New York, 1953); R. M. Adams, *Nil: Episodes in the Literary Conquest of Void During the Nineteenth Century* (New York, 1966); F. Baldensperger, *Le Mouvement des idées dans l'émigration française, 1789–1815* (1925); A. Béguin, *L'Âme romantique et le rêve* (1963, new ed.); J. Bousquet, *Les Thèmes du rêve dans la littérature romantique* (1964) and *Anthologie du dix-huitième siècle romantique* (1972); R. Bray, *Chronologie du romantisme (1804–30)* (1932); M. J. Durry, *La Vieillesse de Chateaubriand, 1830–48* (1933); L. Emery, *L'Âge romantique*, 2 vols (Lyon, 1960); D. O. Evans, *Social Romanticism in France, 1830–48* (Oxford, 1951); L. Guichard, *La Musique et les lettres au temps du romantisme* (1955); P. Guiral, *La Société française 1815–1914, vue par les romanciers* (1969); H. J. Hunt *Le Socialisme et le romantisme en France* (Oxford, 1935) and *The Epic in Nineteenth Century France* (Oxford, 1941); H. Lefebvre, *Musset dramaturge* (1955); M. Milner, *Le Diable dans la littérature française*, 2 vols (1960) and *Le Romantisme, I (1820–43)* (1973); A. Monglond, *Le Préromantisme français* (Grenoble, 1930); P. Moreau, *Le Classicisme des romantiques* (1932) and *Le Romantisme* (1957); D. Mornet, *Le Romantisme en France au XVIIIe siècle* (1912); A. R. Oliver, *Nodier Pilot of Romanticism* (Syracuse, 1964); H. Peyre, *Literature and Sincerity* (New Haven, 1963) and *Qu'est-ce que le romantisme?* (1971); M. Praz, *The Romantic Agony* (Oxford, 1951; first ed. in Italian in 1930).

THE NOVEL

The novel of the nineteenth century has been studied from many a point of view in all the standard volumes on the craft of fiction, such as the well-known ones by P. Lubbock, E. M. Forster, G. Lukács. Among more recent ones, the most useful may be the following: P. Castex, *Le Conte fantastique en France de Nodier à Maupassant* (1951); I. Howe, *Politics and the Novel* (New York, 1964); H. Levin, *The Gates of Horn* (New York and London, 1963); M. Turnell, *The Art of French Fiction* (London, 1951, and New York, 1958). Stendhal has been the subject of a great many works since 1920 or so. Among them those by L. Blum, *Stendhal et le beylisme* (1930, new ed.); V. Brombert, *Stendhal et la voie oblique* (1954); A.

Caraccio, *Stendhal, l'homme et l'œuvre* (1951); G. Durand, *Le Décor mythique de la Chartreuse de Parme* (1961); F. C. Green, *Stendhal* (Cambridge, 1939); F. Hemmings, *Stendhal, a Study of his Novels* (Oxford, 1964); F. Marill, *Le Naturel chez Stendhal* (1956); J. Prévost, *La Création chez Stendhal* (1951); J. Starobinski, 'Stendhal pseudonyme', in *L'Œil vivant* (1961).

Studies on Balzac have been hardly less numerous: M. Bardèche, *Balzac romancier* (1941); P. Bertault, *Balzac, l'homme et l'œuvre* (1968; first ed. 1948); F. Hemmings, *Balzac, an Interpretation of La Comédie humaine* (New York, 1967); P. Laubriet, *L'Intelligence de l'art chez Balzac* (1961); D. F. McCormick, *Les Nouvelles de Balzac* (1973); A. Maurois, *Prometheus, the Life of Balzac* (London and New York, 1965); G. Picon, *Balzac par lui-même* (1956). On the third of the giants of French fiction before 1870, Flaubert, the best works are those by V. Brombert, *The Novels of Flaubert* (Princeton, 1966) and *Flaubert par lui-même* (1971); C. Digeon, *Flaubert* (1970); J. P. Sartre, *L'Idiot de la famille*, 3 vols (1971–3); E. Starkie, *Flaubert, the Making of the Master* and *The Master*, 2 vols (London and New York, 1967 and 1971); A. Thibaudet, *Flaubert* (1935).

On other novelists, only a few significant titles may be mentioned: A. Oliver, *Benjamin Constant: écriture et conquête du moi* (1970); P. Delbouille, *Genèse, structure et destin d'Adolphe* (1972); B. Jasinski, *L'Engagement de B. Constant* (1971). J. Bornecque, *Les Années d'apprentissage de Daudet* (1951); M. Sachs, *The Career of Daudet, a Critical Study* (Cambridge, U.S.A., 1965).

POETRY

A reappraisal of the French Romantic poets has taken place since 1930 or so, when the centenary of Romanticism was celebrated in France and the lasting impact of the Romantic 'mal du siècle' over the post-Second-World-War generations appeared as giving relevance to the visionary poets of 1820–50. Among the general studies on that poetry, the following are notable: A. M. Boase, *The Poetry of France, Vol. 3, 1800–1900* (London, 1967; first published 1952); A. E. Carter, *The Idea of Decadence in French Literature* (Toronto, 1958); A. Cassagne, *La Théorie de l'art pour l'art en France* (1959; first published 1905); E. Estève, *Byron et le romantisme français* (1929; first published 1907); M. Gilman, *The Idea of Poetry in France* (Cambridge, U.S.A., 1958); J. P. Houston, *The Demonic Imagination: Style and Theme in French Romantic Poetry* (Baton Rouge, Louisiana, 1969); M. Moraud, *Le Romantisme français en Angleterre, 1814–48* (1933); J. P. Richard, *Poésie et profondeur* (1955) and *Études sur le romantisme* (1970); H. Riffaterre, *L'Orphisme dans la poésie romantique* (1970).

A very few among the important works on the individual poets are: H. Guillemin, *Le Jocelyn de Lamartine* (1936) and *Lamartine, l'homme et l'œuvre* (1940); G. Bonnefoy, *La Pensée religieuse et morale d'A. de Vigny* (1944); F. Germain, *L'Imagination de Vigny* (1961); E. Lauvrière, *Vigny*, 2 vols (1946). P. Albouy, *La Création mythologique chez Hugo* (1963); J. B. Barrère, *La Fantaisie de Hugo*, 3 vols (1949–60), *Hugo l'homme et l'œuvre* (1952) and *Hugo devant Dieu* (1965); L. Emery, *Vision et pensée chez Hugo* (Lyon, n.d.); J. Gaudon, *Hugo, le temps de la contemplation* (1969); H. Guillemin, *Hugo par lui-même* (1951); A. Maurois, *Olympio ou la Vie de Hugo*, 2 vols (1954); H. Peyre, *Hugo philosophe* (1972); D. Saurat, *La Religion de V. Hugo* (1929); P. Zumthor, *Hugo poète de Satan* (1929). P. Gastinel, *Le Romantisme de*

Musset (1933). S. Fauchereau, *Th. Gautier* (1972); J. Richardson, *Gautier, his Life and Times* (London, 1958). A. Béguin, *Nerval ou la Descente aux enfers* (1945); P. Bénichou, *Nerval et la chanson folklorique* (1971); P. Castex, *Aurelia* (1971); L. Cellier, *Nerval, l'homme et l'œuvre* (1956); R. Chambers, *Nerval et la poétique du voyage* (1969); R. Jean, *Nerval par lui-même* (1964); J. Richer, *Nerval et les doctrines ésotériques* (1947). E. Estève, *Leconte de Lisle* (1923); A. Fairlie, *Leconte de Lisle's Poems on the Barbarian Races* (Cambridge, 1947); I. Putter, *Le Pessimisme de Leconte de Lisle*, 2 vols (Berkeley, 1954 and 1961). L. Austin, *L'Univers poétique de Baudelaire* (1956); P. Emmanuel, *Baudelaire devant Dieu* (1967); A. Fairlie, *Les Fleurs du mal* (London, 1960); M. Gilman, *Baudelaire the Critic* (New York, 1943); J. Hubert, *L'Esthétique des Fleurs du mal* (Geneva, 1953); C. Pichois and W. Bandy, *Baudelaire devant ses contemporains* (1967, new ed.); J. P. Sartre, *Baudelaire* (1947); E. Starkie, *Baudelaire* (London, 1971, new ed.). M. Blanchot, *Lautréamont et Sade* (1963); R. Faurisson, *A-t-on lu Lautréamont?* (1972).

ESSAYISTS, HISTORIANS AND CRITICS

The nineteenth century has been called the golden age of the essay, critical and historical. The greatest historians of France meditated on the past in order to understand the present and often to prophesy or to prepare the future. Only a very summary selection among the many works dealing with the French thinkers and historians can be attempted here. Among the general surveys and studies, I. Babbit, *The Masters of French Criticism* (New York, 1963; first appeared 1912); D. G. Charlton, *Positivist Thought in France During the Second Empire* (Oxford, 1959) and *Secular Religions in France, 1815–70* (London, 1963); E. Faguet, *Politiques et moralistes du dix-neuvième siècle*, 3 vols (1891–1900; Vol. 3 appeared in English translation, London, 1928); E. Wilson, *To the Finland Station* (New York, 1970). On Sainte-Beuve: R. Fayolle, *Sainte-Beuve et le dix-huitième siècle* (1972); A. G Lehmann, *Sainte-Beuve, a Portrait of the Critic, 1804–42* (Oxford, 1962); M. Leroy, *La Pensée de Sainte-Beuve* (1940); L. F. Mott, *Sainte-Beuve* (New York and London, 1925); H. Nicolson, *Sainte-Beuve* (London, 1957); M. Regard, *Saint-Beuve* (1960). On Renan; R. Chadbourne, *Renan* (New York, 1968) and *Renan as an Essayist* (Ithaca, N. Y., 1959); R. Galand, *L'Âme celtique de Renan* (1959); K. Gore, *L'Idée de progrès dans la pensée de Renan* (1970); G. Guisan, *Renan et l'art d'écrire* (Geneva, 1962); L. F. Mott, *Renan* (New York, 1921); H. Peyre, *Sagesse de Renan* (1966) and *Renan et la Grèce* (1973); J. Pommier, *Renan* (1923); H. W. Wardman, *Renan, a Critical Biography* (London, 1964). On Michelet: R. Barthes, *Michelet par lui-même* (1954); J. Gaulmier, *Michelet devant Dieu* (1968); P. Viallaneix, *La Voie royale* (1959). On Taine: A. Chevrillon, *Taine, formation de sa pensée* (1932); R. Gibaudan, *Les Idées sociales de Taine* (1928); S. J. Kahn, *Science and Aesthetic Judgment: a Study in Taine's Critical Method* (London, 1953); P. Lacombe, *Taine historien et sociologue* (1909); F. C. Roe, *Taine et l'Angleterre* (1923). On Tocqueville: H. Brogan, *Tocqueville* (London, 1973); J. Lively, *The Social and Political Thought of Tocqueville* (Oxford, 1962); J. P. Mayer, *Tocqueville, a Biographical Essay in Political Science* (London and New York, 1940). On Gobineau: J. Buenzod, *La Formation de la pensée de Gobineau* (1967); J. Gaulmier, *Spectre de Gobineau* (1965).

FRENCH LITERATURE
SINCE 1870
John Cruickshank

The date 1870 is more obviously significant for the political evolution
of France than for its literary development. This is the year in which the
Franco-Prussian war brought the Second Empire under Napoleon III
to a no doubt deservedly inglorious end. It saw the crushing nature of
the French defeat highlighted by capitulation at Sedan and the siege of
Paris. Nevertheless, 1870 is also the year in which two contrasting
works, both significant in the history of literature, were completed:
Taine's psychological essay, *De l'intelligence*, and Verlaine's collection of
love poems, *La Bonne Chanson*. Taine wrote from a firm belief in
exact and scientific determinism as the proper basis for a study of human
nature. Verlaine, on the contrary, sought to express human truth
through a private sensibility and conscious imprecision at odds with
rational analysis. The closing decades of the nineteenth century were to
elaborate and diversify further these two attitudes. In terms both of
intellectual debate and literary practice, they received their most
striking expression in naturalism and symbolism respectively.

Naturalism

Nineteenth-century 'scientism' was a broad set of beliefs, materialist,
determinist and atheist in spirit, to which Comte, Renan and Taine
made particularly important contributions. Auguste Comte (1798–1857)
elaborated a 'philosophy of positivism' which divided the development
of the human mind into three historical stages: the theological, the
metaphysical, and the scientific or positivist. In this scheme scientific
positivism clearly represented intellectual maturity and Comte, who
saw evidence of analytical precision already ousting philosophic
generalities in various spheres, was anxious to apply scientific method

to all areas of human speculation. In particular, he argued the need for strict observation and experiment in the study of society ('la physique sociale') and may be seen, for good or ill, as a founding father of modern sociology. In a similar spirit Ernest Renan (1823–92) held science to be the only acceptable religion ('il n'y a pas de surnaturel'), while Hippolyte Taine (1828–93) attributed the determining role of heredity and environment to three factors: 'race', 'milieu' and 'moment'.

These are some of the general ideas, not always fully understood, from which the naturalist movement drew inspiration. Émile Zola (1840–1902), the most gifted novelist of the group and its chief theoretician, was familiar with contemporary scientific ideas (including Darwinism) and also read more specialized works including Prosper Lucas's *Traité philosophique et physiologique de l'hérédité naturelle* (1847–50), Claude Bernard's *Introduction à l'étude de la médecine expérimentale* (1865) and Charles Letourneau's *Physiologie des passions* (1868). He combined these scientific interests with a strong social sense and his novels often apply the conclusions of science to the ills of society in a spirit of radical analysis.

In a theoretical justification of his practice as a novelist (*Le Roman expérimental*, 1880) he refers to himself and his fellow naturalists as 'moralistes expérimenteurs'. He made the extravagant claim that the naturalist novelist places his characters in a particular social milieu and then, like a chemist in a laboratory, observes the interaction of temperament and environment which he finally 'writes up'. Zola sees the novelist as the amanuensis of his characters. More seriously, most of the novels use the temperament/environment interaction to suggest that even the most reprehensible characters are not so much innately 'bad' as victims of hereditary and social conditioning – the only acceptable conclusion for what he called, more chillingly than he intended, 'un siècle de science et de démocratie'.

These ideas had already been applied in *Thérèse Raquin* (1867). In 1871 Zola drew the logical consequences of his theories by planning the twenty-volume 'Rougon-Macquart' cycle (1871–93). He was later to write two further, though smaller, groups of novels, *Les Trois Villes* (1894–8) and *Les Quatre Évangiles* (1899–1903), but these are second rate and overtly didactic works. His reputation rests on the 'Rougon-Macquart' series – a grandiose fresco of the Second Empire in which various members of the two related families experience their inherited taints in a variety of situations that include Parisian slum life (*L'Assommoir*, 1877), the world of the *demi-mondaine* (*Nana*, 1880), a strike in a mining community (*Germinal*, 1885), rural poverty (*La Terre*, 1887) and the Franco-Prussian war (*La Débâcle*, 1892). Such novels combine conscientious documentation with a heavy concentration on the more bestial human manifestations. They were severely condemned as prurient and pornographic, while also being widely read and enjoyed.

No aesthetic formula could satisfactorily accommodate Zola's conception of a strictly 'experimental' novel, and the scientific value of the 'Rougon-Macquart' series is almost nil. At the same time, Zola's failure as a scientist is the source of his artistic strength. By temperament he was a poet and visionary, and if the tension between romance and science encouraged some ill-judged melodramatic writing it also created some of the most powerfully imagined scenes in his work. His strong visual response to physical detail and collective movement helped to expand the scope of late nineteenth-century fiction beyond the traditional limits of internalized and individualized psychological analysis.

The Goncourt brothers (Edmond, 1822–96, and Jules, 1830–70), famous for the *Journal* which they began in 1851, first made a reputation as art critics and historians. In the 1860s they collaborated on a number of novels, clearly naturalist in spirit, published before Zola codified naturalistic doctrine. Their early training enabled them to write carefully documented accounts of contemporary society and they also took a particular interest in analysing mental abnormality, e.g. hysteria in *Germinie Lacerteux* (1865) and religious mania in *Madame Gervaisais* (1869). Their approach is typified by a *Journal* entry for 1860, discussing the novel *Sœur Philomène* (1861) and its hospital setting, in which they resolve to study the background 'sur le vrai, sur le vif, sur le saignant'.

The other major figure associated with naturalism is Guy de Maupassant (1850–93) whose first published story, *Boule de suif,* appeared in Zola's collection of *nouvelles, Les Soirées de Médan* (1880). Other contributors, apart from Zola himself, were Paul Alexis (1847–1901), Joris-Karl Huysmans (1848–1907), Léon Hennique (1851–1935) and Henry Céard (1851–1924) whose novel, *Une Belle Journée* (1881), dealt with what he himself called 'cette loi de la médiocrité universelle qui, pareille à la gravitation et despotique autant que la pesanteur, ploie le monde et le soumet à son ordonnance'. As for Maupassant, he is the genuine entertainer among the naturalists, a cynical, amusing observer of human folly whose 300 or so short stories show an astonishing range of narrative skill and artistic versatility. In the preface to the best of his six novels, *Pierre et Jean* (1888), he rightly describes himself as probing, with detachment, 'le sens profond et caché des événements'.

Mention should also be made of Alphonse Daudet (1840–97) though he is best remembered today for the comic and ironic stories collected in *Lettres de mon moulin* (1866), *Tartarin de Tarascon* (1872). etc. The deliberate naturalism of such novels as *Jack* (1876), *Le Nabab* (1877), *Numa Roumestan* (1881) and *Sapho* (1884) contains an element of sentimentality suggesting that Daudet was attracted to the movement more by human sympathy with naturalist subject-matter than from artistic instinct. He rightly described himself as a *homo duplex*.

In the 1880s naturalism scored some success in the theatre with stage adaptations of novels by Zola, the Goncourts, Daudet and others. Between 1887 and 1896 Antoine's Théâtre Libre developed in the same direction, putting on plays by Alexis, Hennique and Céard and such important foreign 'naturalists' as Hauptmann, Ibsen and Strindberg. Ironically, the one French naturalist play of genuine quality, *Les Corbeaux* (1882) by Henry Becque (1837–99), failed completely when first performed at the Comédie Française.

Symbolism

Daudet's dual output suggests that not all writers classed as naturalists fit completely into this category. A striking example is Joris-Karl Huysmans whose early association with naturalism, seen in such novels as *Les Sœurs Vatard* (1879) and *En ménage* (1881), was prompted less by scientific conviction than by a Céard-like pessimism before the irremediable vulgarity of a world in which 'seul le pire arrive'. A fastidious temperament and refined artistic sense led Huysmans to reject the dominant 'scientism' of the day. His best-known novel, *A rebours* (1884), shows the hero, Des Esseintes, escaping from sordid materialism into aestheticism and recherché 'spiritual' experiences. The opening pages of *Là-bas* (1891) discuss the shortcomings of the naturalist novel and the hero, Durtal, is fascinated and repelled by satanism. Huysmans' own development, through aestheticism and satanism to the Catholic faith, is plotted in these two books and in such later novels as *En route* (1895), *La Cathédrale* (1898) and *L'Oblat* (1903).

Significantly, Des Esseintes in *A rebours* reads Mallarmé's poetry – hinting that the symbolist movement with which Mallarmé is associated, and the revival of religious values of which Huysmans's later novels are only one example, represent a common dissatisfaction with the intellectual and artistic assumptions of naturalism. Symbolist doctrine and the Catholic revival possess fundamental differences, but they share a central belief in an *au-delà* beyond immediate material reality.

Symbolism is primarily associated with poetry and with Baudelaire's description of the world as a 'forêt de symboles'. In its final doctrinal form it is a complicated and sometimes pretentious theory though its effects on poetic technique have been important and lasting. The symbolists held the poet to be uniquely equipped to convey to others the truth of the Idea – a world of transcendent reality symbolized in the more immediately accessible world of material objects. This is so because of the poet's sensibility and because words have magical properties which make possible their use as 'symbols' rather than 'dictionary equivalents'. For the symbolist, therefore, the naturalist both failed to recognize the potential power of language and concentrated, in his subject-matter, on appearance rather than reality.

Among the precursors of symbolism Verlaine and Rimbaud are important figures. Paul Verlaine (1844–96) was originally associated with the Parnassian reaction against Romantic rhetoric and subjectivity but his earliest collections of poems, *Poèmes saturniens* (1866) and *Fêtes galantes* (1869), give evidence of the suggestive evocation of mood and the haunting verbal music which were to become important elements in the symbolists' art:

> Les sanglots longs
> Des violons
>   De l'automne
> Blessent mon cœur
> D'une langueur
>   Monotone.

Perhaps his finest collection is *Romances sans paroles* (1874). In the same year in which it appeared he wrote 'Art poétique', a poem setting out his aesthetic ideas at this period. He emphasizes musicality ('De la musique avant toute chose') and points out another symbolist ideal with his call for a poetry of suggestion rather than statement, creating a reality free from definition or discursive comment ('. . . la chanson grise / Où l'Indécis au Précis se joint'). The religious poems collected in *Sagesse* (1881) mark his conversion to Catholicism and seek atonement for his disreputable life. Some are deeply moving (e.g. 'Ô mon Dieu, vous m'avez blessé d'amour') but many will seem maudlin or tasteless to the average modern reader.

Verlaine and Rimbaud were related on the scandalous level of a stormy homosexual relationship. A more lasting and significant link between them is to be found in their individual contributions to the revolutionizing of late nineteenth-century poetry. Arthur Rimbaud (1854–91) had a brief and meteoric literary career, had turned his back on poetry by the age of twenty ('l'art est une sottise'), and died after ten years in Abyssinia as trader, explorer and gun-runner. His poetry, like his life, was a continuing attack on most forms of convention. The earliest poems hit out indiscriminately at all manifestations of authority from God to the local librarian. A vision of limitless freedom is expressed in poems such as 'Sensation' or 'Ophélie' and reaches a climax in the lurching, fascinating imagery of 'Le Bateau ivre':

> J'ai vu des archipels sidéraux! et des îles
> Dont le cieux délirants sont ouverts au vogueur:
> – Est-ce en ces nuits sans fonds que tu dors et t'exiles,
> Million d'oiseaux d'or, ô future Vigueur? –

Shortly afterwards Rimbaud rejected rhyme and completed the poetic prose of his two major works: *Les Illuminations* (probably written 1872) and *Une Saison en enfer* (written 1873).

Like his symbolist contemporaries, Rimbaud strove in these works to capture the reality which is absent from the familiar world. Characteristically, he chose extreme means. Having asserted that the poet must be a seer, 'un voyant', he added: 'Il s'agit d'arriver à l'inconnu par le dérèglement de tous les sens.' If this disordered sensory ferment is the means of experiencing ultimate reality, its literary expression depends on verbal magic. This explains the quite marvellous use of language in *Les Illuminations* and *Une Saison en enfer*. It also accounts for the failure of his ambitions. Rimbaud walked alone to the utmost frontier of symbolism, found that language could not capture his vision, and renounced poetry.

The life of Stéphane Mallarmé (1842–98) was the opposite of Rimbaud's or Verlaine's in its respectable uneventfulness. A literary ascetic and a master-craftsman, he pursued the absent reality of the Idea through the intellect rather than the senses and wrote poems that are beautifully finished and highly enigmatic verbal structures. A few early poems such as 'Brise marine' are not difficult. Others, including such well-known sonnets as 'Le vierge, le vivace et le bel aujourd'hui' or 'Ses purs ongles très haut dédiant leur onyx', have given rise to many different interpretations. Perhaps his most outstanding achievement is to be found in the longer poems such as the unfinished *Hérodiade* (1864–7),

L'Après-midi d'un faune (1876) and *Un Coup de dés jamais n'abolira le hasard* (1897). He states the theory behind such poems as follows: 'Nommer un objet, c'est supprimer la jouissance du poème, qui est faite du bonheur de deviner peu à peu; le suggérer, voilà le rêve. C'est le parfait usage de ce mystère qui constitue le symbole.' This statement (which Verlaine might have signed), together with Mallarmé's distinction between language as 'signe' and as 'organisme dépositaire de la vie', may remind us that his poetry demands a response that goes beyond the limits of logical discourse and strictly rational meaning.

Among the many other poets associated with the symbolist movement three in particular deserve mention. The Comte de Lautréamont – pseudonym of Isidore Ducasse (1846–70) – wrote a set of strikingly original and hallucinatory prose-poems, *Les Chants de Maldoror* (1868). Their mixture of fantasy and fury, blasphemy and sadism, later caused the surrealists to rehabilitate Lautréamont as a precursor, a 'figure éblouissante de lumière noire' as Breton described him. Tristan Corbière (1845–75) is best remembered for his collection, *Les Amours jaunes* (1873), the work of a 'poète maudit' who wrote of himself: 'Son goût était dans le dégoût'. He wrote sardonic, staccato poems in which love and seafaring are the main themes. As for Jules Laforgue (1860–87), his ironical melancholy, his highly personal and unconventional poetic vocabulary, and his use of free verse – e.g. *Les Complaintes* (1885) – influenced a number of later poets including the young T. S. Eliot.

Symbolism also had an impact on the theatre, partly by way of reaction against commercial plays and *pièces à thèse*. The new drama found a sympathetic response in the 1890s from Paul Fort's relatively short-lived Théâtre de l'Art and Lugné-Poë's Théâtre de l'Oeuvre. The two playwrights of lasting interest associated with the movement are Villiers de l'Isle-Adam (1838–89) and Maurice Maeterlinck (1862–1949). The former's *Axël* (1890) combines symbolist qualities with the trappings of decadent Romanticism. The latter's *Pelléas et Mélisande* (1892) has the strengths and weaknesses of symbolist aesthetics when practised in the theatre.

Public Themes and Private Concerns

Looking back on a given historical period one is struck by the number of writers whose published work fails to fit any of the major categories suggested by historians of literature. This is true of many relatively minor literary figures active during the closing decades of the nineteenth century and the early years of the twentieth. Nevertheless, such novelists as Vallès, Bourget and Renard, while neither naturalists nor symbolists, share an intense dissatisfaction with the public standards of their age.

It has been said of Jules Vallès (1832–85) that 'la bohème et l'anarchie composaient son univers'. He led an impoverished life as journalist and political agitator and his fiercely uncompromising left-wing attitude is reflected in all that he did and wrote – from participation in the Republican 'manifestations' at Nantes in 1848 (at the age of fifteen) to his fictional trilogy, *Jacques Vingtras* (1879–86). In some ways he was a kind of prose Rimbaud, though moved to violent and revolutionary positions by social rather than metaphysical anger. The three 'Jacques Vingtras' novels, *L'Enfant* (1879), *Le Bachelier* (1881) and *L'Insurgé* (1886), express savage indignation at the society of his day and a fierce pity for the socially oppressed.

Paul Bourget (1852–1935) was a very different kind of writer who, towards the end of his life, sympathized with the highly conservative Catholicism of the Action Française. The dominant influence of Taine is clear in his two series of *Essais de psychologie contemporaine* (1883 and 1886), but his subsequent writings, particularly his best-known novels, *Le Disciple* (1889) and *L'Étape* (1902), reject the conclusions of progressive positivism. A certain kind of 'freethinking' ethic, related to materialistic and atheistic assumptions, causes misery and tragedy in both *Le Disciple* and *L'Étape*. It was Bourget's ambitious aim to establish an intellectual position which would reveal 'l'identité entre la loi de l'Église et la loi de la réalité, entre l'enseignement de l'éxpérience et celui de la Révélation'.

We return, with Jules Renard (1864–1910), to social rather than philosophical dissatisfaction, particularly in the one novel by which he is still remembered, *Poil de carotte* (1894). This story of an unhappy boyhood becomes the vehicle for an attack on the adult society of his day. Nevertheless, Renard lacked the energetic anger of a Vallès and his ambiguous position – part critical and part escapist – is illustrated by the *Histoires naturelles* (1896) – portraits of birds and animals to which he brought outstanding gifts of observation, fantasy and humour.

There is an element of Romantic *évasion* in the exotic novels of Pierre Loti – pseudonym of Julien Viaud (1850–1923) – whose career as a sailor took him to many parts of the world. Travel and writing became forms of temporary distraction from the ineluctable fact of death. The two activities resulted in novels which convey a richly poetic picture of faraway settings for unhappy love-affairs, e.g. *Aziyadé* (1879), *Le Mariage de Loti* (1880), *Rarahu* (1880), *Madame Chrysanthème* (1887), *Ramuntcho* (1897) and *Les Désenchantées* (1906). These romantic stories enjoy little favour nowadays, though Loti's novel of Breton fishing life, *Pêcheur d'Islande* (1886), remains a minor classic. Escape of a somewhat different kind into the world of childhood make-believe and adolescent love is found in another, later minor classic. This is *Le Grand Meaulnes* (1913) by Alain-Fournier, pseudonym of Henri-Alban Fournier (1886–1914). Fournier's aim, and eventual achievement, in the novel are put succinctly in a letter of 1906: 'Mon credo en art et en littérature: l'enfance. Arriver à la rendre sans aucune puérilité, avec sa profondeur qui touche les mystères.'

Two poets who developed along very different paths are the Belgian Verhaeren and the Béarnais Jammes. Émile Verhaeren (1855–1916) has often been compared with Walt Whitman both on account of his handling of free verse and his vision of democratic fraternity. He wrote some fine love poetry towards the end of his life but is usually associated with more public themes, inspired by socialist ideals and the problems and achievements of industrial progress, to be found in such collections as *Les Villes tentaculaires* (1895), *Les Forces tumultueuses* (1902) and *La Multiple Splendeur* (1906). He was a poet who could justifiably claim: 'Mon cœur, je l'ai rempli du beau tumulte humain.' Francis Jammes (1868–1938), on the contrary, is above all a poet of private simplicities filtered through a tender, melancholy, humorous and original sensibility. He writes of humble people and country life in *De l'angélus de l'aube à l'angélus du soir* (1898). A rediscovered Christian faith adds a further dimension to *Les Géorgiques chrétiennes* (1911) which seek to convey 'la beauté que Dieu donne à la vie ordinaire'.

In the history of the French theatre the closing years of the nineteenth century were a relatively impoverished period. One may mention the well-made, essentially superficial, plays of Victorien Sardou (1831–1908), the sometimes pretentious psychological dramas of Georges de Porto-Riche (1849–1930), the mechanical, farcical comedies of Georges Courteline (1858–1929) and Georges Feydeau (1862–1921), and the neo-Romantic theatre of Edmond Rostand (1868–1918) including *Cyrano de Bergerac* (1898) and *L'Aiglon* (1900).

Politics and Polemics

In 1894 Captain Alfred Dreyfus was arrested, tried and convicted on a charge of passing French military secrets to the Germans. The famous 'Affair' which followed lasted until 1906. In the years leading up to the quashing of the 1894 verdict Dreyfus, who was Jewish, became a symbol around which the contending forces of Left and Right waged a fierce ideological battle. The anti-military, anti-clerical Left – the Dreyfusards – pressed for revision. Zola, Proust, Renard, Péguy and Anatole France, among many others, were identified in varying degrees with Dreyfusism. The conservative, Catholic Right defended authority and the honour of the army, claiming that the nation was in danger of being undermined by atheists, Jews and freemasons. Among prominent anti-Dreyfusards were Barrès, Déroulède, Maurras and the critic Jules Lemaître. The turn of the century thus became a period of intense social and political conflict and its leading literary figures were France, Péguy, Barrès and Bloy.

It has never been seriously questioned that Anatole France, pseudonym of Anatole-François Thibault (1844–1924), was a master of clear and stylish French prose. Nevertheless he has often been dismissed – perhaps too easily – as a shallow, smiling sceptic of very limited moral and intellectual qualities. There is some justification for this judgement in his early work, but a notable change occurred after 1895 under the impact of the Dreyfus case. Apart from L'Affaire Crainquebille (1902), a novel about wrongful imprisonment, the four novels forming L'Histoire contemporaine (1896–1901) pillory the army, the Church, royalist politics and the anti-Semitism of the day. However, France's humane and rational socialism itself became qualified, in the three major novels of his maturity, by increasing pessimism about man. L'Île des pingouins (1908) despairs of social progress; Les Dieux ont soif (1912) finds an appalling human capacity for fanatical cruelty exemplified by the Jacobins during the French Revolution; La Révolte des anges (1914) bitterly satirizes Christianity.

Charles Péguy (1873–1914) was also prominent in the Dreyfusard cause and lived through the intellectual confrontations of the age with exemplary honesty. It was in fact this honesty, not lack of integrity, which compelled him to step across party divisions and espouse apparently opposite causes: internationalism and patriotism, anti-clericalism and devout Catholicism, republicanism and political conservatism. This pluralism of outlook marks the Cahiers de la quinzaine (1900–14) in which he published work by Anatole France, Romain Rolland and others, as well as his own major journalism and poetry. In *Notre Jeunesse* (1910) he defended the Dreyfusism of his earlier years while attacking those Dreyfusards who reduced this *mystique* to a *politique*, i.e. to the vulgar level of political manœuvring. Before his death in battle in 1914 he gave passionate mystical expression to his patriotism and deep religious sense in poems of epic length such as *Ève* (1914), and in three prose poems: *Le Mystère de la charité de Jeanne d'Arc* (1910), *Le Porche du mystère de la deuxième vertu* (1911) and *Le Mystère des saints innocents* (1912).

The most influential and gifted writer in the anti-Dreyfusard camp was Maurice Barrès (1862–1923). His journalism and novels confront socialist collectivism with a passionate defence of individual independence (in his trilogy, *Le Culte du moi*, 1888–91) and later of traditionalist and nationalist values (in a second trilogy, *Le Roman de l'énergie nationale*, 1897–1902). Though not possessing Péguy's profound religious sense, Barrès saw Catholicism as a necessary element both of traditionalism and nationalism. Also, as a Lorrainer, he preached a war of revenge for the lost provinces of Alsace and Lorraine. The articles written during World War I were in the same spirit. Barrès was instrumental in providing his generation with a partly rational, partly mystical, basis for right-wing views. The genuinely original literary gifts which he brought to this task are seen at their best in one of his later and finest novels, *La Colline inspirée*.

Like Péguy and Barrès, Léon Bloy (1846–1917) was a man of passionate conviction. Though much less directly involved in political polemics, his unorthodox Catholicism proved fiercely intransigent in social and moral matters. He stigmatized contemporary society as 'athée, renégate, apostate, sacrilège, parricide, infanticide'. When a fire at the Bazar de la Charité in 1897 resulted in 125 members of high society being burned alive, he only regretted that the number of victims had not been greater. Such violent hatred can be explained, though not excused, by his horror of contemporary materialism, his feeling for the despair of the socially oppressed, his mystical cult of poverty as necessary to salvation. These themes dominate his chaotic and visionary novels, *Le Désespéré* (1886) and *La Femme pauvre* (1897). In this last novel Clotilde Maréchal formulates Bloy's own conviction when she exclaims: 'Il n'y a qu'une tristesse, c'est de N'ÊTRE PAS DES SAINTS'. His conception of sanctity, however, was the reverse of the *bien-pensant*'s cosy vision.

Four New Masters

Proust, Gide, Valéry and Claudel, all born within four years of one another, came to maturity in the 1890s and dominated the first three decades of this century. With the possible exception of Gide, they are all major writers of European importance.

The early life of Marcel Proust (1871–1922) gave little indication that he was destined to become the greatest French novelist of the twentieth century. During the 1890s he appeared to be a rather affected frequenter of various fashionable Parisian *salons*, an aesthete and dilettante who suffered from ill-health and wrote intelligent but essentially ephemeral essays on art, literature and high society. These articles were eventually collected in *Les Plaisirs et les jours* (1896), *Pastiches et mélanges* (1919) and the posthumously published *Chroniques* (1927). He also underwent a period of intense enthusiasm for Ruskin's 'religion of beauty'. His translations of Ruskin, done with considerable difficulty, are *La Bible d'Amiens* (1904) and *Sésame et les lys* (1906). We now know that during this early period Proust was also observing, with a sharp and often satiric eye, the very social circles with which he himself was most closely identified. They were to provide much of the material for his study of the transformation of French society between the 1880s and the end of World War I – a study which is an important element in his vast novel. With his mother's death in 1905, and his own increasing ill-health, he retired to the famous cork-lined room in the Boulevard Haussmann and wrote the fifteen volumes of *A la recherche du temps perdu*.

The relatively late discovery of two collections of manuscripts – a novel, *Jean Santeuil* (1952) and some critical essays and imaginative prose, *Contre Sainte-Beuve suivi de Nouveaux mélanges* (1954) – makes it clear that Proust had actually begun work on his masterpiece some time in the 1890s. His deep emotional relationship with his mother probably proved an inhibiting factor, and he experienced other problems, but after 1905 he worked with increasing success, finished a first version in 1912 and published the opening section (*Du Côté de chez Swann*) at his own expense in 1913. Further publication was interrupted by the war but he revised his text until it grew from something like 1,200 pages to approximately 4,000. He continued to work on it right up to his death.

Proust's purpose in *A la recherche du temps perdu* (1913–27) can be summed up by Ruskin's phrase in *Stones of Venice*: '. . . what we want art to do for us is to stay what is fleeting, and to enlighten what is incomprehensible, to incorporate the things that have no measure, and immortalize the things that have no duration.' The Proustian world is one of flux and mystery, reflecting in artistic terms the contemporary rejection of rationalism and scientism by Bergson. The novel's narrator gradually learns to arrest time through the phenomenon of involuntary memory and, eventually, through his art. As he elucidates the previously hidden associations of some sense impression (eating a *madeleine* dipped in tea, gazing at a hawthorn hedge, etc.) he solves a mystery, relives a piece of the past, establishes the enduring nature of the self, and later discovers the creative principle of his novel. The self is also explored in relation to the phenomenon of love (both heterosexual and homosexual) which Proust analyses as a supreme form of self-deception rendered more bitter by inevitable jealousy and the failure to make genuine contact with another human being. As these explorations and discoveries progress through the novel they are linked with many counterpointed themes: art and life, society and the self, impressionism and symbolism, painting and music. Satire and humour, poetry and analytical intelligence, are used to create a remarkable range of fictional characters. Above all, Proust displays his greatness as a novelist through his creation of an autonomous, imaginative world to which we readily surrender yet which also illuminates profoundly our everyday experience. This illumination depends on language and style, as well as on vision. The importance which Proust gives to style, and his conception of it as an integral part of truth in art, are both evident when he writes in the final volume of his novel: '. . . la vérité ne commencera qu'au moment où l'écrivain prendra deux objets différents, posera leur rapport . . . et les enfermera dans les anneaux nécessaires d'un beau style'.

Proust and Gide (in common with Valéry) possessed outstanding gifts of intellectual analysis and artistic sensibility. Inevitably, these gifts took different forms. Whereas Proust died in his early fifties yet suggests a prematurely old man recapturing and reinterpreting the past, Gide died in his eighties yet possesses the attitudes and interests of a permanently young man probing and anticipating the future. Ironically, however, it was the reputation of the apparently forward-looking Gide which declined shortly after his death. Fashionable radicalism is notoriously transient and public attitudes, as well as public events, have overtaken Gide. His arguments against puritanism and colonialism, and in favour of sexual and social freedom, are now largely taken for granted. The 'liberator of youth' appears irrelevant to those who have long since lost their chains.

André Gide (1869-1951) had a strict Protestant upbringing and his frequently stated desire to 'disturb' his readers springs from a need to free himself from the inhibitions and prohibitions of a late nineteenth-century adolescence. His earliest writings show affinities with the symbolists, and his work of 'moral subversion' is first explicit in *Les Nourritures terrestres* (1897). Visits to North Africa in the preceding years had contributed much to his liberation from asceticism, and in the lyrical pages of *Les Nourritures* he exhorts an imaginary young man, Nathanaël, to rid himself of the Christian sense of sin and cultivate the life of the senses. He also teaches intensity of living ('Nathanaël, je t'enseignerai la ferveur'), horror of settled habits ('Ne *demeure* jamais, Nathanaël') and a comprehensive individualism ('Assumer le plus possible d'humanité'). Some assertions made by Gide in the book (e.g. 'Les idées nettes sont les plus dangereuses' or 'Il faut agir sans juger si l'action est bonne ou mauvaise') appear naïve or irresponsible viewed from the post-Auschwitz, post-Hiroshima world.

The puritan conscience is not easily eradicated, however, and Gide did not liberate himself completely. Much of his best writing, in fact, reflects a tension between the pagan and the puritan, between the teachings of Nietzsche and of the Bible. Two of his best *récits*, *L'Immoraliste* (1902) and *La Porte étroite* (1909), deal respectively with the themes of self-indulgence and self-denial. The conflict between them, causing a mixture of hypocrisy and self-deception, is movingly and delicately explored in *La Symphonie pastorale* (1919). The play, *Le Roi Candaule* (1901), swings right away from the viewpoint of *Les Nourritures* whereas the satirical and sometimes farcical tales which Gide termed *soties* – *Paludes* (1896), *Les Caves du Vatican* (1914), etc. – praise moral nonconformity. The latter work also contains the most notorious example of the famous Gidean *acte gratuit* – a murder committed for reasons of emotional and intellectual curiosity.

The term *roman* is applied to only one of the fictional works: *Les Faux-Monnayeurs* (1926). This is a clever, indeed over-clever, novel in which Gide breaks away from traditional French forms by means of a deliberately loose, untidy structure and characters which he refuses to 'explain' comprehensively to his readers. Distinctions between art and life are blurred by the fact that one of the characters, Édouard, is himself writing a novel entitled *Les Faux-Monnayeurs* and is keeping a literary diary which has the same title as that which Gide himself actually published: *Journal des faux-monnayeurs* (1926). Despite a determination to convey the 'openness' and disorder of actual experience, Gide's literary pyrotechnics finally produces an impression of extreme artificiality.

Gide's social conscience was first seriously stirred by his experience as a juror at a Criminal Assize Court in Normandy (*Souvenirs de la cour d'assises*, 1914). His conscience was further sharpened by ten months spent in Central Africa and his *Voyage au Congo* (1928) is sharply critical of European colonialism. The book has since been attacked for criticizing the *results* of colonialism rather than the *system* as such, and most of the judgements made are more moral than political, e.g. 'Moins le blanc est intelligent, plus le noir lui paraît bête'. The disillusion following Gide's short-lived admiration for communism is explained in *Retour de l'U.R.S.S.* (1936) and *Retouches à mon Retour de l'U.R.S.S.* (1937). Fundamentally, Gide was intensely self-absorbed and, in addition to an indirect apologia for his own homosexuality in *Corydon* (1923), he wrote a fascinating autobiography, *Si le grain ne meurt* (1926), and noted his reflexions on his reading and on his contemporaries in the *Journal* extending from 1889 to 1949.

Among the major European poets of this century – Rilke, Yeats, T. S. Eliot, etc. – Paul Valéry (1871–1945) is not the least important figure. It was due to the encouragement of Gide and Pierre Louÿs that he moved to Paris from his native Midi in the early 1890s. This was a crucial moment in his life since it brought him into direct contact with Mallarmé. The latter was to exercise a potent influence on Valéry's work and his early poems, later collected in *Album des vers anciens* (1920), display the intricate verbal melody and severe intellectuality of symbolism:

> Été, roche d'air pur, et toi, ardente ruche,
> Ô mer! Éparpillée en mille mouches sur
> Les touffes d'une chair fraîche comme une cruche,
> Et jusque dans la bouche où bourdonne l'azur . . .

Lines such as these remind us that Valéry's Apollonian severity does not exclude Dionysian elements containing a rich sensuality.

Despite some early success, Valéry was dissatisfied both with his own poetry and with literature in general. In 1892 he underwent an intellectual crisis in Genoa, the so-called 'nuit de Gênes', and for the next twenty years wrote almost no poetry. This 'silence' has been explained in several ways, but it seems most likely that Valéry decided to explore and cultivate the resources of his own mind rather than continue writing poetry. From an early date he had been interested in a wide range of subjects including psychology, mathematics and architecture; he even attempted to unify all human knowledge by means of mathematics. He possessed formidable intellectual tastes ('Les choses du monde ne m'intéressent que sous le rapport de l'intellect') and, though he produced no philosophical system, the workings of his mind can be followed in detail in the famous *Cahiers* (twenty-nine large volumes) begun in 1894. Two prose works, *Introduction à la méthode de Léonard de Vinci* (1895) and *La Soirée avec Monsieur Teste* (1896), show how much he was fascinated by intellectual universality. Other prose writings include two fine dialogues on Socratic lines, *Eupalinos ou l'architecte* (1921) and *L'Âme et la danse* (1921), while ten years later he published his acute *Regards sur le monde actuel*. In 1919 he had written a brief but penetrating essay on the contemporary world, 'La Crise de l'esprit', with its famous opening sentence: 'Nous autres, civilisations, nous savons maintenant que nous sommes mortelles.'

In 1912, under pressure from Gide among others, Valéry began to revise his early poems for collective publication (the eventual *Album des vers anciens*). He also started work on a long poem published in 1917 as *La Jeune Parque* and dedicated to Gide. This has been called the most difficult poem in the French language. According to its author, it is an attempt to achieve in words something akin to modulation in music. Verbal modulations catch the changes of a human consciousness during the course of a night, partly through the figure of a young woman ('La Jeune Parque') faced with problems of love and death. The kind of poetry that results, and the impossibility of reducing it to rational, discursive terms, are both suggested by Valéry's statement: '. . . plus un poème est conforme à la Poésie, moins il peut se penser en prose sans périr.'

Apart from some verse passages in *Mon Faust* (1941), Valéry's last significant poetry is contained in *Charmes* (1922). The title comes from the Latin *carmina*, songs or incantations, and the collection consists of twenty-one poems including such famous pieces as 'Fragments du Narcisse', 'Ébauche d'un serpent' and 'Le Cimetière marin'. Valéry considered that eight lines from the first of these three poems represented his most successful attempt to reach his own ideal of 'la poésie pure':

> Ô douceur de survivre à la force du jour,
> Quand elle se retire enfin rose d'amour,
> Encore un peu brûlante, et lasse, mais comblée,
> Et de tant de trésors tendrement accablée
> Par de tels souvenirs qu'ils empourprent sa mort,
> Et qu'ils la font heureuse agenouiller dans l'or,
> Puis s'étendre, se fondre, et perdre sa vendange,
> Et s'éteindre en un songe en qui le soir se change.

Generally, the poems of *Charmes* have a classical regularity justified by Valéry's claim that 'les exigences d'une stricte prosodie sont l'artifice qui confère au langage naturel les qualités d'une matière résistante'. They are poems written to endure by conferring formal perfection on a profound response to experience.

It is through his discovery of a completely satisfying spiritual and artistic inspiration within the limits of Roman Catholic orthodoxy that Paul Claudel (1868–1955) differs most significantly from his three distinguished contemporaries. The great certainties of the faith, as well as its central mysteries, pervade his best work both as poet and dramatist. According to his own account, Claudel was first made conscious of the *existence* of a supernatural world, and incidentally freed from nineteenth-century scientism, by reading Rimbaud's *Les Illuminations* and *Une Saison en enfer*. He found the *meaning* of this supernatural world in the Bible and Catholic teaching, particularly during the four years following a mystical experience in Notre-Dame-de-Paris while the 'Magnificat' was being sung on Christmas Day 1886. Later, his careful study of Thomist philosophy was to have a profound influence on his work. He also acknowledged different forms of indebtedness to Aeschylus, Dante, Shakespeare, Dostoevsky, etc.

Claudel was a diplomat by profession and his experience of the Far East prompted an outstanding prose-poem, *Connaissance de l'Est* (1900). This kind of writing, rather than the self-imposed formal severity of a Valéry, suited his genius best, and his poetry is almost all written in *versets*, irregular and cunningly used lines of which he wrote: 'Le verset est une ligne qui s'arrête, non parce qu'elle est arrivée à une frontière naturelle, et que l'espace lui manque, mais parce que son chiffre intérieur est accompli et que sa vertu est consommée.' The use to which he put the *verset* can be studied at its best in *Cinq Grandes Odes* (1910) and *Cantate à trois voix* (1914). In the following lines from the first of these collections Claudel's rich and buoyant lyricism issues in praise of God's immanence in the beauty and wonder of the physical and human worlds:

> Je vous salue, ô monde libéral à mes yeux!
> Je comprends par quoi vous êtes présent,
> C'est que l'Éternel est avec vous, et qu'où est la Créature,
>   le Créateur ne l'a point quittée.
> Je suis en vous et vous êtes à moi et votre possession est la
>   mienne,

Et maintenant en nous à la fin
Éclate le commencement,
Éclate le jour nouveau, éclate dans la possession de la source
   je ne sais quelle jeunesse angélique!

Though a gifted lyric poet, Claudel is admired above all as an epic
dramatist, combining the spoken exchanges of the theatre with high
rhetorical forms in the tradition of Corneille. In view of the 'dialectic of
salvation', the struggle between the flesh and the spirit which is central
to Christianity, it is not surprising that he should have found the theatre
a congenial medium. He writes in the interesting *Positions et propositions
I* (1928): 'La foi fait vivre tout homme moderne dans un milieu
essentiellement dramatique. . . . La vie est pour lui, non pas une série
incohérente de gestes vagues et inachevés, mais un drame précis qui
comporte un dénouement et un sens.' Of the dozen or so plays which
he wrote (sometimes in two versions), the best are probably *Partage de
midi* (1906), *L'Annonce faite à Marie* (1912) and *Le Soulier de satin* (1929
and 1944). These are not so much 'realistic' works as rhetorical meditations on religious themes. Although some of the plays fail to convince
us as psychology, *Partage de midi* is both a moving portrayal of adulterous love and an exploration of the means whereby sexual love may be
transmuted into love of God. Mesa's return to God, through Ysé,
causes him to exclaim in Act III:

Ah! je sais maintenant
Ce que c'est que l'amour! et je sais ce que vous avez
   enduré sur votre croix, dans ton Cœur,
Si vous avez aimé chacun de nous
Terriblement comme j'ai aimé cette femme, et le râle,
   et l'asphyxie, et l'étau . . .

This 'evangelization of the flesh' is also a central theme in *Le Soulier de
satin* – a lengthy, ambitious work which projects the drama of body and
spirit on to an enormous canvas that includes sixteenth-century Europe,
Africa and America. The beautifully written *L'Annonce faite à Marie*
has a medieval setting of miracles, mysteries and exemplary self-
immolation. The events of the play are held together by the doctrine of
substitution, the idea that all human beings live in a state of spiritual
interdependence which gives purpose and meaning to suffering and
evil.

The Growth of the Avant-Garde

The closing years of the nineteenth century are notable for change and innovation in many spheres of French life. With the founding of the trade-union movement, the Confédération Générale du Travail, in 1895, industrial society came of age. By the end of the century the bitter conflicts and unsavoury revelations of the Dreyfus Affair had dealt severe blows to the authority of both the army and the Church. At the same time, applied science was making rapid progress. In 1900, when the Eiffel Tower had already dominated the Parisian skyline for eleven years, the electric light bulb appeared at the International Exhibition and the Paris *métro* began its underground life. Significant co-operation between technology and art dates from the same year when Georges Méliès set up a film studio at Montreuil.

In the early 1870s Rimbaud had declared: 'Il faut être absolument moderne.' Even earlier, Lautréamont had given lessons in modernity to a restricted audience. Nevertheless, the growth of the artistic avant-garde is chiefly associated with the decade preceding World War I. In music, Satie and Roussel were active. In painting, the Salon d'Automne of 1905 revealed fauvism, Picasso completed 'Les Demoiselles d'Avignon' in 1907, and almost immediately afterwards he and Braque developed their particular forms of cubism. In literature, modernism was chiefly associated with poetry. New attitudes and new forms were cultivated by Jacob, by Cendrars and, above all, by Apollinaire. Literary innovation was made easier, however, by the earlier work of Alfred Jarry (1873–1907) whose play *Ubu Roi* (1896) remains a notable avant-garde landmark.

Ubu Roi, one of several 'Ubu' works, has the virtues and faults of a certain kind of avant-garde writing. It is a violent farce which caricatures human greed, cruelty and cowardice. The atmosphere suggests both the blind destructiveness and the freewheeling imagination of an ungovernable child. Ferocity and fantasy, crude language and lavatory jokes, combine to place it in a curious no-man's-land between precocious adolescence and retarded manhood. Jarry's posthumously published *Gestes et opinions du Docteur Faustroll* (1911) is his other claim to fame. This 'neo-scientific' prose fantasy outlines his doctrine of 'pataphysics' (a science going as far beyond metaphysics as metaphysics extends beyond physics) and was later much admired by the surrealists.

The work by Jarry was enthusiastically acclaimed by Guillaume Apollinaire (1880–1918) for its 'débauches de l'intelligence'. This response was in keeping with his own role as, in André Billy's phrase, 'prince de l'esprit moderne'. As prose-writer and art critic, as well as poet, Apollinaire sought to understand and reflect the scientific advances and intellectual innovations of the new century. His collection of stories, *Le Poète assassiné* (1916), explores the significance and status of poetry in the modern world. Essays such as *Les Peintres cubistes* and *L'Esprit nouveau et les poètes* explain and advocate modernism. Surrealist fantasy, recalling Jarry, animates his play *Les Mamelles de Tirésias* (1917).

Apollinaire's first collection of poems, *Alcools* (1913), apart from its experimental aspect, also contains traditionalist poetic forms with symbolist overtones and reveals him as a major love poet. His range varies from the lyric perfection of 'Le Pont Mirabeau' to the positive modernity of 'Zone' ('Bergère ô tour Eiffel le troupeau des ponts bêle ce matin'). Unexpected juxtapositions, simultaneity and discontinuity, a conversational tone and surrealist imagery, are all techniques of modernism carried over into *Calligrammes* (1918) which, as the title suggests, contains poems set out typographically in pictorial form. The final poem of the collection, 'La Jolie Rousse', is a moving poetic testament suggesting that Apollinaire wished to be a 'modern' without vilifying an earlier literary tradition:

> Soyez indulgents quand vous nous comparez
> A ceux qui furent la perfection de l'ordre
> Nous qui quêtons partout l'aventure
>
> Nous ne sommes pas vos ennemis
> Nous voulons vous donner de vastes et d'étranges domaines
> Où le mystère en fleurs s'offre à qui veut le cueillir

Apollinaire's innovations were later surpassed by those of the Dadaist and surrealist movements. Nevertheless, he invented the term 'surrealism' and Breton's *Manifeste du surréalisme* (1924) was dedicated to him. He is a genuine experimenter who deservedly became a classic.

Two other poets, Max Jacob (1876–1944) and Blaise Cendrars – pseudonym of Frédéric Sauser (1887–1961) – should be mentioned. Jacob was an early friend of Apollinaire and Picasso, sharing their avant-garde struggles. He opposed reason and tradition in art with irony and humour, parody and burlesque. He is best known for the prose poems of *Cornet à Dès* (1917). Conversion to a highly personal and unconventional faith prompted him to live in seclusion from 1921 onwards. His otherworldliness is summed up in the last two lines of a poem written some time before his death in the Drancy concentration camp:

Je suis mourant d'avoir compris
que notre terre n'est d'aucun prix.

Cendrars wrote a number of novels including *Moravagine* (1926) and *Les Confessions de Dan Yack* (2 vols: 1927, 1929). Many of his poems, like his novels, reflect his wide travels. The title poem of the collection *Prose du Transsibérien* (1913) is also a literary collage using techniques of juxtaposition, discontinuity and simultaneity which recall Apollinaire. These techniques create an impression of confused and animated city life in the following lines:

Il pleut des globes électriques
Montrouge Gare de l'Est Métro Nord-Sud bateaux-mouches
    monde
Tout est halo
Profondeur
Rue de Buci on crie *l'Intransigeant* et *Paris-Sports*
L'aérodrome du ciel est maintenant, embrasé, un tableau
    de Cimabué.

Literature and World War I

World War I broke out at a moment when intensive patriotism was already a notable theme among some of the most influential French writers. In an earlier section reference was made to Péguy's mystical love of France and Barrès's call for the return of Alsace and Lorraine. To these names should be added that of Ernest Psichari (1883–1914) whose novels, particularly *L'Appel des armes* (1913), seek a common order and tradition in the established values of the army and the Church. *L'Appel des armes* was dedicated to Péguy and owes a clear literary debt both to him and to Barrès. The fact that patriotic and military sentiments were widespread among young Frenchmen in the immediate pre-war years was confirmed and analysed in *Les Jeunes Gens d'aujour-d'hui* published by Henri Massis and Alfred de Tarde in 1913. It is not surprising that the effect of war itself was to sharpen such feelings. Patriotic verse and prose became the order of the day. On the other hand, such writing rarely achieves high literary quality. In particular, poetry and patriotism coexist at the expense of the former – at least in the modern world – and evidence of this can be found in such collections as Jammes's *Cinq Poèmes pour le temps de la guerre* (1916), Verhaeren's *Les Ailes rouges de la guerre* (1917), Rostand's *Le Vol de la Marseillaise* (1919) and Claudel's *Poèmes de guerre 1914–1916* (1922). The fact that Claudel attempted to read a fundamental spiritual meaning into the conflict between France and Germany did not save him from either bombast or bathos.

Poetry of protest against the war, such as that written in England by Wilfred Owen or Siegfried Sassoon, scarcely existed in France. There is no major French war poet and the best poetry written on the battlefield turns out, surprisingly perhaps, to be that of Apollinaire. The poems he wrote at the front are mainly collected in *Calligrammes* (1918) and the posthumously published *Ombre de mon amour* which appeared in 1948. The experience of war heightened Apollinaire's sense of mortality, intensified his love affairs, and provided a new range of aesthetic experiences. The opening stanza of a poem from this period brings together his pathos and his aestheticism:

> Si je mourrais là-bas sur le front de l'armée,
> Tu pleurerais un jour, ô Lou, ma bien-aimée,
> Et puis mon souvenir s'éteindrait comme meurt
> Un obus éclatant sur le front de l'armée,
> Un bel obus semblable aux mimosas en fleur.

The last three lines of the same poem show that Apollinaire, the conscious manipulator of words and typography, could also express with simplicity and economy the fearful destiny of his generation:

> ᴚa nuit descend,
> On y present
> ᴄn long, un long destin de sang.

It is clear that something at once as unique and appalling as trench warfare provided novelists with a new subject for realistic description as well as arousing moral horror and revulsion. These two responses are present in what was undoubtedly the major French novel of warfare at this period – *Le Feu* (1916) by Henri Barbusse (1873–1935). It is a violent book on a violent subject, containing a Zola-like sense of physical detail together with anger at 'des choses épouvantables faites par 30 millions d'hommes qui ne le veulent pas'. Later, Barbusse developed much further the mixture of pacifism and revolutionary Marxism already implicit in this novel. His post-war writings, however, stayed at the level of radical journalism and ended ingloriously with adulatory biographies of Lenin and Stalin. Another war novel which made a considerable impact on publication is *Les Croix de bois* (1919) by Roland Dorgelès – the pseudonym of Roland Lecavelé (b. 1886). Dorgelès's descriptive powers recall those of Barbusse though they are accompanied by a certain sentimentality foreign to *Le Feu*. Authentic non-heroism also has its place, summed up by the statement: 'J'trouve que c'est une victoire, parce que j'en suis sorti vivant.' Perhaps the most humane protest – one which saw the war as a terrible failure on the part of Western civilization – is to be found in *Vie des martyrs* (1917) and the ironically entitled *Civilisation* (1918) by Georges Duhamel (1884–1966). Such novels illustrate 'l'illusion perdue d'une culture européenne' of which Valéry wrote. Among the many other novelists who published during the war, mention should be made of Maurice Genevoix (b. 1890). Five of his novels were collected and reprinted in 1950 under the title *Ceux de 14*.

Inevitably, a number of writers preferred to digest their experiences more slowly and published retrospective novels aiming at something more intellectually ambitious than direct reportage or instant protest. Three such writers are Henry de Montherlant (b. 1896), Jules Romains (the pseudonym of Louis Farigoule, b. 1855) and Roger Martin du Gard (1881–1958). Montherlant's *Le Songe* (1922) is a distinctive, often lyrical, meditation on the themes of love, war and death as well as an exploration of the relationship between thought and action. Character-istically, his reaction to the experience of war combines the contrasting emotions of exultation and horror. War provides the main descriptive set-pieces of *Le Songe*, yet something of its wider scope is suggested by the question on which it ends: 'Le désir est incomplet. L'amitié manque de viscères. L'amour tel qu'on l'entend d'ordinaire est une infériorité. Qui me tirera une tendresse qui vient du fond de mes entrailles et que j'approuve pourtant de toute ma raison?' In the case of Jules Romains, the novels *Prélude à Verdun* (1937) and *Verdun* (1938) form part of an enormous *roman-fleuve* – *Les Hommes de bonne volonté* (1932–46) – in which the war is related to wider aspects of French society and history between 1908 and 1933. Roger Martin du Gard was also the author of a *roman-fleuve* – *Les Thibault* (1922–40). The section of this work entitled *L'Été 1914* (1936) dramatically evokes Europe on the brink of war. For Martin du Gard the experience of 1914–18 both made him an ardent pacifist and destroyed the faith in progressive rationalism which had characterized his first major novel, *Jean Barois* (1913).

Surrealism

The fact that Apollinaire invented the adjective *surréaliste* serves as a reminder that this movement of conscious irrationality had its roots in the pre-war avant-garde. The further fact that the most glorious days of surrealism spanned the decade following World War I suggests a connection between this attack on logic and reason and the crisis of confidence in the established order brought about by the events of 1914–18. In fact, as early as 1916, a group of young writers and artists, mostly pacifists and revolutionaries by instinct, had launched the so-called Dadaist movement from Zürich in neutral Switzerland. The *Manifeste Dada 1918* by Tristan Tzara (1896–1963) proclaimed the liberation of literature and art from all logic, scorned bourgeois notions of order and meaning, and characterized the contemporary world as one of disaster and decomposition. These now familiar ideas were warmly welcomed by André Breton (1896–1966), the future leader of French surrealism, and his associates including Philippe Soupault (b. 1897) and Louis Aragon (b. 1897). After the war Breton and Tzara joined forces in Paris but disagreements developed between them. In 1924 the first issue of the periodical *La Révolution surréaliste* (1924–9) marked both the end of Dadaism and the foundation of surrealism as a distinctive movement.

Breton's first *Manifeste du surréalisme* (1924) is a statement, appropriately iconoclastic and incoherent, of the movement's aims. These were neo-Dadaist in so far as they sought to ridicule the cultural certainties of a society which had ended in the cataclysm of 1914–18. The inherent violence and absurdity of this rational, ordered society were to be countered by violence and absurdity in art. More particularly, Breton had been influenced by Freud's ideas and he elaborated a theory of the truth and freedom to be obtained by automatic writing (liberated from all moral and aesthetic constraints) and the cultivation of dreams. Later, in *Le Surréalisme et la peinture* (1928), Breton extended his theories to the visual arts and with his second manifesto a year later identified the surrealist adventure with the aims of Marxism. This manifesto, published in the only issue of *La Révolution surréaliste* to appear in 1929, marks the beginning of Breton's ultimately unsuccessful attempt to reconcile the authoritarian programme of the French Communist Party with the mysticism and imaginative freedom inherent in surrealist theory and practice. This mysticism is indicated – it could hardly be precisely defined – in a famous passage in the manifesto:

> Tout porte à croire qu'il existe un certain point de l'esprit d'où la
> vie et la mort, le réel et l'imaginaire, le passé et le futur, le communi-
> cable et l'incommunicable, le haut et le bas, cessent d'être perçus
> contradictoirement. Or c'est en vain qu'on chercherait à l'activité
> surréaliste un autre mobile que l'espoir de détermination de ce point.

In fact, Breton's later theoretical works stick to this position and move
away from that 'conformisme stalinien' with which he taxed the
Communist Party in 1935. Similarly, when Aragon broke with
surrealism to become a totally committed Communist, Benjamin
Peret – co-editor with Pierre Naville of *La Révolution surréaliste* –
described the move as one from the status of *poète* to that of *agent de
publicité*.

As might be guessed, the temperaments of writers attracted by
surrealism tended to break them up into warring factions or encouraged
them to pursue highly individual paths. Individuals differed a good deal
in their ideas and in the manner in which these ideas were expressed.
In many ways, the movement remains more impressive as a collective
phenomenon than as a series of separate, individual achievements.
Indeed, the movement has tended to denounce the cult of personal
authorship. It may also be said that the chief manifestations of surrealism
have been in poetry, painting and the cinema. Nevertheless, a tradition
of novel-writing also exists. Raymond Roussel (1877–1933) laid the
foundations of the surrealist novel (and drama) with such early works
as *Impressions d'Afrique* (1910), *Locus solus* (1914) and *L'Étoile au front*
(1925). The tradition was continued by Aragon's *Le Paysan de Paris*
(1926) and Breton's *Nadja* (1928), while more recent surrealist fiction
includes *Au Château d'Argol* (1939), *Un Beau ténébreux* (1945), *Le Rivage
des Syrtes* (1951) by Julien Gracq (b. 1910) and *Le Lis de mer* (1956)
and *La Motocyclette* (1963) by André Pieyre de Mandiargues (b.
1909).

As regards poetry, one of the most constant features has been the
bringing together of unexpected and apparently unconnected images.
In *L'Amour la poésie* (1929) Paul Éluard (1895–1952), the major poet of
the movement, wrote: 'Les ressemblances ne sont pas en rapport. Elles
se heurtent.' Something of his own achievement can be seen in a short
love poem from an earlier collection, *Capitale de la douleur* (1926):

> Ta chevelure d'oranges dans le vide du monde,
> Dans le vide des vitres lourdes de silence
> Et d'ombre où mes mains cherchent tous tes reflets.

La forme de ton cœur est chimérique
Et ton amour ressemble à mon désir perdu.
Ô soupirs d'ambre, rêves, regards.

Mais tu n'as pas toujours été avec moi. Ma mémoire
Est encore obscurcie de t'avoir vue venir
Et partir. Le temps se sert de mots comme l'amour.

Such poetry does not simply reflect a mood; it creates an independent, self-authenticating aesthetic structure. It also creates a 'surreality' which is offered as the royal road to a new knowledge spanning (as in much primitive art) the traditional gap between subjective and objective reality.

Surrealism has always had both its serious and its leg-pulling aspects. Writers as diverse as Breton and Éluard, Roussel and Soupault, René Crevel (1900–35) and Robert Desnos (1900–45) have produced pessimism and *le merveilleux*, blasphemy and *humour noir*, praise of insanity and a *beauté convulsive*. Today, the success of surrealism may be measured by the extent to which it has become an integral part of our contemporary sensibility. Its failure lies in the fact that it has proved a symptom rather than a cure, reflecting and reinforcing the social and moral confusion against which it originally reacted.

Inter-War Theatre

The period 1918–39 was one of original producers and enterprising dramatists. The former category includes Jacques Copeau, Jacques Hébertot and the anti-naturalist 'Cartel des quatre': Georges Pitöeff, Charles Dullin, Louis Jouvet and Gaston Baty. The dramatists who have lasted best are Jean Giraudoux (1882–1944), Jean Cocteau (1889–1963) and Jean Anouilh (b. 1910). Producers and playwrights combined to encourage poetic drama, fantasy and mime, to simplify or stylize stage scenery, to regard the 'well-made' play with suspicion, to create what Baty called 'une zone de mystère'.

It is no exaggeration to say, however, that the French stage was dominated, at least during the 1930s, by Giraudoux and Jouvet – a collaboration that began with the production of *Siegfried* (1928) and extended to *La Folle de Chaillot* (1945). It also included *Amphitryon 38* (1929), *Intermezzo* (1933), *La Guerre de Troie n'aura pas lieu* (1935), *Électre* (1937) and *Ondine* (1939). Giraudoux's qualities are indicated by the adjectives most commonly used by French critics to describe his talent: 'paradoxal', 'raffiné', 'précieux'. His is above all a theatre of verbal magic, a literary theatre clothed in original, poetic language. Beneath a brilliant surface created by irony and wit, verbal subtlety and delicate, luminous speech, there exist a preoccupation with fundamental human qualities and what is often a tragic vision. Such concerns are fed by the subject-matter which Giraudoux mostly derived from mythological, classical or biblical sources. The conflict between human and supernatural values is the central theme of *Amphitryon 38*, while questions of war and peace, of sacred and profane love, of freedom and compromise, pervade *La Guerre de Troie*, *Judith* (1931) and *Électre* respectively. Something of Giraudoux's pride in human limitation is seen in the opening lines of Alcmène's statement to Jupiter in *Amphitryon 38*:

> Je ne crains pas la mort. C'est l'enjeu de la vie. Puisque ton Jupiter, à tort ou à raison, a créé la mort sur la terre, je me solidarise avec mon astre. Je sens trop mes fibres continuer celles des autres hommes, des animaux, même des plantes, pour ne pas mourir tant qu'il n'y aura pas un légume immortel. Devenir immortel, c'est trahir, pour un humain . . .

This passage, though incomplete, also reminds us that Giraudoux created a theatre of eloquent monologues. The lengthy *tirade* has a major role in his work as in the verbal encounters between Hector and Ulysse that are a memorable feature of *La Guerre de Troie*. In many of the plays these long speeches exchanged between characters are less a debate than what has been called 'an aesthetic equilibrium between contrary definitions'. Ultimately, the characters use language to account for the world in terms that reach the mind through the imagination.

Jean Cocteau possessed an astonishingly rich diversity of talents. His achievements include those of poet, playwright, actor, film director, choreographer, book illustrator and artist in glass and ceramics. He fulfilled a variety of innovating roles on the inter-war scene and must be regarded as an important and gifted *animateur* who finally lacked that intense concentration of talent which characterizes most of the greatest artists. As a man of the theatre, he began with a number of ballets, particularly *Parade* (1917) of which he wrote the scenario with settings by Picasso, music by Satie and choreography by Massine. For *Les Mariés de la Tour Eiffel* (1921) Cocteau himself provided the choreography with music by 'les Six' (i.e. Auric, Durey, Honegger,

Milhaud, Poulenc and Taillefer). In *La Machine infernale* (1934) – a witty reworking of the Oedipus legend – and in other plays such as *Les Chevaliers de la Table Ronde* (1937) and *Les Parents terribles* (1938), as well as in a series of experimental films from *Le Sang d'un poète* (1932) to *Orphée* (1949), Cocteau displays imagination, sophistication and technical ingenuity as he explores the role of the poet, the tragic nature of love, the traps set by life for youth, purity and idealism.

It was from Giraudoux rather than Cocteau that Anouilh learnt 'qu'on pouvait avoir au théâtre une langue poétique et artificielle qui demeure plus vraie que la conversation sténographique.' Inventiveness and stylization mark his plays and, although a less gifted poet than either of his seniors, Anouilh outstrips them in terms of a quite brilliant mastery of stage technique. In splendidly constructed plays he uses comedy and tragedy, wit and cynicism, to convey his disenchanted vision – and particularly the imperious, yet finally fruitless, rebellion of the young on behalf of purity and against mediocrity, ugliness and compromise. Characteristic works among the earlier plays are such 'pièces roses' or 'pièces brillantes' as *Le Bal des Voleurs* (1932), *Le Rendez-vous de Senlis* (1937), *La Répétition* (1950) and such 'pièces noires' as *La Sauvage* (1934) and *Antigone* (1944). In some other plays, particularly *Le Voyageur sans bagage* (1937), *Léocadia* (1939) and *L'Invitation au château* (1947), the bitterness, whether expressed as comedy or tragedy, gives way to what appears as a scarcely logical happy ending – a reflection of Anouilh's claim that art itself can impose satisfactory form on a fatally flawed existence. Plays written after 1950 and deserving mention are *L'Alouette* (1952), a lyrical treatment of the Joan of Arc theme, *Pauvre Bitos* (1956), an attack on ideological murder by tyrants of both Left and Right, and *Becket, ou l'Honneur de Dieu* (1959), a superficial work when compared with Eliot's *Murder in the Cathedral*.

Among the many other plays written during this period, mention should be made of the comedies of Jules Romains – e.g. *Monsieur Le Trouhadec saisi par la débauche* (1923), *Knock, ou le Triomphe de la médecine* (1923) and *Donogoo* (1930); the farces of Fernand Crommelynck (b. 1888) – e.g. *Le Cocu magnifique* (1921); the delicate, understated 'theatre of silence' of Jean-Jacques Bernard (b. 1888) – *Le Feu qui reprend mal* (1921); the homely yet poetic handling of biblical material by André Obey (b. 1892) – e.g. *Noé* (1931) and *Lazare* (1952); the fantasy, satire and metaphysical unease of Armand Salacrou (b. 1899) – e.g. *L'Inconnue d'Arras* (1935), *La Terre est ronde* (1938) and *Les Nuits de la colère* (1946).

An Age of Fiction

Both Giraudoux and Cocteau also wrote a number of novels. In the case of Giraudoux, his fiction possesses many of the qualities of his drama. His satire and wit are at their best in *Bella* (1926), a devastating picture of the French political scene of his day. His gifts of poetry and humorous fantasy give a very distinctive flavour to such novels as *Simon le pathétique* (1918), *Suzanne et le pacifique* (1921) and *Juliette au pays des hommes* (1924). *Siegfried et le limousin* (1922), a novel on Franco-German relations, reached the stage as *Siegfried* in 1928. As regards Cocteau, he wrote fewer novels than Giraudoux and is best remembered for *Thomas l'imposteur* (1923), *Le Grand Écart* (1923) and *Les Enfants terribles* (1929). A short passage from the first of these novels, describing military defences on the Belgian coast during World War I, is typical of Cocteau's amusing inventiveness:

> On se trouvait ému devant ce paysage féminin, lisse, cambré, hanché, couché, rempli d'hommes. Car ces dunes n'étaient désertes qu'en apparence. En réalité, elles n'étaient que trucs, décors, trompe-l'œil, trappes et artifices. La fausse dune du colonel Quinton y faisait un vrai mensonge de femme. Ce colonel, si brave, l'avait construite sous une grêle d'obus, qu'il recevait en fumant dans un rocking-chair. Elle dissimulait, en haut, un observatoire d'où l'observateur pouvait descendre en un clin d'œil, par un toboggan. En somme, ces dunes aux malices inépuisablement renouvelées, côté pile, présentaient, côté face, aux télescopes allemands, un immense tour de cartes, un bonneteur silencieux.

A different kind of lyricism, focused on the world of sense impressions, on young love, on animals and on life in the theatre, is to be found in the novels of Sidonie-Gabrielle Colette (1873–1954). Thinly veiled autobiography provides the subject-matter of the 'Claudine' series, of which *La Maison de Claudine* (1922) is perhaps the best, and *Sido* (1930). More objective novels include *La Vagabonde* (1910), *Chéri* (1920) and *La Fin de Chéri* (1926), *Le Blé en herbe* (1923) with its delicate portrait of adolescent love, *La Chatte* (1933) in which a cat significantly affects the life of a young married couple, and *Gigi* (1945). Colette registered the world of physical sensation, both inside and outside human beings, with poetic precision. She has been described as an 'amie de l'instinct' and wrote of what she herself called 'mon désir de posséder par les yeux les merveilles de la terre'. With that honesty which was one of her most obvious qualities, she also wrote – in elegiac rather than tragic terms – of physical decay and the relative brevity of sensual life. Her talent, if minor, was perfect of its kind, and she possessed outstanding gifts as a stylist.

Whereas Colette lived to be more than eighty, Raymond Radiguet (1903–23) died at the age of twenty. He was an astonishingly precocious youth, known by his friends as 'le miracle de la Marne' because of his talent and the place of his birth. Although owing much to the friendship of Cocteau and Max Jacob, Radiguet had distinct literary views of his own. He wrote two novels which have been widely admired, *Le Diable au corps* (1923) and *Le Bal du comte d'Orgel* (1924). Both show his mastery of a 'classical' prose style – at once precise and analytical. In each novel there is an admirable woman who loves two men in different ways. However, whereas the emphasis in *Le Diable au corps* is on the confusion and pain of an adolescent's love for an older woman, *Le Bal du comte d'Orgel* is a conscious reworking of the dilemma posed in the seventeenth century by Madame de La Fayette's *La Princesse de Clèves*.

With Henri Bosco (b. 1888) and Jean Giono (b. 1895) we return, though in a somewhat different spirit, to Colette's 'merveilles de la terre'. Bosco and Giono have deep roots in different parts of the Midi and write of the countryside and its peasant inhabitants with profound understanding. A few lines from Bosco's best novel, *Le Mas Théotime* (1945), sum up his basic attitude: 'Cette terre est forte et nourricière d'âme . . . car elle satisfait à ce besoin inné de lenteur solennelle et d'éternel retour que seuls la croissance du blé ou le verdissement des vignes offrent à l'homme qui est aux prises avec la grandeur et les servitudes agricoles.' The gifts of poetic evocation and mythic patterning which distinguish other novels by Bosco, including *L'Âne culotté* (1937) and *Malicroix* (1948), are sometimes accompanied by weaknesses of plot. Despite inevitable individual differences, Giono's early work was similar in spirit with its study of primitive peasants in the Basses-Alpes seen against a background of elemental powers and what he calls 'cette force qui ne choisit pas, mais qui pèse d'un poids égal sur l'amandier qui veut fleurir, sur la chienne qui court sa course, et sur l'homme.' The most remarkable novels of this type are those forming the 'Pan' trilogy: *Colline* (1928), *Un de Baumugnes* (1929) and *Regain* (1930). After World War II Giono's novels underwent a considerable change in substance and form. Such works as *Le Hussard sur le toit* (1951) and *Le Moulin de Pologne* (1952) show a broadening of scope, as well as a concision of style, that contrast sharply with the earlier lyrical paganism.

A very different group of novelists is constituted by those who wrote between the wars from a position of firm religious belief. Major novelists of the period whose fiction reflects their Catholic convictions are François Mauriac (1885–1970), Georges Bernanos (1888–1948) and Julien Green (b. 1900). These writers were all faced with a particular difficulty – that of doing justice to their belief in divine oversight of human affairs while making such a belief acceptable, at least within the terms of their novels, to the generality of readers. They were aware of the problem facing them as they attempted to portray what Green calls 'la région secrète où Dieu travaille'. Bernanos asserted that 'l'expérience de l'amour divin n'est pas du domaine du roman' while Mauriac found 'rien de moins saisissable que le doigt de Dieu dans le cours d'une destinée'. Nevertheless, all three are the authors of an impressive body of fiction which, while hardly constituting what could be called 'the Catholic novel', indicates the rich variety of forms that can be taken by 'novels written by Catholics'.

For Mauriac, as for Proust, the memory of childhood impressions is a major creative principle. His best works are set in the Landes surrounding his native Bordeaux. A striking sense of place is achieved by repeated references to vineyards, pine forests, the flatness of the countryside, sultry weather, heavily shuttered houses, etc. These physical details create an appropriate atmosphere for his study of human sinfulness ('l'abîme qu'ouvre, dans le monde moderne, l'absence de Dieu'). Young people are torn between purity and evil, while the 'middle-aged' sins of complacency, materialism, insensitivity, hypocrisy and scandal-mongering are attributed to the *bien-pensants* – Mauriac's 'worm-eaten pillars of the Church'. Up to 1930 he appears to side, against the *bien-pensants*, with characters who remain outside the Church – e.g. the heroine in *Thérèse Desqueyroux* (1927) who attempts to poison her husband. Other major novels of the same period – *Le Baiser au lépreux* (1922), *Genitrix* (1923), *Le Désert de l'amour* (1925) – attack Catholic conformism with almost anti-clerical vehemence while also emphasizing the vanity of human love and displaying Mauriac's reaction to what he regards as the bestial nature of sex. Some of his later novels, including *Le Mystère Frontenac* (1933) and *La Fin de la nuit* (1936), are artistic failures precisely because Mauriac attempted to 'purify the source' and treated bourgeois Catholic orthodoxy much more sympathetically. Even as good a novel as *La Pharisienne* (1941) suffers from an overtly 'improving' conclusion. *Le Nœud de vipères* (1932), however, remains a remarkably successful attempt to portray the process of religious conversion in psychologically convincing and spiritually moving terms.

The fictional world of Georges Bernanos is the work of a powerful, visionary gift. He renders experience in terms of a titanic struggle between good and evil which is more uncompromising and dramatic than in Mauriac. Miracles occur, Satan takes human form, heroic individuals struggle to the utmost limits of pure grace or pure malignity, and violence – in both its moral and physical forms, including murder, suicide and rape – is an integral part of the characters' life. All these features are present in two of Bernanos' best-known novels, *Sous le soleil de Satan* (1926) and *Journal d'un curé de campagne* (1936). Also, each has as its central figure a priest of little practical competence, but possessing great spiritual power, recalling the 'saintly fools' of Dostoevsky. Sainthood is also achieved by Chantal de Clergerie, the heroine of *La Joie* (1929), whereas single-minded evil characterizes Abbé Cénabre in *L'Imposture* (1927) and the horrifying, haunting hero of *Monsieur Ouine* (1943). In these novels, as in the starkly impressive *Nouvelle Histoire de Mouchette* (1937), extreme suffering is often part of a pattern through which Bernanos suggests modern versions of Christ's Passion and the way in which the torment of one individual may possess redemptive power for another.

Julien Green also writes of violence – murder and rape, madness and suicide – in a way that recalls Bernanos. At the same time, and although he writes in a distinctly personal idiom, his reaction to sexuality and his picture of a loveless, faithless world remind one of Mauriac. Such novels as *Adrienne Mesurat* (1927), *Léviathan* (1929) and *Épaves* (1932) powerfully convey this 'monde de désespérés'. Green had an early Protestant upbringing, became a Catholic convert but lost the faith, was deeply influenced by Buddhism, and finally embraced Catholicism in 1939. The main novels reflecting his Buddhist phase – *Le Visionnaire* (1934), *Minuit* (1936) and *Varouna* (1940) – added a dimension of mysticism and fantasy to his earlier vision. His specifically Christian preoccupations are central to one of his best-known novels, *Moïra* (1950), with its American student hero who tragically fails to sustain the consequences of his belief in God. Conflict between the flesh and the spirit is also present in *Chaque homme dans sa nuit* (1960) where, for once, the atmosphere of gloom is lightened by a suggestion of meaning and hope extending beyond the suffering and solitude, cruelty and fear. which characterize his view of the human condition.

It should be added that Mauriac, Bernanos and Green have all had success in the theatre. Of Mauriac's five plays, *Asmodée* (1938) and *Les Mal Aimés* (1945) are perhaps the best. Two of Green's three plays, *Sud* (1953) and *L'Ennemi* (1954), have been particularly admired, while Bernanos wrote a moving film script, *Dialogues des Carmélites* (1949), based on the guillotining of a community of nuns during the French Revolution and set to music by Poulenc.

A novelist who is attracted by the more austerely contemplative demands of religion and art, yet also strongly solicited by action and sexuality, is Henry de Montherlant. Reference has already been made to his early novel, *Le Songe*, but he is the author of numerous other works of fiction insufficiently appreciated outside France. Bullfighting and adolescent love are humorously counterpointed in *Les Bestiaires* (1926); irony and compassion create memorable characterization in *Les Célibataires* (1934); the artist's need both for sexual stimulation and ascetic detachment is explored with wit and intelligence in the four volumes of *Les Jeunes Filles* (1936–9). Major novels appearing more recently are *Le Chaos et la nuit* (1963), an imaginative study of an aged Spanish anarchist exiled in France; *La Rose de sable* (1968), an indictment of French colonialism in North Africa; *Les Garçons* (1969), a moving evocation of a liberal Catholic school in Paris on the eve of World War I.

Three other novelists who have combined action and contemplation in their work are André Malraux (b. 1901), Antoine de Saint-Exupéry (1900–44) and Louis-Ferdinand Céline – pseudonym of Dr L.-F. Destouches (1894–1961). Malraux is the major figure among these three. His work marks the coming of age of what might be called 'the novel of the human condition', and this metaphysical dimension has proved a major influence in modern French fiction. Malraux's novels, with the exception of *La Voie royale* (1930), have also reflected some of the major political events of his lifetime: revolution in China in *Les Conquérants* (1928) and *La Condition humaine* (1933); Nazi Germany in *Le Temps du mépris* (1935); the Spanish Civil War in *L'Espoir* (1937); World Wars I and II in *Les Noyers de l'Altenburg* (1948). In an early essay, *La Tentation de l'Occident* (1926), a young Chinese expresses Malraux's own view when he writes to his French correspondent: 'La réalité a été pour vous Dieu, puis l'homme; mais *l'homme est mort*, après Dieu, et vous cherchez avec angoisse celui à qui vous pourriez confier son étrange héritage.' This is the post-Nietzschean drama which Malraux has explored in his novels and lengthy writings on art, a drama intensified by Spengler's pessimistic view of Western civilization. In turbulent novels of fresh psychological insight and outstanding narrative skill Malraux probes beneath the political surface of his story to uncover human solitude in the face of death and what he terms the 'royaumes métalliques de l'absurdité'. These metallic kingdoms are peopled by characters vainly seeking self-validation in heroism, collective political action, drugs, eroticism, mythomania and art.

The world of action in Saint-Exupéry's novels is that of the commercial pilot, pioneering routes to West Africa and South America – *Courrier Sud* (1928), *Vol de nuit* (1931), *Terre des hommes* (1939) – and that of the combat pilot in World War II – *Pilote de guerre* (1942). Like Malraux, Saint-Exupéry considered the life of thought to be sterile without the accompaniment of difficult or dangerous action. His novels combine stories of his own and his friends' adventures with lyrical passages on the wonder of life, the dignity of human beings, and what he calls the authentic luxury of human relations. These are loosely constructed but beautifully written works in which ideas of sacrifice and duty, heroism and fraternity, contribute to a mystical humanism rather less attractively presented in the posthumously published collection of notes and impressions, *Citadelle* (1948).

A very different atmosphere pervades Céline's novels. He sees no salvation for man (whom he judges to be cowardly, hypocritical, selfish) and considers the truth of the world to be death. The title of his first and finest novel, *Voyage au bout de la nuit* (1932), is an apt description of Céline's literary and spiritual journey. He was a romantic nihilist who made literature out of his disgust for human beings and developed a scathing, colloquial prose style which has influenced a number of later writers. After *Mort à crédit* (1936) he produced a series of increasingly strident, often anti-Semitic, and virtually self-parodying novels including *Bagatelles pour un massacre* (1938), *Féerie pour une autre fois I* (1952), *Normance (Féerie pour une autre fois II)* (1954), and a horrifying trilogy reflecting the collapse of Nazi Germany: *D'un château l'autre* (1957), *Nord* (1960) and the posthumously published *Rigodon* (1969).

In this 'age of fiction' in inter-war France many other novelists were active. Georges Duhamel extended his immediate post-war reputation with two novel cycles: *Vie et aventures de Salavin* (1920–32) and *Chronique des Pasquier* (1933–44). Jacques de Lacretelle (b. 1888) achieved popular success with *Silbermann* (1922) and *Retour de Silbermann* (1930). Marcel Jouhandeau (b. 1888) is a self-tormenting and unorthodox Catholic whose many novels analysing marriage and human relations include *Monsieur Godeau intime* (1926), *Monsieur Godeau marié* (1933) and *Chamindour* (1934). Drieu la Rochelle (1893–1945) reflected the moral malaise of the twenties and thirties in various novels and collections of short stories including *L'Homme couvert de femmes* (1925), *Le Feu follet* (1931) and *Gilles* (1939), while Marcel Aymé (1902–67) first achieved success as a comic satirist with a robust account of provincial and peasant *mores* in *La Jument verte* (1933).

Two other novelists, both of strong left-wing views, should be mentioned. Paul Nizan (1905–40) had his reputation renewed by Sartre's preface to the 1960 edition of *Aden Arabie* (1931). A member of the Communist Party, Nizan wrote fluent political novels, including *Antoine Bloyé* (1933), *Le Cheval de Troie* (1935) and *La Conspiration* (1938), designed to show that 'toute la société bourgeoise est en proie à la mort'. A more wide-ranging novelist is Louis Guilloux (b. 1899), a non-Marxist revolutionary whose novels express the metaphysical and social anger and scepticism of Cripure in *Le Sang noir* (1935): 'Je détruis toute idole, et je n'ai pas de Dieu à mettre sur l'autel. . . . Les paradis humanitaires, les Édens sociologiques, hum!' Guilloux's earlier novels, including *La Maison du peuple* (1927), were autobiographical and populist. Much later, in *Le Jeu de patience* (1949), he showed a readiness to combine social preoccupations with interesting technical experiments.

World War II: Resistance and Liberation

The successive experiences of military defeat, enemy occupation, resistance to this occupation, and final liberation inevitably had a profound effect on the population of France, including French writers, between 1940 and 1944. A mood of moral and social guilt under the Vichy regime gradually gave way to patriotic affirmation and heroism. This, in its turn, was followed by the memoirs and apologias, the explanations and radical revisions, of the post-Liberation period.

Political and moral confusion and uncertainty, already evident in the years immediately preceding World War II, were intensified by the signing of the armistice in France and the establishment of the Vichy government. Its supporters included patriotic traditionalists who put their faith in Marshal Pétain (e.g. the aged Charles Maurras), anti-Semites and Fascists who admired Nazi ideology, pacifists who preferred occupation to war, ideologues who regarded Hitler as the only effective bulwark against the spread of Communism in Europe,

religious traditionalists who hoped for much-needed moral regenera-
tion and a Catholic revival. Inevitably, these were not the views of a
majority of intellectuals and the literature associated with these various
attitudes is limited in both quantity and interest. Writers already
mentioned who favoured collaboration with Nazism include Drieu la
Rochelle and Céline. Two other novelists should be mentioned.
Alphonse de Châteaubriant (1877–1951) responded with a kind of
romantic lyricism to Nazi mythology and directed the collaborationist
journal *La Gerbe*. Much earlier he had published two widely praised
novels, *Monsieur des Lourdines* (1911) and *La Brière* (1923). Robert
Brasillach (1909–45) wrote some good literary criticism and several
novels including *Les Sept Couleurs* (1939). With Drieu la Rochelle he is
the most admirable figure associated with collaboration – honest,
idealistic, courageous. He was tried, imprisoned and shot in 1945 and
his *Poèmes de Fresnes* were posthumously published in 1949.

Under the Occupation certain symbolic gestures were possible.
Parisian audiences were able to interpret Sartre's *Les Mouches* (1943) and
Anouilh's *Antigone* (1944) in Resistance terms. Generally speaking,
however, the clandestine conditions imposed on dissident writers by
the fact of enemy occupation did not make for large output or lasting
quality. Writing often took the form of polemics or patriotic essays
contributed to such initially roneo-typed periodicals as *Résistance*, *La
Pensée libre* and the important *Lettres françaises*. Contributors included
Aragon, Éluard, Mauriac and Sartre. A clandestine publishing house,
Les Éditions de Minuit, had also been established. It published such
texts as Mauriac's *Le Cahier noir*, a *nouvelle* by Elsa Triolet, *Les Amants
d'Avignon*, poems by Aragon and Éluard, and *33 Sonnets composés au
secret* by Jean Cassou. The most famous publication was a short novel,
Le Silence de la mer (1942), by Vercors – pseudonym of Jean Bruller
(b. 1902). This is a humane and finely drawn study of the relations
between two French people and a German officer billeted on them
during the Occupation.

It is not surprising that much clandestine literature took the relatively
intense and economical form of poetry. Aragon and Éluard became
outstanding Resistance poets, the former in *Le Crève-cœur* (1941) and
Le Musée Grévin (1943), the latter in *Poésie et vérité* (1942), *Au rendez-
vous allemand* (1944), and particularly in his famous litany to 'Liberté'.
Among many other poets writing at this time were Robert Desnos who
had broken with surrealism before his death in a concentration camp in
1945, and Pierre Emmanuel (b. 1916). Emmanuel is a Catholic poet

whose wartime collections include *Jour de colère* (1942) and *La Liberté guide nos pas* (1943) and who wrote: 'La guerre me révéla cette *sensibilité spirituelle* que je n'ai pas cessé de traduire depuis.'

With the Liberation the novelists came back into their own with a vast amount of fiction dealing with war, deportation, occupation and resistance. There is only space to list a few of the more interesting works. On the war itself, Robert Merle gave a tough, graphic account of Dunkirk in *Week-end à Zuydcoote* (1949) and Jules Roy, in *La Vallée heureuse* (1946), provided the bomber pilot's pendant to Saint-Exupéry's *Pilote de guerre*. Roger Nimier's *Le Hussard bleu* (1950) covered the final phases of the war in Europe. Deportation and the world of the concentration camps is the subject of David Rousset's *L'Univers concentrationnaire* (1946) and *Les Jours de notre mort* (1948) as well as of Francis Ambrière's *Les Grandes Vacances* (1946) and Robert Antelme's *L'Espèce humaine* (1947). Moving poetry born of these experiences will be found in Jean Cayrol's *Miroir de la Rédemption* (1944) and *Poèmes de la nuit et du brouillard* (1946). Occupation and resistance are treated in many different ways in *Drôle de jeu* (1945) by Roger Vailland, *Les Forêts de la nuit* (1947) by Jean-Louis Curtis, *Les Épées* (1948) by Roger Nimier, *Uranus* (1948) by Marcel Aymé, *Bande à part* (1951) by Jacques Perret, and *Au bon beurre* (1952) by Jean Dutourd.

Humanism and Existentialism

The search for an authentic humanism which Albert Camus shared in some measure with Gide and Malraux, and the brand of atheistic existentialism which Jean-Paul Sartre described as a form of humanism, both have their roots in a tradition of intellectual dissent and rebellion of which the outrage of Lautréamont and Rimbaud, or the anti-rationalism of the surrealists, offer particularly striking literary expressions. Perhaps it is therefore not surprising that Camus (1913–60) and Sartre (b. 1905) were both classed as existentialists in 1945 although Camus explicitly rejected this classification and Sartre pointed out important differences between them. What they had most obviously in common was a sense of the absurd or irrational nature of man's experience of the world and an acute feeling of his solitary, isolated position facing the finality of death in a universe without God. At the same time, whereas Camus located irrationality not in the world as such but in the confrontation between the human mind and that world, Sartre argued that the physical universe itself is absurd in the sense that it can be given no *a priori* philosophical justification. These ideas are reflected in different ways in the essays, novels and plays of both writers. They led Camus to look for an alternative philosophy to both Christianity and Marxism; they have prompted Sartre to regard Marxism as alone providing a coherent set of solutions.

After an honourable career in clandestine journalism during the Occupation, Camus rapidly emerged as a major literary figure with two plays, *Le Malentendu* (1944) and *Caligula* (1945), and a striking first novel, *L'Étranger* (published in 1942 but only widely read after 1945). All these works explored, in terms of individual experience, that sense of 'the absurd' which Camus also discussed on a more philosophical level in a long essay, *Le Mythe de Sisyphe* (1942). The plays proved less successful than the novel in which, through the personality of Meursault, Camus conveyed the 'feeling' of a contemporary brand of nihilism with which he had undoubted temperamental affinities yet which he was mainly concerned to overcome. His own rebellion against nihilism, in the name of justice and human fraternity, is given imaginative form in his second major novel, *La Peste* (1947), with its elaborate and suggestive symbolic structure, and in two further plays, *L'État de siège* (1948) and *Les Justes* (1950). In another influential essay, *L'Homme révolté* (1951), he contrasted his own idea of moral and metaphysical rebellion with the Marxist doctrine of violent politico-historical revolution which he saw as running counter to true humanism. He achieved an outstanding measure of moral and artistic integrity which perhaps reached their culminating point in his third novel, *La Chute* (1956), and in the short stories – which are also a set of fascinating stylistic exercises – collected under the title *L'Exil et le royaume* (1957).

By professional training Sartre is a teacher of philosophy. His earliest published works, which appeared before World War II, consisted of philosophical papers together with his best-known novel, *La Nausée* (1938), and a collection of short stories, *Le Mur* (1939). From this point onwards his novels and plays continued to centre around certain themes first set out at great length in *L'Être et le néant* (1943), a philosophical work which remains the major statement in French of atheistic existentialism. For Sartre there is no God, no objective system of universal values, and therefore no 'given' or established religious or secular morality. The individual is totally free and therefore totally responsible. He must exercise his freedom by constant, responsible choice, avoiding the pitfalls of evasive 'bad faith' and refusing to fulfil roles which others seek to impose upon him in order to deprive him of his freedom.

Unlike Camus, Sartre has been a more successful playwright than novelist and some of the ideas just mentioned are given dramatic form, and handled with considerable theatrical skill, in *Les Mouches* (1943), *Morts sans sépulture* (1946), *La Putain respectueuse* (1946), *Les Mains sales* (1948), *Les Séquestrés d'Altona* (1959), etc. In what is probably his most ambitious play, *Le Diable et le bon Dieu* (1951), existentialist themes are combined with an imaginative projection of the conflict between ends and means which reminds us of his political preoccupations and of the fascination which Communism holds for him. Existentialism and Communism are also central to his most ambitious work of fiction, the three volumes of *Les Chemins de la liberté* (1945–9). Thus in *L'Âge de raison* (1945) the central figure, Mathieu, is pulled in opposite directions by his demand for individual freedom and his sense of collective efficacy. Of the other two volumes, *Le Sursis* (1947) uses techniques of simultaneity to convey a complex picture of Europe during the Munich crisis while *La Mort dans l'âme* (1949) has the Fall of France as its subject. Sartre's most sustained – and opaque – attempt to relate existentialism and Marxism at a philosophical level will be found in *Critique de la raison dialectique* (1960).

The literary status of Simone de Beauvoir (b. 1908), closely associated with Sartre both personally and intellectually, has been the subject of some debate. A long, untidy novel, *Les Mandarins* (1954), evokes the Parisian intellectual circles of the 1940s to which she belonged and contains thinly fictionalized portraits of Camus and Sartre among others. Like Sartre, she has written philosophical essays on existentialism and on the need to divorce ethics from religious or metaphysical absolutes – *Pour une morale de l'ambiguité* (1947), etc. – as well as a lengthy and sometimes alarmingly humourless book on the status and rights of women, *Le Deuxième Sexe* (1949). Her best novels are *L'Invitée* (1943) and *Le Sang des autres* (1944). The former deals with the existentialist idea of the individual achieving freedom through a genuinely autonomous act. It is not without significance that the act in this particular instance is the murder of another human being. The latter is a dramatic and sometimes moving novel about the 1930s and the French Resistance movement. The intellectual world which Sartre and Simone de Beauvoir represent, and which Camus came to reject with increasing firmness, is portrayed in her three autobiographical volumes, *Mémoires d'une jeune fille rangée* (1958), *La Force de l'âge* (1960) and *La Force des choses* (1963).

New Forms in the Theatre

Montherlant's plays belong to this section more by historical accident than aesthetic affinity. Although he had established his reputation as a novelist and essayist in the inter-war period, he did not begin his public career as a dramatist until the writing and production of *La Reine morte* in 1942. This play immediately struck what was to become the authentic Montherlantian note in the theatre – a searching account of psychological and moral dilemmas associated with exaltation and grandeur and expressed in richly rhetorical terms. These qualities, together with the fact that he has written a number of 'costume' tragedies, place Montherlant in a tradition that goes back through Claudel, and the Musset of *Lorenzaccio*, to the plays of Corneille and Racine. His conception of the theatre, and the world created by his drama, are unique in the post-war period and represent a new form in this sense, however far removed they may be from the 'theatre of the absurd' and the laconic anti-heroism of Beckett or Ionesco.

Montherlant's main 'costume' tragedies, in addition to *La Reine morte*, are – with their dates of publication rather than performance – *Malatesta* (1946), *Le Maître de Santiago* (1947), *Port-Royal* (1954), *Don Juan* (1958), *Le Cardinal d'Espagne* (1960) and *La Guerre civile* (1965). In all these plays character polarities predominate and Montherlant matches the tragic inevitability inherent in his historical material with a tightly woven theatrical structure. His non-historical plays, written in less lyrical and more everyday language, include *Fils de personne* (1944) and *La Ville dont le prince est un enfant* (1951). The former is a moving tragedy of the failure of a father and (illegitimate) son to understand each other despite goodwill on both sides. The latter dramatizes material skilfully reworked eighteen years later in the novel *Les Garçons*.

Although he differs from Montherlant in almost every respect, Jean Genet (b. 1910) shares with him the ability to manipulate language with outstanding skill and to clothe his ideas in rich and sonorous prose. Genet uses this gift of language, however, to praise evil and hymn the virtues of murder, betrayal, theft and violent crime generally. He spent much of his early life in jail in various European countries and faced life imprisonment in 1947. He was eventually pardoned, largely through the intervention of the Parisian literary world. By this time he had written a number of novels glorifying his criminal associations and homosexual relationships. Artistic skill and often repulsive subject-matter come together in *Notre-Dame des fleurs* (1944), *Miracle de la rose* (1946), *Pompes funèbres* (1947) and *Querelle de Brest* (1947).

It was also in 1947 that Genet first turned to the theatre and it is Genet the dramatist who speaks most convincingly with an original and authentic literary voice. He condemns Western drama for its trivial realism and seeks to create a ritualized theatre inspired by Japan, Bali and China. The result is a theatre of ceremony in which, at least in the later plays, symbols in human form take the place of traditional, psychologically motivated characters. It was ideas like these which prompted him to describe the elevation of the host during the Mass as a piece of genuine theatrical effectiveness. His own first play, *Haute Surveillance* (1947), can in fact be interpreted as a perverse Mass acted out by three prisoners. *Les Bonnes* (1947) was a breakthrough in his work in so far as it moved away from the world of homosexually obsessed criminals. In common with *Le Balcon* (1956) it introduces a number of existentialist themes including the human tendency towards role-playing and the acting out of private fantasies. *Le Balcon*, with its brothel or 'house of illusions', also mirrors the falseness and hollowness of society. Two later plays, *Les Nègres* (1958) and *Les Paravents* (1961), are violent, ritualistic pieces closer to Voodoo ceremonies than to Noh theatre.

The writings of Samuel Beckett (b. 1906), with their bitter sense of the absurdity of existence and of a world predicated on death and physical decay, suggest a desperate rewriting of some of Camus's earliest work. Unlike the fundamentally classical Camus, however, Beckett sees language itself as a manifestation of irrationality. This fact both contributes to the distinctive resonance of his plays and links them in terms of expression as well as attitude to the 'theatre of the absurd' in general. The play which made Beckett a world-renowned figure, *En attendant Godot* (1952), opens on a deserted country road with a single, stunted tree. Under this tree two tramps talk to one another, achieve no meaningful communication, and await the mysterious Godot who fails to appear. This play creates talk without meaning, and movement without development. The wit, the humour and the punning are often tragic and painful. With some justification Beckett's plays have been described as constituting a 'théâtre-limite' and most of them, since *En attendant Godot*, show a progressive paring down of character, action and speech. *Fin de partie* (1957) takes place in a bare room; Hamm cannot stand, Clov cannot sit, and Hamm's legless parents, Nagg and Nell, occupy two dustbins. In *Krapp's Last Tape* (1959), translated into

French as *La Dernière Bande* (1959), man-become-animal confronts a machine. *Happy Days* (1961), translated into French as *Oh! les beaux jours* (1963), has a heroine who is buried up to the waist in earth. The crude, the farcical and the incoherent are all essential elements in Beckett's desperate and despairing response to life. His sometimes barely human characters, subject to extremes of physical humiliation, drag out a meaningless existence in a physical waste dominated by the fact of suffering and the eroding action of time.

The plays of Eugène Ionesco (b. 1912) also reflect a world in which man is dehumanized and alienated. Again, they mirror the breakdown of language. However, Ionesco differs from Beckett in his response to this situation which often takes the form of wildly funny and 'absurd' fantasy. He emphasizes his own conception of the theatre as one based on the private imagination and in which inventiveness is much more important than any specific message: 'C'est dans mes rêves, dans mes angoisses, dans mes désirs obscurs, dans mes contradictions intérieures que, pour ma part, je me réserve le droit de prendre cette matière théâtrale.' From this personal basis, which provides him with a set of near-surrealist images, he exposes the mechanical and the ready-made in behaviour and speech. Thus his first major play, *La Cantatrice chauve* (1950), shows up the routine conformity and pomposity of an English couple through the inanities of their conversation:

M. SMITH. Un médecin consciencieux doit mourir avec le malade s'ils ne peuvent pas guérir ensemble. Le commandant d'un bateau périt avec le bateau, dans les vagues. Il ne lui survit pas.

MME SMITH. On ne peut comparer un malade à un bateau.

M. SMITH. Pourquoi pas? Le bateau a aussi ses maladies; d'ailleurs ton docteur est aussi sain qu'un vaisseau; voilà pourquoi encore il devait périr en même temps que le malade comme le docteur et son bateau.

MME SMITH. Ah! Je n'y avais pas pensé . . . C'est peut-être juste . . . et alors, quelle conclusion en tires-tu?

M. SMITH. C'est que tous les docteurs ne sont que des charlatans. Et tous les malades aussi. Seule la marine est honnête en Angleterre.

MME SMITH. Mais pas les marins.

M. SMITH. Naturellement.

Among Ionesco's numerous plays *La Leçon* (1951), *Les Chaises* (1952), *Amédée, ou Comment s'en débarrasser* (1954), *Le Nouveau Locataire* (1957),

Tueur sans gages (1959) and *Rhinocéros* (1960) all bear testimony to his imagination and inventiveness – and to his outstanding gift for making tragedy comic and comedy tragic. *Rhinocéros*, in particular, points to another aspect of his theatre – the fact that his inventiveness is sometimes a means of making social or political comment in symbolical terms. Thus Bérenger, who appears in other plays in addition to *Rhinocéros*, is the lone survivor in a society of men that has become a herd of dangerous rhinos, i.e. an authoritarian society lacking intellectual refinement but possessing potentially lethal power. The application to twentieth-century dictatorships, whether of the Right or the Left, is obvious.

Other writers for the theatre who may be classed in the same avant-garde tradition as Beckett and Ionesco include Jacques Audiberti (1899–1965), author of *Quoat-Quoat* (1946), *Le Mal court* (1947), *La Fête noire* (1948) and *Les Naturels du Bordelais* (1953); Jean Tardieu (b. 1903), whose *Théâtre de chambre* was published in 1955 and his *Poèmes à jouer* in 1960; Arthur Adamov (b. 1908), author of *Le Professeur Taranne* (1953) and *Le Ping-Pong* (1955); Fernando Arrabal (b. 1932), whose *Théâtre I* and *Théâtre II* were published in 1958 and 1961 and his *Théâtre panique* in 1965. One can find in most of these dramatists, as in Genet, Beckett and Ionesco, traces of the theories set out so forcibly by Antonin Artaud (1896–1948) – theories to do with ritual, spectacle and anti-rationalism – in *Le Théâtre et son double* (1938).

Some Post-War Poets

One of the most accessible French poets still writing after World War II was Jules Supervielle (1884–1960). Within the general development of twentieth-century poetry he saw himself as pioneering 'une poésie moins ardue, plus proche de chacun de nous'. At the same time, this poetry was calculated to lead the reader 'dans les lointains et les abîmes'. In fact, Supervielle was a spiritual idealist who wrote about the mysterious beauty of the physical world and the organic relationship between man and nature. Many poems are devoted to this theme and the opening stanza of 'Arbres dans la nuit et le jour', published in 1945, is typical:

> Candélabres de la noirceur,
> Hauts-commissaires des ténèbres,
> Malgré votre grandeur funèbre
> Arbres, mes frères et mes sœurs,

> Nous sommes de même famille,
> L'étrangeté se pousse en nous
> Jusqu'aux veinules, aux ramilles,
> Et nous comble de bout en bout.

Delicacy and charm, simplicity and humour, are features of Super-vielle's poetry as of his short stories on mythical and biblical themes (e.g. *L'Arche de Noé* (1938) and *Le Petit Bois et autres contes* (1947)). Some of his most characteristic verse – poems on animals which recall La Fontaine and whimsical poems on the relationship between God and man – will be found in *Gravitations* (1925), *Le Forçat innocent* (1930), *La Fable du monde* (1938) and *Oublieuse mémoire* (1949). Another collection, *Poèmes de la France malheureuse* (1941), consists of poems written in Uruguay (where he was born) and passed from hand to hand in Occupied France.

With Pierre-Jean Jouve (b. 1887) we approach more closely to the mainstream of modern French poetry since he recognizes a considerable debt to Baudelaire and has in turn influenced poets younger than himself – e.g. Emmanuel and Bonnefoy. Jouve dates his poetic maturity from *Les Mystérieuses Noces* (1925). He had become a convert to Roman Catholicism shortly before, as well as showing a deep interest in psychoanalytic theory, and much of his verse from this point onwards centres around the problem of good and evil interpreted by means of a distinctive, and fundamentally pessimistic, mixture of theological and Freudian imagery. His poems reveal the 'neuves férocités et lâchetés anciennes' of man. Apart from *Les Mystérieuses Noces*, his many volumes of poetry include *La Symphonie à Dieu* (1930), *Sueur de sang* (1934), *Gloire* (1940) and *La Vierge de Paris* (1945). Although his poetic vigour sometimes leads to formlessness, Jouve is often a master of language and something of his ability to transmute his faith into memorable verse can be seen in these lines from the final poem in *La Symphonie à Dieu*:

> Témoin des lieux insensés de mon cœur
> Tu es né d'une vierge absolue et tu es né
> Parce que Dieu avait posé les mains sur sa poitrine,
> Et tu es né
> Homme de nerfs et de douleur et de semence
> Pour marcher sur la magnifique dalle de chagrin

Et ton flanc mort fut percé pour la preuve
Et jaillit sur l'obscur et extérieur nuage
Du sang avec de l'eau.

Saint-John Perse – pseudonym of Alexis St Léger Léger (b. 1887) –
published his first book of verse as long ago as 1909. His best-known
long poem, *Anabase* (1924), was translated into English by T. S. Eliot
in 1930, yet his world-wide reputation only dates from the award of the
Nobel Prize for Literature in 1960. With ceremonious formality, and in
often difficult imagery, Saint-John Perse celebrates the rich variety of
the natural world. He writes: '. . . par son adhésion totale à ce qui est,
le poète tient pour nous liaison avec la permanence et l'unité de l'Être' –
and he adds: 'Poète est celui qui rompt pour nous l'accoutumance.'
Both these poetic functions are typically present in this short extract
from *Amers*:

Ô mon amour au goût de mer, que d'autres paissent loin de mer
l'églogue au fond des vallons clos – menthes, mélisse et méliot,
tiédeurs d'alysse et d'origan – et l'un y parle d'abeillage et l'autre y
traite d'agnelage, et la brebis feutrée baisse la terre au bas des murs
de pollen noir. Dans le temps où les pêches se nouent, et les liens sont
triés pour la vigne, moi j'ai tranché le nœud de chanvre qui tient la
coque sur son ber, à son berceau de bois. Et mon amour est sur les
mers! et ma brûlure est sur les mers! . . .

Saint-John Perse's celebration of Being emphasizes plenitude, regenera-
tion, purification, energy and love in *Éloges* (1911), *Pluies* (1943),
Neiges (1944), *Vents* (1946) and *Amers* (1957). Exile in America during
World War II inspired *Exil* (1942) and old age *Chronique* (1960).

If a poet with as individual a voice as Saint-John Perse had to be
classified we should probably place him, at least technically, in the
symbolist tradition. Pierre Reverdy (1889–1960), on the other hand,
owes a clear debt to surrealism like so many of his contemporaries. Both
these poets shunned publicity and left their poetry to speak for itself.
Reverdy, indeed, lived the life of a recluse at Solesmes from 1926 until
his death, vainly seeking a solution to his religious problems. The
circumscribed but very real quality of Reverdy's verse was only generally recognized with the republication of his poems for the period
1915–22 in *Plupart du temps* (1945). Other major collections include *Les
Épaves du ciel* (1924) and *Liberté des mers* (1960). Reverdy's characteristic

combination of haunting sadness and a strong plastic sense is seen in
'Fausse porte ou portrait' from *Les Épaves du ciel*:

> Dans la place qui reste là
> Entre quatre lignes
>   Un carré où le blanc se joue
> La main qui soutenait ta joue
>   Lune
> Une figure qui s'allume
>   Le profil d'un autre
>   Mais tes yeux
> Je suis la lampe qui me guide
> Un doigt sur la paupière humide
>   Au milieu
> Les larmes roulent dans cet espace
>   Entre quatre lignes
>   Une glace

Like Reverdy, René Char (b. 1907) served an apprenticeship to
surrealism, and the collection *Artine* (1930) has been called a 'classic' of
the movement. His poems published since 1945 are different in manner
and mood though a certain obscurity, and a sometimes dazzling use
of imagery, recall his literary origins. Char is both the poet of that
sensibility which his friend and admirer Camus called 'the absurd' (he
defines the poet as a 'magicien de l'insécurité'), and a writer whose
humanity and sensibility have deep and permanent roots in his native
Vaucluse. The following lines, from a poem on the river Sorgue in
the collection *Fureur et mystère* (1948), indicate something of his
qualities:

> Rivière de l'âme vide, de la guenille et du soupçon,
> Du vieux malheur qui se dévide, de l'ormeau, de la compassion.
>
> Rivière des farfelus, des fiévreux, des équarisseurs,
> Du soleil lâchant sa charrue pour s'acoquiner au menteur.

Char has increasingly used the prose-poem as a medium for taut,
aphoristic writing with which to illuminate deep and elusive truths
about human experience. An excellent anthology of his poems, chosen
by himself, was published as *Commune Présence* in 1964.

Inevitably, the five poets named so far, while they are probably
major figures in post-war French poetry (along with Éluard), do not

exhaust either the number or variety of poets whose work deserves to be mentioned. At one extreme of sensibility there is the radical pessimism of Henri Michaux (b. 1899) for whom: 'Tout enfonce, rien ne libère / Le suicidé renaît à une nouvelle souffrance'. He sees the world in Kafkaesque terms and has sought to exorcize it through mescalin and art. Representative collections of his work are *Épreuves, Exorcismes* (1945) and *Passages* (1950). At another extreme Francis Ponge (b. 1899) devotes many prose poems to physical objects, particularly in *Le Parti pris des choses* (1942), in a manner recalling the *chosisme* of the 'new novelists'. Indeed, Ponge might be speaking for Robbe-Grillet when he writes: '. . . je me fais tirer, par les objets, hors du vieil humanisme, hors de l'homme actuel et en avant de lui.' Very different again, both from these poets and from one another, are Jacques Prévert (b. 1900) and Raymond Queneau (b. 1903) who have both written clever, witty and humorous verse and who made their names with *Paroles* (1946) and *Si tu t'imagines* (1952) respectively. We return to the expression of nihilism, often vigorously and memorably expressed, in the poetry of André Frénaud (b. 1907). The title of his most representative collection of poems, *Il n'y a pas de paradis* (1962), is significant.

Two other poets have established considerable reputations: Patrice de la Tour du Pin (b. 1911) and Yves Bonnefoy (b. 1923). La Tour du Pin has been underrated by some critics, perhaps because of the largely traditionalist and classical qualities of his verse. An enormous work, *Une Somme de poésie* (1946), to which he added further lengthy volumes in 1959 and 1963, is inevitably of uneven quality though impressive in scope and ambition. The best passages reveal an outstanding ability to handle religious themes and the experience of love. La Tour du Pin is also acutely conscious of the spiritual paucity of the post-Christian world.

> Nous n'avons plus d'idoles . . .
> Après celles de pierre ont croulé celles d'âme.
> Les derniers sens d'adoration se sont défaits.
> D'ailleurs, qui s'en étonne?
> Plus on touche à la mort et plus on prend ses traits.

As regards Bonnefoy, he is also a less consciously avant-garde poet than many of his contemporaries, but he carries out an anguished interrogation of a world in which death is the overriding reality. His best-known collections are *Du mouvement et de l'immobilité de Douve* (1954) and *Hier régnant désert* (1958).

Towards a New Novel

The various terms *nouveau roman, anti-roman, école du regard* or *chosisme* suggest that the phenomenon to which they refer is neither obviously homogeneous nor easily defined. The novelists in question share the conviction that it is inappropriate today, for social, philosophical or aesthetic reasons, to write novels indistinguishable in form and attitude from those of the nineteenth century. Nevertheless, there is a vast difference between the fierce nihilism of Beckett, the psychological subtleties of Sarraute or Duras, the objectivity and formalism of Robbe-Grillet.

A clear break with the traditional novel, and one which anticipates later ideas, is to be found in a work on the theory of fiction, *Lazare parmi nous* (1950), by Jean Cayrol (b. 1911). Cayrol's experiences during three years spent in prisons and concentration camps during World War II convinced him that suffering is a necessary precondition of redemption. He entertains some ultimate hope for man, but sees him as conditioned by solitude, dereliction and estrangement. A social outcast, resembling a secular Christ taking on himself the world's misery, is the protagonist of his trilogy *Je vivrai l'amour des autres* (1947–50). Themes of estrangement and absence continue to haunt such later novels as *La Noire* (1949), *Le Vent de la mémoire* (1952), *L'Espace d'une nuit* (1954), *Les Corps étrangers* (1959), etc.

The world of the human or sub-human outcast is something which Cayrol and Beckett have in common though Beckett, as we saw in the case of his plays, wholly lacks that belief in the possibility of redemption which is central to Cayrol. Another surface similarity between their desolate fictional worlds is the fact that the balance between people and objects is precarious in two senses: people are often reduced by these novelists to the status of 'things' haunting the very fringes of existence; furthermore, objects can take on major significance in this world of depersonalized human creatures. Neither Cayrol nor Beckett treats objects with the scientific detachment aimed at by Robbe-Grillet or Butor. Rather, material things are necessary points of reference in a world of desolation and flux – a pair of old socks, riddled with holes, in the opening volume of Cayrol's *Je vivrai l'amour des autres*, or the sucking-stones in Beckett's *Molloy* (1951). This last work forms part of a trilogy of which the other volumes are *Malone meurt* (1951) and *L'Innommable* (1953). The increasing tendency in these novels to withdraw from the physical world of bodies and objects into the flux of demented consciousness and confusions of language reaches a climax in *Comment c'est* (1961) in which the elemental Bom and Pim crawl naked through the slime and darkness of existence.

The nineteenth-century conception of the novel is challenged in a different way in the fiction of Nathalie Sarraute (b. 1902). Plot and character portrayal are replaced by situations existing between people whose inner movements and underlying reactions compose a network of relationships beyond the reach of any socio-psychological approach to character. One is reminded of Dostoevsky, and more particularly of Virginia Woolf. In a collection of literary essays, *L'Ère du soupçon* (1956), Nathalie Sarraute explains her 'suspicion' of traditional accounts of human nature and therefore of the fictional characters portrayed by most nineteenth-century novelists. In the early *Tropismes* (1939), and in later novels such as *Portrait d'un inconnu* (1946), *Martereau* (1953), *Le Planétarium* (1959) and *Les Fruits d'or* (1963), she shows authentic personality expressing itself, and true relations between people being established, by silences, gestures, inflections and oblique meanings often totally at variance with the words spoken.

The network of relationships between people is also explored, with a distinctive dialectic of absence and presence, silence and words, passivity and revolt, by Marguerite Duras (b. 1914). Tone, texture and subtle counterpointing are brilliantly handled in such novels as *Les Petits Chevaux de Tarquinia* (1953), *Le Square* (1955), and *Moderato cantabile* (1958) in which a laconic workman and his boss's wife act out in imagination an adulterous passion shot through with the obsessive overtones of a *crime passionnel* which each had witnessed separately. Later works include the film scenario *Hiroshima mon amour* (1960) and the novels *Le Vice-consul* (1966) and *L'Amante anglaise* (1967).

Claude Simon (b. 1913), Alain Robbe-Grillet (b. 1922) and Michel Butor (b. 1926) are generally regarded as the quintessential 'new novelists'. Simon is a distinctive writer concerned with the destructive nature of time in novels of dizzying chronology and confused consciousness that recall the American William Faulkner. Difficulties and uncertainties assail the reader of such novels as *Le Vent* (1957), *L'Herbe* (1958), *La Route des Flandres* (1960) and *Le Palace* (1962).

Difficulties and unresolved doubts are also created by the novels of Robbe-Grillet and Butor. Coherence and meaning, characters and plot, give way to a puzzling pattern of inconsistencies and ambiguities, hints and half-truths. Robbe-Grillet argues that 'coherent' nineteenth-century forms of character and plot reflected a social order which no longer exists and a set of social values in which we no longer believe. With character and plot lacking intellectual respectability, we must find different forms while being forced to concern ourselves increasingly with objects. Such objects will be seen as 'being present' rather than as 'having meaning beyond themselves'. Hence the detached formalism and the ambiguities of character and story in *Les Gommes* (1953), *Le Voyeur* (1955), *La Jalousie* (1957), *Dans le labyrinthe* (1959) and *La Maison de rendez-vous* (1963).

Michel Butor's novels have contained more varied types of experiment. An early novel such as *L'Emploi du temps* (1956) has many of the characteristics attributed to Robbe-Grillet above. With *La Modification* (1957), however, although the plot has an almost traditional clarity, unusual effects are achieved by the use of the vocative form throughout the whole narrative. Ambitious experiments with the presentation of space and time are made in *Degrés* (1960) and in the literary collage entitled *Mobile* (1962).

It may be argued that most 'new novelists' are too self-consciously intellectual, and too much in love with technique and theory, to be truly creative. One is tempted to suggest that their theoretical writings provide more entertaining fiction than is found in many of their novels. Generally speaking, the middle decades of the twentieth century have been a period of intelligent agitation in literature rather than one of permanent accomplishment. Even novels as well contrived as *La Route des Flandres*, *La Jalousie* or *La Modification* may become curios, not classics. Nevertheless it is on experiment in drama and poetry, no less than in fiction, that genuine growth and future achievement in literature depend.

Bibliography

The development of French literature since 1870 is a complex subject as well as a lengthy one. This has two obvious results where the present bibliography is concerned. In the first place, general studies of the period are inevitably selective and tend to present their material in terms of somewhat arbitrary patterns. Secondly, it has only been possible to mention a few of the most helpful titles from among the many critical works devoted to various sections into which the preceding chapter has been divided.

General Studies

A detailed, traditional literary history in English will be found in P. E. Charvet, *A Literary History of France: the Nineteenth and Twentieth Centuries, 1870–1940* (London, 1967). This book, which does not deal with post-war writing, extends from naturalism to existentialism and includes accounts of all the main literary figures. The best French history of the subject is H. Clouard, *Histoire de la littérature française du symbolisme à nos jours*, 2 vols (Paris, 1962). Particularly valuable is the attention paid to philosophy, history, literary criticism and memoirs during the period. A wider canvas, in the sense that it deals with Europe generally and not only France, can be found in R.-M. Albérès, *L'Aventure intellectuelle du XXe siècle, 1900–1950* (Paris, 1950). A more selective approach is contained in J. Cruickshank (ed.), *French Literature and its Background*, Vols 5 and 6 (London, 1969 and 1970). Vol. 5 *The Late Nineteenth Century*, includes chapters on 'Symbolism and Mallarmé' and 'Literature and Ideology, 1880–1914'; Vol. 6, *The Twentieth Century*, apart from essays on the main authors, contains chapters on such subjects as 'The Birth of the Modern, 1885–1914', 'Surrealism', 'Vichy France, 1940–1944' and 'The "Nouveau roman"'. W. Fowlie, *Climate of Violence* (London, 1969), is still more selective and includes an interesting section on poets and painters at the turn of the century.

NATURALISM

One of the leading French authorities on naturalism (and realism) is R. Dumesnil. His *Le Réalisme et le naturalisme* (Paris, 1955) is a large and comprehensive treatment of the subject. As regards naturalism, parts 3–6 are particularly relevant, especially the sections dealing with 'scientisme', 'naturalisme' and the theatre between 1850 and 1890. P. Martino is perhaps a more old-fashioned historian of literature but his *Le Roman réaliste sous le Second Empire* (Paris, 1913) and his *Le Naturalisme français* (Paris, 1923) are very informative and worth consulting. Another sound and detailed work is C. Beuchat, *Histoire du naturalisme français*, 2 vols (Paris, 1949).

SYMBOLISM

The theory and practice of the symbolist movement in France are well set out and discussed in A. G. Lehmann, *The Symbolist Aesthetic in France, 1885–1895*, 2nd ed. (Oxford, 1968). The same subject is dealt with at length, and in considerable detail, in two works by G. Michaud. His *La Doctrine symboliste* (Paris, 1947) and *Message poétique du symbolisme*, 3 vols (Paris, 1947) are essential reading for a scholarly understanding of symbolism. This is also true of M. Décaudin, *La Crise des valeurs symbolistes* (Paris, 1960), which is only useful for those who are already familiar with basic symbolist doctrine. As regards the theatre, its development through the phases of naturalism and symbolism is excellently studied in J. A. Henderson, *The First Avant-Garde (1887–1894): Sources of the Modern French Theatre* (London, 1971). Apart from accounts of Antoine, Paul Fort and Lugné-Poe, attention is paid to mime, marionettes, etc.

PUBLIC THEMES AND PRIVATE CONCERNS

Several of the ideas and authors mentioned in this section are very readably discussed in V. Brombert, *The Intellectual Hero: Studies in the French Novel, 1880–1955* (Philadelphia and New York, 1961). This book also contains an interesting essay on the development of the concept of 'the intellectual' in France. Those who seek more detailed knowledge of Bourget or Loti should consult M. Mansuy, *Paul Bourget* (Paris, 1961), or K. G. Millward, *L'Œuvre de Pierre Loti et l'esprit fin de siècle* (Paris, 1955). The drama of the period is discussed in J. R. Taylor, *The Rise and Fall of the Well-Made Play* (London, 1967).

POLITICS AND POLEMICS

M. Tison-Braun, *La Crise de l'humanisme*, Vol. I (Paris, 1958), offers a very full and challenging account of the major writers of the second half of the nineteenth century who also had some political importance or, like Bloy, were passionate critics of Belle Époque society. Much of the same subject-matter, but with an emphasis on the main Catholic polemicists of the period, is covered in R. Griffiths, *The Reactionary Revolution: the Catholic Revival in French Literature, 1870–1914* (London, 1966). The anti-rationalism and political conservatism of the period are excellently described and analysed. These ideas are also briefly but usefully discussed in chapter 3 of P.-H. Simon, *L'Esprit et l'histoire* (Paris, 1954).

FOUR NEW MASTERS

One of the best introductory approaches to Proust remains A. Maurois, *A la recherche de Marcel Proust* (Paris, 1949). A short but illuminating study in English is A. King, *Proust* (London, 1968). We are presented with a most intelligent and sophisticated analysis of *A la recherche du temps perdu* by I. Bersani, *Marcel Proust: the Fictions of Life and of Art* (New York, 1965), and mention should also be made of J. M. Cocking, *Proust* (London, 1956), and J. Mouton, *Proust* (Paris, 1968).

G. W. Ireland, *Gide* (London, 1963), offers a clear and concise general guide to Gide's work. As further reading on the subject both G. Brée, *André Gide, l'insaisissable Protée* (Paris, 1953), and A. J. Guérard, *André Gide*, 2nd ed. (Cambridge, Mass., 1969), are to be recommended. J. Delay has made an impressive psychological study of the young Gide in *La Jeunesse d'André Gide*, 2 vols (Paris, 1956–8).

Among the many books on Valéry, helpful general works include H. A. Grubbs, *Paul Valéry* (New York, 1968), W. N. Ince, *The Poetic Theory of Paul Valéry* (London, 1961), F. Scarfe, *The Art of Paul Valéry* (London, 1954), and P. O. Walzer, *La Poésie de Valéry* (Geneva, 1953).

As regards Claudel, essential reading would include J. Madaule, *Le Drame de Paul Claudel* (Paris, 1947), H. Colleye, *La Poésie catholique de Claudel* (Liège, 1945), and J. Chiari, *The Poetic Drama of Paul Claudel* (London, 1954).

THE GROWTH OF THE AVANT-GARDE

The development of the early avant-garde theatre is comprehensively and authoritatively studied in H. Béhar, *Étude sur le théâtre dada et surréaliste* (Paris, 1967). A more general, somewhat journalistic, but thoroughly entertaining account of the early avant-garde is R. Shattuck, *The Banquet Years: the Arts in France, 1885–1918* (London, 1958). There are chapters on the paintings of Henri Rousseau and the music of Satie, as well as on Jarry and Apollinaire.

LITERATURE AND WORLD WAR I

This is a relatively neglected topic, though two books deal with the subject in considerable detail: J. N. Cru, *Témoins* (Paris, 1929), and M. Tison-Braun, *La Crise de l'humanisme*, Vol. II (Paris, 1967). There is also a useful chapter on World War I literature in P.-H. Simon *L'Esprit et l'histoire* (Paris, 1954).

SURREALISM

A very readable account of the phenomenon of surrealism will be found in A Balakian, *Surrealism: the Road to the Absolute* (New York, 1959). An essential work is M. Nadeau, *Histoire du surréalisme*, 2 vols (Paris, 1945–7). The second of these volumes contains a fascinating collection of documents, manifestos, broadsheets, etc. Other helpful and important contributions to the subject include M. Raymond, *De Baudelaire au surréalisme* (Paris, 1933), F. Alquié, *Philosophie du surréalisme* (Paris, 1955), and M. Carrouges, *André Breton et les données fondamentales du surréalisme* (Paris, 1950).

INTER-WAR THEATRE

Most immediately relevant are P. Brisson, *Le Théâtre des années folles* (Geneva, 1943), and D. Knowles, *French Drama in the Inter-War Years, 1918–1939* (London, 1967). This latter work is a mine of factual information enthusiastically presented. Among many other books which include sections on this period, mention should be made of J. Guicharnaud, *Modern French Theatre* (New Haven, Conn., 1961), D. I. Grossvogel, *Twentieth Century French Drama* (New York, 1958), J. Jacquot (ed.), *Le Théâtre moderne:* Vol. I, *Hommes et tendances* (Paris, 1958), and P. Surer, *Le Théâtre français contemporain* (Paris, 1964).

AN AGE OF FICTION

All the novelists mentioned in this section are the subject of many separate studies, either whole books or substantial essays. Attempts to cover more generally the most significant fiction of the period are also numerous. The most full and detailed treatment will be found in H. Peyre, *The Contemporary French Novel* (New York, 1955), and G. Brée and M. Guiton, *An Age of Fiction* (London, 1957). An important work in French is P. de Boisdeffre, *Métamorphoses de la littérature*, 2 vols (Paris, 1963). There is a section on the French novel between the two World Wars in M. Raimond, *Le Roman depuis la Révolution* (Paris, 1967), and essays on Bernanos, Malraux and some theoretical aspects of the age of fiction in J. Cruickshank (ed.), *The Novelist as Philosopher: Studies in French Fiction 1935–1960* (London, 1962).

WORLD WAR II: RESISTANCE AND LIBERATION

Essential to a general understanding of the Resistance are H. Michel, *Histoire de la*

Résistance, 2nd ed. (Paris, 1958), and the same author's *Les Courants de pensée de la Résistance* (Paris, 1962). Resistance writing is discussed in Vercors, *La Bataille du silence: souvenirs de minuit* (Paris, 1967), and, more narrowly and at second hand, in H. Josephson and M. Cowley, *Aragon, Poet of the French Resistance* (London, 1945). It is perhaps worth adding that the writings of collaborators are dealt with in P. Sérant, *Le Romantisme fasciste* (Paris, 1959).

HUMANISM AND EXISTENTIALISM

The general literature on this subject is vast. Among general studies, mention should be made of P. Foulquié, *L'Existentialisme* (Paris, 1949), R. Grimsley, *Existentialist Thought* (Cardiff, 1955), R. Pierce, *Contemporary French Political Thought* (London, 1966), and C. Smith, *Contemporary French Philosophy* (London, 1964). It is only possible to list a very few of the many books published on Sartre and Camus. Two of the clearest and most penetrating shorter books on Sartre are: I. Murdoch, *Sartre* (London, 1953), and M. Cranston, *Sartre* (London, 1962). Among longer studies A. R. Manser, *Sartre: a Philosophic Study* (London, 1966), and P. Thody, *Sartre: a Literary and Political Study* (London, 1960), are both to be recommended. On Camus, two of the first studies in English are J. Cruickshank, *Albert Camus and the Literature of Revolt* (London, 1959), and P. Thody, *Albert Camus 1913–1960: a Biographical Study* (London, 1961). A sound general treatment will be found in P. H. Rhein, *Albert Camus* (New York, 1969), and Camus is excellently studied as a 'committed' writer in E. Parker, *Albert Camus: the Artist in the Arena* (Madison, 1965). In connection with French existentialist writing, mention should also be made of G. Gennari, *Simone de Beauvoir* (Paris, 1959).

NEW FORMS IN THE THEATRE

Two basic introductory studies in English are M. Esslin, *The Theatre of the Absurd* (London, 1961), and L. C. Pronko, *Avant-Garde: the Experimental Theatre in France* (Berkeley and Los Angeles, 1962). Other books well worth consulting include L. Abel, *Metatheatre: a New View of Dramatic Form* (New York, 1963), P. L. Mignon, *Le Théâtre d'aujourd'hui de A jusqu'à Z* (Paris, 1966), G. Serreau, *Histoire du nouveau théâtre* (Paris, 1966), and G. E. Wellworth, *The Theatre of Protest and Paradox* (London, 1964).

SOME POST-WAR POETS

Selections from all the leading post-war French poets, together with some most illuminating critical comments, will be found in C. A. Hackett, *An Anthology of French Poetry* (Oxford, 1952), and the same editor's *New French Poetry: an Anthology* (Oxford, 1973). Other useful introductions to this general field are A. M. Boase (ed.), *The Poetry of France, Vol. 4: 1900–1965* (London, 1969), and J. Rousselot, *Panorama critique des nouveaux poètes français* (Paris, 1953). There are some outstanding critical insights in J.-P. Richard, *Onze études sur la poésie moderne* (Paris, 1964), and there are articles on Jouve, Reverdy, Aragon, Desnos and the modern *poème en prose* in E. M. Beaumont, J. M. Cocking and J. Cruickshank (eds), *Order and Adventure in Post-Romantic French Poetry: Essays presented to C. A. Hackett* (Oxford, 1973).

TOWARDS A NEW NOVEL

The best introduction in English is undoubtedly J. Sturrock, *The French New Novel* (London, 1969). Another highly intelligent book, and one which is also sympathetic towards the aims of the *nouveaux romanciers*, is L. Janvier, *Une Parole exigeante* (Paris, 1964). A more hostile view is taken by J. Bloch-Michel, *Le Présent de l'indicatif* (Paris, 1963). The whole phenomenon is discussed, useful factual information is given, and brief extracts in English translation from more than a dozen 'new novelists' are provided by L. Lesage, *The French New Novel: an Introduction and a Sampler* (Pennsylvania, 1962).

INDEX